MAKING AN IMPACT

FACILITATING STUDENT SUCCESS WITH LESSONS FROM INSTRUCTIONAL COMMUNICATION AND EDUCATIONAL PSYCHOLOGY

SAN BOLKAN
California State University, Long Beach

Kendall Hunt
publishing company

Cover image © Shutterstock.com

Kendall Hunt
publishing company
www.kendallhunt.com
Send all inquiries to:
4050 Westmark Drive
Dubuque, IA 52004-1840

ISBN 978-1-5249-1372-4

Published in the United States of America

CONTENTS

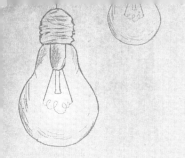

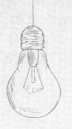

INTRODUCTION

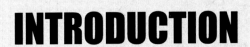

So you decided to read this book, huh? Good for you. I wrote this book to help people like you become better at teaching others by changing the way you communicate with them. Importantly, you don't have to be a teacher to appreciate the information in the pages that follow. In fact, just about anyone can benefit from understanding what promotes adult learning. Are you a sales associate with the need to improve your persuasive abilities? This book should help. Are you a spokesperson for your organization? This book will tell you what aspects of your speeches are beneficial for promoting your cause and what aspects might be detrimental. Perhaps your role as a communicator is to simply present information to others at meetings. Why not learn how to increase the probability that people will understand and want to listen to you? Although I wrote this book from the perspective of improving instruction, just about anybody can benefit from the work of researchers who have dedicated their professional careers to figuring out how to facilitate adult learning.

At this point you may be wondering why you should listen to me. Of course, you don't have to, but I have done a lot of work synthesizing the vast literature related to human learning to explain some of the most important concepts in this field of research. And, you can rest assured knowing that I have the credentials to help you learn this information. I have a Ph.D. in Communication Studies from the University of Texas at Austin (class of 2007!) and, since graduating, the focus of my research has been on instructional communication. In essence, I spend most of my days reading about, and conducting research relating to, the ways teachers can improve their instruction to enhance student learning. I have more than 30 peer-reviewed publications on the topic, and I have read (literally) thousands of articles and dozens of books dedicated to the study of human learning. Now, I admit that there are more accomplished scholars out there who know more than I do about this subject. However, I do know a fair amount, and I am confident that what I know and what I can teach you will be helpful in your instructional endeavors. Moreover, and crucially, none of the experts who know more than I do have written books like this one that summarize the extensive literature while also translating these complex topics into lessons that are easy to understand and delivering them in a format that is fun to read. So, for now at least, if you want an enjoyable and practical text that focuses on improving instruction, you are going to have to learn from me. That said, you should feel confident knowing that I am at least the 100th best scholar to write this book (based on my own, unofficial ranking system).

So what's the point of this book? Of course, there are several. However, the majority of my focus is dedicated to helping you understand the fundamental principles of adult learning so you can communicate in ways that increase the probability that people understand and remember the material you present. In addition to helping you understand the principles of adult learning, I will also provide concrete advice regarding several things you can do to improve your teaching. Importantly, I am going to try to do all of this while writing in a tone that makes you actually want to read this book. This is no easy task. However, I am going to work hard to do it because it would be ironic to make you read a book about effective teaching if I did not follow my own rules for making teaching effective. That would be like making you watch the television show *Finding Bigfoot* on Animal Planet where, after several seasons on the air, no one has done anything even remotely close to finding a bigfoot. I am not going to do to you what Animal Planet has been doing to me for almost a decade. Instead, I am going to practice what I preach by doing my best to make this book both informative and enjoyable.

Alright, so that is my job, what about yours? Your job is to learn. By learning about what behaviors lead to student success, and what behaviors do not, you should develop an understanding of what it takes to be a good instructor. And, as someone famous once said, when it comes to being a good instructor "knowing is half the battle." Let me explain why this is important . . .

The quote noted in the previous paragraph is attributed to the cartoon character, G.I. Joe, who at the end of his television show would tell little kids watching his program that knowing how to be safe or how to be kind to others is half the battle in the fight for personal success. For instance, at the end of the cartoon viewers would be shown a vignette such as a little boy playing with a kite. Suddenly a gust of wind would take the kite up and into a telephone pole with electric wires everywhere. The little boy would yell to his friend that he was going to climb the pole to retrieve the kite and, just as he was about to do so, we would see G.I. Joe burst onto the scene to stop the kid from climbing. Then, G.I. Joe would say something like, "Hey kid, climbing power lines is dangerous and can hurt you. Better leave that kite where it is and go play with something else." Of course, the kid would be shocked at his coming close to being harmed and would say, "Thanks, G.I. Joe. Now I know." To which Joe would reply, "Good, and knowing is half the battle." Then the scene would cut to black, and you would be sitting at home thinking "Holy smokes, G.I. Joe just saved that kid's life."

Admittedly, I am not certain that this is exactly how it went down. That is how I remember it though and in reality it doesn't really matter because I am simply trying to make a point. Why do I recount this story about G.I. Joe and his message to little kids around the world? Because G.I. Joe was right! You *do* have to know what you are doing in order to do it right. And, that's where this book comes in. I have worked hard to gather some of the most important research related to instructional communication and educational psychology to help you understand the ideas behind what scholars have suggested leads to student learning. You might be a good teacher already, or you might be a terrible one so far. Either way, this book was designed to help you learn what it takes to help facilitate student success and, as G.I. Joe would say, knowing this information is half the battle when it comes to effective instruction.

Now, the thing about G.I. Joe's message that always bugged me is that he forgot to tell us about the other half of what it takes to succeed. Although he told us about the importance of knowing things, he left it there. So, let me see if I can help G.I. Joe out on this matter: When it comes to personal success, while half the battle includes knowing what to do, the other half involves actually *doing* it. Here's what I mean . . . If G.I. Joe was in a battle and knew how to use his weapons to defeat the bad guys, we would be glad. However, if Joe never actually did anything with that knowledge and the bad guys got away, we would be sad. As it relates to effective instruction, knowing what it takes to be a good teacher is really only half the battle because the other half necessitates that you put what you know into practice. Thus, the second part of your job is to do just that. To this point, in each chapter I will give you concrete advice pertaining to how you can employ specific behaviors in your classrooms (and elsewhere) to ensure that, in addition to understanding why good teachers do certain things, you can also do those things yourself.

Having said all of the above, I want you to know that I have chosen to write about some of the most important variables known to influence students' academic outcomes. This information is derived from my experience as a researcher, a teacher, and as a consumer of information. I did my best to include what I (and others) consider to be the most important ideas in instructional communication and educational psychology to date so I hope you enjoy the book and I hope you learn a lot!

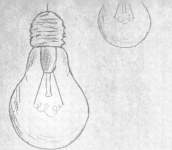

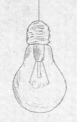

ABOUT THE AUTHOR

San Bolkan (Ph.D., University of Texas at Austin, 2007) is an Associate Professor in the Department of Communication Studies at California State University, Long Beach. His research has been published widely and covers subjects related to instructional communication including topics such as teacher clarity, student motivation, and transformational leadership in the classroom.

ONE

COWs

OBJECTIVES

By the end of this chapter, you should be a changed person in the following ways:

1. You should know about the four general dimensions of knowledge
2. You should know the definition of learning
3. You should have an understanding of what it means to "elaborate" and how elaboration is linked to learning
4. You should know what three factors need to be present in order to ensure elaboration
5. You should be able to wrestle a full-sized pig to the ground with only your bare hands (Just joking about this one. But seriously, if you could do this by the end of the chapter I would be 100% impressed)

COWs

What does it take to become a great teacher? A lot. If you read the journals dedicated to educational psychology or instructional communication you would almost certainly become overwhelmed. In fact, just one issue of the journal *Communication Education* is likely to have several important topics to consider. For example, perusing one issue of the journal (volume 65, issue 1) reveals studies focused on topics such as: students' use of technology in class, student complaints, student-to-student communication, classroom civility, and students' oral participation. That's a lot to wrap your head around; it would be difficult to study any of those ideas in their entirety. And, that's just one issue of one volume of one journal! Taking this route to becoming a better teacher might prove to be very time-consuming. To get yourself up to speed on instructional issues might take weeks, months, or even years (there are Ph.D. programs dedicated to the study of this subject).

Instead of reading about it, maybe there is another route to becoming a good teacher. For example, some people might tell you that becoming good at anything just takes practice. The 10,000-hour rule (see Ericsson, Krampe, & Tesch-Romer, 1993) made famous by one of my favorite authors, Malcolm Gladwell (2008), would suggest that to become an expert in your field you must spend 10,000 hours, or about 10 years for those of us who do not want to count up our hours of practice, deliberately practicing a skill to become proficient at it. You read that correctly, 10 years. I know, holy smokes! By the time you master 10 things, you are dead! Choose wisely!

So, perhaps if you practiced teaching for 10 years, you would be a terrific teacher. If you have already taught for 10 years, you might even be a pro by now. Well, maybe. To be fair, various scholars question the necessity of such a long period of sustained practice and note that other factors might be important for determining expertise as well (see Macnamara, Hambrick, & Oswald, 2014, for example). This makes sense to me—practice can't be the only thing that matters. I mean, think about it: If you put someone who does not know how to swim, has never swam, and has never seen someone swim before into a body of water with no way to escape, do you think that he or she would become an expert swimmer in 10 years? Probably not. Come to think of it, that person would probably drown. Okay, bad example. Let me try again. Let's think about an example related to the focus of this book. Just because I practice teaching for 10 years, do you think that guarantees I will end up being a good teacher? I don't think so. In fact, in my experience as a student, some of the best instructors I had were people who just started in their careers. On the other hand, I have had several instructors who were terrible at what they did despite the fact that they had been practicing for more than the requisite 10,000 hours.

While I am not discounting the importance of practice, my point is that just because you practice something for a long time does not mean you are going to get good at it. Instead, and in addition to other important factors, you must practice it correctly if you are going to do it well. Practicing bad habits over a period of 10 years will simply make you really good at being bad (aren't those the lyrics to a Rihanna song?). That's where coaching, instruction, and other methods of help come in. If you want to get good at something, you must learn how to do it the right way. In other words, if you want to be good at something, you must first learn what it means to be good at doing that thing. That said, considering you are reading about how to become a better teacher, let's figure out what it means to be good at instruction.

Okay, what do you need to know in order to help your students learn at their highest potential? As I already mentioned, the list of known effective (and ineffective teaching) behaviors would be impossibly long to manage so I am not going to try to tell you everything you need to do. Instead, at this point, let's figure out what it means to learn in the first place. Perhaps after that we will have some direction regarding what we need to do to facilitate this process. So what is learning? Learning refers to the process of creating a lasting change in a person's knowledge base as it pertains to some aspect of his or her life. When it comes to student learning, we might categorize the process by thinking about it in terms of the dimensions of knowledge a student might develop. According to researchers Lorin Anderson and David Krathwohl (2001), there are four dimensions to consider: these dimensions include factual knowledge, conceptual knowledge, procedural knowledge, and metacognitive knowledge.

Factual knowledge refers to knowing isolated facts and is exemplified by the simple retention of specific information. Examples of factual knowledge might include students knowing where to locate the radiator on a car, or the function of a fuel pump. Although learning factual knowledge is important for setting the foundation of expertise (see Brown, Roediger, & McDaniel, 2014), most teachers probably also want their students to develop conceptual knowledge. *Conceptual knowledge* includes an understanding of how basic facts work together to form principles, models, or theories. As just mentioned, developing factual knowledge about car mechanics, for example, might include learning about the various parts of a car engine. Conceptual knowledge, on the other hand, would reflect an understanding of how these parts function together to create systems that allow the engine to work.

Next, *procedural knowledge* refers to students' knowledge of how to actually do something. This might include their knowledge of how to use a computer program to complete various tasks, for example. Knowing what to do and when to do it are included in Anderson and Krathwohl's (2001) definition of procedural knowledge. Finally, *metacognitive knowledge* refers to students' knowledge of learning strategies (e.g., effective note-taking and memorization techniques) and when to use these. Metacognitive knowledge also refers to students' understanding of their own strengths and weaknesses as they pertain to their learning.

We now know that learning involves creating a change in some aspect of students' knowledge which might include factual, conceptual, procedural, or metacognitive knowledge. That said, this change is supposed to be lasting. So, how do we ensure that students actually learn something instead of simply memorizing it for the time being and then forgetting it later down the road? Well, as it pertains to student outcomes, scholars examining differences in student learning often emphasize the importance of individual differences in the depth of their thinking about course material (this is sometimes called elaboration).

According to the levels of processing framework, information that is processed in a deep manner (i.e., information that is elaborated) is associated with longer-lasting memories compared with information that is processed in a shallow manner (e.g., Craik & Lockhart, 1972). Specifically, compared to students who do not, students who spend time thinking about course material by adding details to what is being learned, clarifying ideas in a lesson, highlighting relationships between concepts, or connecting new information to material already learned are more likely to experience higher message recall and comprehension (King, 1992).

Essentially, what's going on when students elaborate is that they are making information more meaningful. Thus, if we want to ensure that students learn to the best of their ability, we have to help them elaborate and make sense out of the material we are teaching them. By making information more meaningful, it becomes easier for students to remember and comprehend their course lessons (King, 1992; Levin, 1988; Pressley, McDaniel, Turnure, Wood, & Ahmad, 1987). As researchers Craik and Lockhart (1972) note, elaboration is crucial in education because, in the end, it is the effort spent deeply analyzing information that leads to better learning, not simply the time spent studying.

Got it! We now know that in order for students to learn successfully, they need to experience a lasting change in one of their dimensions of knowledge, and to do this well they need to think deeply about course concepts and link what they learn to things they already know. Now, the next question we need to answer is "what predicts students' elaboration and deep thinking?" According to several scholars (e.g., Chaiken, Liberman, & Eagly, 1989; Eagly & Chaiken, 1993; Petty & Cacioppo, 1986), individuals need to have two things if they are going to think deeply about information—*ability* and *motivation*. And, that's where you come in. Although it could be argued that students should do their best to elaborately process instructional messages, scholars note that students may not have the ability or the motivation to think deeply about course concepts on their own (Dornisch, Sperling, & Zeruth, 2011; King, 1992). Because they cannot do it, or are unwilling to do it, instructors play a significant role in promoting students' ability and motivation to think deeply about course concepts (King, 1992).

Yes! Now that we know how to help our students learn, all we need to do is encourage their ability and motivation to deeply process our course materials. We're done, right? Not so fast. Before we get too excited about promoting students' ability and motivation to think deeply about course concepts, I have to tell you that these two ideas are not the end of the story. In fact, according to some researchers, these ideas might only explain about two-thirds of what students need to do to learn.

Specifically, researchers claim that if we want students to learn, then in addition to having the ability and motivation to think about their course concepts, students also need the *opportunity* to do so. Opportunity reflects the breaking of ability into internal (e.g., personality, intelligence) and external aspects (e.g., educational opportunities) that might influence human behavior, with opportunity representing the latter—I guess that means there's one more thing to learn.

It took a while for us to get here, but based on what you just read, you now know that if you want to facilitate student learning you need to help create some type of lasting change in students' base of knowledge. You also know that this will occur to the extent that students think deeply about, or elaborate on, their course material. Finally, you learned that, as a teacher you can help students elaborate on class concepts to the extent that you influence students' abilities, opportunities, and motivation to think deeply about their course lessons. Because promoting students' abilities, opportunities, and motivation is of the utmost importance in educational settings, the rest of the chapter is devoted to going over these topics in more detail . . . to do that, I'm going to talk to you about the idea of nurturing students' COWs.

COWs

Our goal as teachers is to help students perform at their best. That said, although there are a variety of methods we might employ to help students perform to their highest potential, it is difficult to tell what, exactly, we should focus on when we walk into our classrooms. I think that one of the reasons for this confusion is because researchers who study the subject of student success often fail to put their findings into a bigger picture. For example, there are plenty of academic papers that will tell you it is important to be clear when teaching. However, these articles often fail to articulate how clarity works with other teacher behaviors (such as an enthusiastic delivery method) and student characteristics (such as self-discipline) to influence student learning. Because this is the case, studies that focus on one teaching behavior tend to paint an overly simplistic picture of effective instruction. When I read articles like the one being described I think to myself, "I get it, being clear is important, but *how* important is it in the grand scheme of things. And, crucially, how does it work *with* other variables to predict student success?" That said, I think it is important that we try to think about our teaching from a holistic perspective so we can focus on specific effective instructional behaviors all the while keeping in mind how these behaviors relate to student learning in its totality. To this point, this book is organized around three major concepts that help put individual teaching behaviors into a larger, more comprehensive framework.

The framework that I want to introduce relates to the concept of nurturing COWs and stems from an article examining predictors of job performance published in 1982 and authored by researchers Melvin Blumberg and Charles Pringle. In this article, Blumberg and Pringle noted that when it comes to performance at work, there are a variety of issues that predict success. For example, some of these predictors include job satisfaction, attitude about the job, and motivation to do well at the job, among many others. However, Blumberg and Pringle were unhappy with the variable-analytic approach to studying job performance one issue at a time and wanted to couch the study of performance at work in a bigger context. Essentially, these researchers were frustrated with the lack of organization related to the many predictors of task performance and believed that this way of looking at things made it unwieldy to understand what it takes to be one's best at work. As the writers argued, when it comes to human performance, people seemed to be focusing on studying individual trees instead of looking at the more important patterns that make up the forest.

Thus, the authors set out to articulate a general theory of human task performance by looking for various relationships in the many predictors. Long story short? Blumberg and Pringle argued for three general categories that predict performance. Specifically, the three categories are: the *capacity* to perform, the *opportunity* to perform, and a person's *willingness* to perform. I underlined the first letter of each word because it creates an acronym I can remember—COW. Thus, according to Blumberg and Pringle, if we want to understand what it takes to help people perform their best at work, we should take into consideration people's capacity to do something well, their opportunity to do something well, and their willingness to do something well. Of course, the same thing is true in an academic context: in order for students to learn their best, they must have the capacity, opportunity, and willingness to do so. Therefore, as a teacher, you might say that your job is to be a farmer, rancher, or performer of animal husbandry and to nurture students' COWs.

Capacity

According to Blumberg and Pringle, the first idea in the COWs framework is capacity, which refers to a broad conceptualization of ability. In the context of learning, we can think of capacity as anything inside students that allows them to do well in our courses. Included under the notion of capacity are the ideas of knowledge, skills, intelligence, levels of education, and anything else that might be internal to a person that would help them perform well in an academic environment. In the classroom, the question we need to ask related to capacity is this: does the student have the personal ability to perform in the way he or she is being asked?

So, how important is capacity? Very. In fact, in our lives, the capacity to do something is often a requirement for our doing it, or even trying it. Why don't I jump off the roof of my building and try to fly around like some type of superhero professor? Because I can't fly and I know how the movie ends if I jump off the building in an attempt to do so. The same is true in other aspects of our lives, let me explain with an example. When I was a little kid, I loved playing soccer. My dad was my coach, my friends were often on my team, and I enjoyed a reasonable amount of success as a player. I liked the sport quite a bit (still do), and I would practice after school even if my team did not have a scheduled training session. I loved soccer so much that I dreamed of being a professional soccer player. And, I truly believed my dream would come true until I was crushed one night when, during a sleepover, my friend told me that I would never play professional soccer. I thought he was being a jerk. Turns out he was being realistic. I was okay at the sport as a kid. But, compared to the really talented players, I wasn't anywhere close to putting on a professional jersey. As I grew up, I remember making a decision not to pursue a professional soccer career—with my (lack of) skills, I simply was not going to cut it. Instead, I decided to focus on academics to help me find my professional calling. So, the moral of this story is that despite my motivation to do it, and despite my having the opportunity to develop my skills, I was never even close to being good enough to play professional soccer. And, as you might reasonably assume based on your reading my book about teaching, because of my lack of ability, I never became a professional soccer player.

The point I am trying to make here is that when people are asked to perform some type of behavior, they must have the ability to do it. Of course, the same is true in education: capacity matters. In support of this notion, research points to the conclusion that the students who do the best in college are the ones who have the highest ability to do so. For example, researchers Coyle and Pillow (2008) have demonstrated that SAT and ACT scores tap into underlying characteristics of students' general intelligence and that both standardized tests, along with intelligence, help predict students' first-year college grade point averages (GPAs). Similar results have been reported by other researchers (e.g., Robbins, Allen, Casillas, Peterson, & Le, 2006).

Despite the information presented above, a reasonable person might argue that intelligence alone (and certainly the SAT and ACT tests alone) is not the only predictor of student success. Even an unreasonable person like me might make a similar argument. In fact, several researchers who study student learning take the position that intelligence is not the only factor that predicts success—there are other components of a student's ability that matter as well. Self-control (sometimes called self-discipline) is one of these components.

According to Duckworth and Gross (2014), the ability to exercise self-control "entails aligning actions with any valued goal despite momentarily more-alluring alternatives" (p. 319). Put more simply, self-control refers to people's ability to make themselves do something they should do, or avoid something they know they should not do. On a diet? Avoiding delicious chips and dip at a party (and eating celery sticks instead) takes self-control. Trying to save money? Not buying tickets to that concert you want to see takes self-control. What about if you are trying to exercise more? Putting on your running shoes and going for a jog even when you are tired or hungover takes, for some people, monumental amounts of self-control.

Experts agree that students who demonstrate better self-control tend to experience more academic success. In fact, according to researchers Duckworth and Seligman (2005), highly disciplined students tend to outperform their less disciplined peers on pretty much every academic performance variable that exists. Furthermore, studies of self-control in relation to academic achievement consistently show a positive association between the two variables even after controlling for factors such as students' intelligence (Conard, 2006; Duckworth & Seligman, 2005; Noftle & Robins, 2007). So what's the point? The point is that the ability to control their impulses is another aspect of students' capacity to do well that matters when it comes to their academic performance and learning.

Although it could be argued that the ability to exercise self-control is a choice, researchers who study the subject claim that self-control is related to people's genetic makeup (Kool, McGuire, Wang, & Botvinick, 2013; Moffitt et al., 2011). This means that self-control is a trait-like personality characteristic kind of like a person's level of extraversion or outgoingness (Kochanska & Knaack, 2003; Tangney, Baumeister, & Boone, 2004). As such, self-control gets classified in our COWs system as a part of students' capacity to perform well in educational contexts. This is because the ability to exercise self-control is something inherent in students that enables them to excel in their courses.

So, back to where we started with our conversation about students' ability to do well in school. Obviously, intelligence matters when it comes to student success. However, other components of students' capacity matter as well. Thus, our goal as teachers should be to identify how we can help students maximize their inherent potential by creating situations that allow them to be the best students they can be. In this book, we will cover three aspects related to students' capacity to do well in our courses; these topics include a more thorough investigation of self-control, a breakdown of students' achievement motivation (i.e., reasons for working hard in school), and a discussion of the behaviors teachers enact that ultimately prove detrimental to students' capacity to learn at their best.

Opportunity

Recently, I was walking down Main Street in my home town of Seal Beach when I heard the delightful sounds of a guitarist strumming an interesting and provocative tune. As I listened, my eye stumbled upon a man who was playing his guitar outside a local restaurant in the hopes of earning a few tips. What caught me off guard was not the fact that he was playing on a sunny Sunday—there are several people who regularly play music around town to earn money. Instead, what caught me off guard was that he had a little device in his guitar case that looked like a credit card reader. Curious, I stopped to ask him what it was that I was looking at. In fact, he told me, it was a credit card reader. The gentleman, Jim, proceeded to tell me that when he plays guitar and then asks for money, people sometimes tell him that they wish they could provide him with a tip but are unable to do so. When pressed, these people tell him that they would be happy to spare a few dollars . . . if only they had the cash on them. Essentially, Jim communicated to me that one of the reasons people fail to donate to his cause is because they tell him they do not have the opportunity to give. So, to help facilitate their ability to donate, Jim invested in a credit card reader to attach to his phone. "It's great," Jim told me. "Donations go straight into my checking account and people no longer have to worry about not having cash on them if they want to give." I thought the idea was a good one.

According to Blumberg and Pringle, Jim's reasoning is spot on. Opportunity is another element that predicts performance, and refers to the environmental factors that influence a person's ability to perform an act. Opportunity is different from capacity insofar as it relates to forces that are thought to be external to the person performing an action (remember that capacity refers to a person's internal ability). Specifically, Blumberg and Pringle define opportunity as any outside force that enables or constrains a person's task performance including natural conditions or the behaviors of other people.

Perhaps an example will help make the notion of opportunity clearer. In their article, Blumberg and Pringle provide an example of opportunity by recounting a story about miners attempting to work in a coal mine. They report that although the individuals were scheduled to work, no one was mining on one particular occasion. Basically, despite the miners being physically able to work and being motivated to do so, they were unable to mine on the day being observed because a cave-in had occurred. Thus, despite having the capacity and willingness to do so, the external environment prohibited the performance of the men who would otherwise be mining coal—in other words, they had no opportunity to mine.

I can imagine that not many of us have much mining experience, so let me give you another example. I used to live in Santa Monica, which is a part of Los Angeles. When I lived in Santa Monica, I would occasionally run into celebrities because of my proximity to places like Beverly Hills, Venice Beach, and Malibu. It was cool bumping into celebrities until you realized that they are just regular people, except slightly more recognizable. Anyway, one of the things that always struck me about Los Angeles is how many people I have met who, although they were not celebrities yet, wanted to be celebrities in the future. Most of the people I have met like this are not from Los Angeles and did not grow up here. Instead, most of these individuals are transplants from other parts of the world. Interestingly, when I speak to these people they inevitably tell me that the decision to move here was a no-brainer: if you want to be in the entertainment business, Los Angeles is the place to be. Their rationale is something along the lines of the title of a British lottery game show . . . you have to be in it to win it. Because living in Los Angeles provides more opportunities to be "discovered," aspiring celebrities tend to move here instead of hoping to hit it big while living in their parents' basements in Dubuque, Iowa.

We have spent the last few pages developing the idea of opportunity as it relates to performance and prosperity. Of course, opportunity plays other roles in our lives as well. Think about the first person you fell in love with. For most of us, it was probably somebody who happened to be nearby. Typically, we don't fall in love with someone across the world because it is unlikely that we would have an opportunity to interact with persons living in a galaxy far far away (although, admittedly, this is changing with the opportunities provided for meeting people through the Internet). The helping hand of opportunity is often overlooked by people who seek to explain the success of others as well. This seems to be particularly true in American society where, as an individualistic culture, we tend to believe that people are responsible for their own successes and failures. But, without opportunity, even the most qualified and motivated individual cannot succeed. For example, it is no mistake that the top surfers in the world tend to come from places like Brazil, Australia, and the United States. These are places that have lots of coastline and a healthy market for surfing. When's the last time you heard of a professional surfer hailing from Tajikistan?

Of course, as it pertains to the focus of this book, opportunity is important in education as well. Certainly, the macroeducational opportunities matter quite a bit when it comes to academic achievement (e.g., what school you go to, if you even have the chance to go to school). However, as teachers, we might not have much control over those forces. Instead, our impact may have more to do with the microeducational opportunities we provide within the classroom. For instance, based on some of my own research (e.g., Bolkan, Goodboy, & Kelsey, 2016), my colleagues and I have shown that if you do not give students the opportunity to learn their course lessons because you fail to provide clear lectures, students will be unable to learn the material you present.

The truth is, just like in other performance scenarios, the opportunities present for student success matter quite a bit as well. As you will learn in this book, there are a variety of things you can do as an instructor to ensure that your students have the best possible opportunity to learn at their maximum potential. Specifically, in this book we will cover opportunities related to improving students' abilities to retain and transfer the information you provide in your courses, the cognitive load students experience that makes it difficult for them to remember and transfer the information you provide, and we will discuss what you can do to reduce the load placed on students' cognitive processing through the provision of clear lessons.

Willingness

The third aspect of the Blumberg and Pringle COWs model is willingness. In order to do something and to do something well, a person needs to want to do it; in other words, he or she must be motivated. Let me give you an example. As I mentioned, I live in Seal Beach, California, and I am lucky enough to be approximately half a block from the Pacific Ocean. In the summer, I like to take my surfboard out and surf the waves at my local break. Whenever I go out I have fun: the water is warm, the sun feels good, and being in nature is refreshing after a long day of working on my computer. The thing is, however, when winter comes around, I do not get into the water at all. This is despite the fact that I still like to surf, the sun is still warm on most winter days in Southern California, and the waves are even better than in the summer. So why don't I go into the water? The reason I do not get into the water is because the water is significantly colder in the winter, and I would freeze my butt off if I got in. I have the capacity to get into the water, and I have the opportunity to do so. However, the reason I do not get in the water in the winter is simply because I do not want to. When people mention getting into water when it is in the 50-degree range, I usually look at them and shake my head in a mixture of fear and disgust. I know they have wetsuits for this kind of stuff, still . . . that water is so cold it literally hurts to touch it, and I just don't want to get in.

Obviously, this is just one example, and it comes from my own experience. However, I am sure you can think of instances in your own life where a lack of willingness to perform an activity has stopped you from actually performing it. If you are having a hard time coming up with examples, let me just ask why you don't poop in public places with the door open or put a spider on your face before you fall asleep. The answer to these questions is probably because, like most normal human beings, you simply do not want to do those things.

Let's see how this pertains to education. To help make my point, I want to ask you an important question: why don't we have robots teaching our students? Robots presumably have the ability to store more information than humans can remember, and they should also be able to disseminate that information to students without any mistakes. Robots would never show up late to class, would have the ability to grade tests on the spot, and would never cancel class due to family emergencies. Moreover, robots would teach curriculum consistently. This means that students in section 1 with Robot 43 would learn the exact same material as students in section 2 with Robot 82. This idea is important if we expect students to come away from their college experience with a specific set of knowledge. Think about the administrative savings colleges would enjoy as well! Faculty salaries are a major expense in the operating budget of a university. Instead of paying professors a living wage, administrators could simply buy the robots and then pay technicians and programmers to upload course material. You could even make the robot friendly looking or, better yet, cute so that when the website "Rate my Robot Professor" pops up, you can still rate your mechanical instructor with a smoking hot chili pepper.

So, are you ready to sign your students up at robot-university yet? Maybe you should be. Although universities have not adopted widespread robotic teaching systems, they have developed ways to automate the delivery of course content in the form of online courses. As it pertains to our discussion, researchers claim that these types of classes show no significant differences in student learning outcomes compared to face-to-face instruction (see Cavanaugh & Jacquemin, 2015; Means, Toyoma, Murphy, & Bakia, 2013). And, in some cases, researchers even claim that learning can be enhanced with the presence of an online pedagogy (Means et al., 2013). Prepare for the robot-revolution!

Well, maybe not just yet. Research still points to the importance of teachers in online learning environments. For example, the superiority of online courses tends to stem from hybrid classes, not classes that are offered online only. Moreover, you might not be surprised to learn that successful online classes are not those where students log onto vague learning platforms filled with masses of unorganized information. No, successful online platforms are those that mimic the varied experiences and interactions students enjoy in physical classrooms. For example, students tend to learn more online when they are exposed to sources of information as opposed to text only (Means et al., 2013). In addition, instructor preparation, guidance, and assistance, among other things, still matter in the online world (Ma, Han, Yang, & Cheng, 2015).

Despite students' abilities to do well in online contexts, there is an important reason why we might want to avoid the robotic teaching apocalypse for the time being, and that reason relates to students' willingness. Let me give you an example to make the point . . . Sometimes I help students understand the importance of teachers in academic contexts by asking them to tell me what they would do if, instead of having classes where students interact with teachers like most universities typically do, the university simply handed them a book and told them to go over the information and learn it. That is, I ask them to imagine that instead of having teachers in classrooms, the university simply supplied books and places to sit and read. Then I ask my students how much information they think they would learn by the end of the semester if we implemented the new system. Do you know what they tell me? Without fail, most students tell me that they would not study at all! Essentially, without instructors to motivate them, my students tell me they would not be very likely to learn on their own. Admittedly, maybe some would, but many would not. And why not? Because the information in books can be dull, unclear, or otherwise difficult to manage, and most students need help getting motivated to do the things they are supposed to do to learn. That's where teachers come in.

The foregoing information reflects the notion that teachers can help their students become more willing to engage with various learning activities. And that's the point: Blumberg and Pringle's third element of productivity is willingness to perform a task, and for our purposes it is related to the motivation, satisfaction, involvement, and relevance students experience in class. Getting back to our question about robot teachers, the reason we should not be switching to robotic teaching any time soon is because robotic teachers that simply disseminate information would be terribly impersonal, boring, and, as a result, demotivating. Having said all of that, you should now know that as a teacher you play a major role in creating learning environments that help get students excited about the content of their courses.

But, is getting students excited about learning really that important? Well, let's see what happens when they are not . . . Almost 30 years ago, Keller (1987) noted that "no matter how motivated learners are when they begin a course, it is not too difficult to bore them, if not kill their interest totally" (p. 2). And, boredom continues to be a problem in learning environments to this day. For example, according to researchers Pekrun, Goetz, Daniels, and Stupinsky (2010), students report being bored approximately 42% of the time when attending class or studying. Nett, Goetz, and Hall (2011) would argue that this number should be higher. In their study, the researchers found that students reported experiencing some degree of boredom in their classrooms roughly 58% of the time. These results are similar to those reported by Mann and Robinson (2009) who found that 68% of students sampled in their study thought their lectures were boring some or half of the time, while 30% of students found their lectures to be boring most or all of the time. In support of these conclusions, Goetz and Hall (2014) noted that for students, "boredom is one of the most commonly experienced emotions in educational settings" (p. 314).

So why does any of this matter? Because according to Larson and Richards (1991), students report less interest and pay less attention to activities when they are bored. Likewise, when they are bored, students become easily distracted from focal tasks, and both their motivation to learn and the quality of their studying are reduced (Pekrun et al., 2010). It may be no surprise then for readers to learn that researchers have found that students who experience boredom in the classroom tend to experience lower academic achievement as well (Goetz, Frenzel, Pekrun, Hall, & Ludtke, 2007; Pekrun et al., 2010).

After reading the foregoing paragraph, let's ask the question again: is getting students excited about learning important? I think it is. Thankfully, getting students motivated does not mean that teachers have to put on a dog and pony show just to make sure students do not get bored in their classrooms. Scholars suggest that boredom tends to arise from situations that demand attention but offer low stimulation, variety, significance, and autonomy (Fisher, 1993), and also from unchallenging, undifferentiated, and repetitive tasks (Larson & Richards, 1991; Pekrun et al., 2010). That said, there are a variety of things instructors can do to get their students motivated about the learning process, and many of these do not involve delivering entertainment at the expense of providing high-quality instruction. It will be my job in this book to teach about a few of your options for making this happen. Specifically, in this book you will read: a chapter dedicated to promoting autonomous motivation through the fulfillment of students' fundamental needs, a chapter written to explain how you can help meet students' needs for motivation by teaching in a charismatic fashion, and a chapter dedicated to helping you facilitate intellectual stimulation in the classroom.

Which aspect?

Okay, now that you know about COWs (capacity, opportunity, and willingness) and their relationships with student learning, you should know that Blumberg and Pringle suggest that you concentrate on the entire COW if you want students to learn: a person must have modicum of all three elements working for them if he or she is to perform at all. The best way to think of this is as a math problem: performance = capacity × opportunity × willingness. I know you, you are good at math, so you know what this means. If any of the values for an element is zero, the total equation equals zero (Andrews, 1988).

Of course, as long as any one element is not at zero, the more you have of any element, the better the results will be. That is to say, within the elements, Blumberg and Pringle state that performance increments are summative. Stated differently, within the element of capacity, for example, each of the variables related to this element (skills, intelligence, self-control, etc.) add up to determine a person's potential. The reason this is important is because this tells me that the specifics of the individual items matter less than their cumulative effect. In other words, the major components of the COW are what are important. Therefore, regardless of the specific ideas you choose to promote, try to remember that the bigger picture of nurturing students' COWs is what is most crucial.

Still, could it be the case that one element of the COW reigns supreme? Should you focus on one element instead of the others? The answer is: it depends. First, different contexts might lead to different conclusions. I can imagine a scenario where I ask a student to perform a simple or mundane task and in this case his or her capacity to perform the behavior would probably matter less than the student's willingness to do it. However, in other situations, capacity might play a bigger role. For example, a student might be willing to participate in a task involving quantitative data analysis, but not have the training to do it. Of course, the same might be said for varying scenarios linked to opportunity. Second, influencing any dimension in the COW framework most likely influences the others. Think about it—if you are given motivation to pursue a goal (willingness), you may be more self-disciplined when working toward that goal (capacity). Thus, working on one element of the COW is likely to influence the other elements as well. That said, my advice is that instead of worrying about which aspect of student learning to focus on, it is probably easier and more productive to focus your efforts on all three aspects of the COWs framework.

Summary

Before we move on let's go through what you learned in this chapter. First, we mentioned that we want our students to learn at their best. To do this we learned that we should help students create a lasting change related to four aspects of their knowledge. Do you remember what those were? They were factual knowledge, conceptual knowledge, procedural knowledge, and metacognitive knowledge. In addition, we discovered that students tend to enjoy lasting changes in their memories when they think deeply about their course lessons and make them meaningful in some way. Second, we were introduced to the idea that in order to think deeply about their course concepts, students need to have the capacity (ability), opportunity, and willingness (motivation) to do so. We learned that if students come to class without any one of the three aspects, they are unlikely to learn at all. Finally, we discovered that, as long as one element of learning is not zero, the more we can facilitate of each component, the better.

So are we done yet? For this chapter, we are. But our journey to learn about teaching is just getting started. In this book, we will talk about each of the elements related to student learning in its own section, and I will detail what you can do as a teacher to ensure that you nurture students' COWs to enhance their learning.

END-OF-CHAPTER QUESTIONS

1. The COWs framework can be applied to a variety of performance behaviors across several of life's domains. Can you think of a situation (or situations) in your own life where your capacity, opportunity, and willingness to perform a behavior have affected your outcomes?

2. Out of the three ideas discussed in this chapter (i.e., capacity, opportunity, and willingness), which one has the biggest impact on your performance at school or work? Why do you think this is the case?

3. As far as students are concerned, which of the three ideas discussed in this chapter (i.e., capacity, opportunity, or willingness) do you think you have the most potential to influence? What are some concrete ways you might influence student performance in this regard?

KEY TERMS

10,000 hours: The time some scholars believe it takes to practice a skill and master it

Factual knowledge: Knowledge of isolated facts

Conceptual knowledge: Knowledge of how basic facts work together to form principles and theories

Procedural knowledge: Knowledge related to specific skills and how to perform various behaviors

Metacognitive knowledge: Knowledge of learning strategies and an understanding of one's own strengths and weaknesses when using these strategies

Elaboration: Thinking deeply about course material by adding details to what is being learned, clarifying ideas in a lesson, highlighting relationships between concepts, or connecting new information to material already learned

Learning: Acquiring knowledge and skills and having them readily available from memory

Capacity: Anything inside people that gives them the ability to perform well (e.g., intelligence, self-control)

Opportunity: External forces that either inhibit or enable performance

Willingness: Motivation to perform a behavior

REFERENCES

Anderson, L. W., & Krathwohl, D. R. (Eds.) (2001). *A taxonomy for learning, teaching, and assessing: A revision of Bloom's taxonomy of educational objectives: Abridged edition.* New York, NY: Addison Wesley Longman.

Andrews, J. C. (1988). Motivation, ability, and opportunity to process information: Conceptual and experimental manipulation issues. *Advances in Consumer Research, 15,* 219–225.

Blumberg, M., & Pringle, C. D. (1982). The missing opportunity in organizational research: Some implications for a theory of work performance. *The Academy of Management Review, 7,* 560–569. doi:10.5465/AMR.1982.4285240

Bolkan, S., Goodboy, A. K., & Kelsey, D. (2016). Instructor clarity and student motivation: Academic performance as a product of students' ability and motivation to process instructional material. *Communication Education, 65,* 129–148. doi:10.1080/03634523.2015.1079329

Brown, P. C., Roediger, H. L. III, & McDaniel, M. A. (2014). *Make it stick: The science of successful learning.* Cambridge, MA: Harvard University Press.

Cavanaugh, J. K., & Jacquemin, S. J., (2015). A large sample comparison of grade based student learning outcomes in online vs. face-to-face courses. *Online Learning Journal, 19,* 1–8.

Chaiken, S., Liberman, A., & Eagly, A. H. (1989). Hueristic and systematic information processing within and beyond the persuasion context. In J. S. Uleman & J. A. Bargh (Eds.), *Unintended thought* (pp. 212–252). New York, NY: Guilford Press.

Conard, M. A. (2006). Aptitude is not enough: How personality and behavior predict academic performance. *Journal of Research in Personality, 40,* 339–346. doi:10.1016/j.jrp.2004.10.003

Coyle, T. R., & Pillow, D. R. (2008). SAT and ACT predict college GPA after removing g. *Intelligence, 36,* 719–729. doi:10.1016/j.intell.2008.05.001

Craik, F. I. M., & Lockhart, R. S. (1972). Levels of processing: A framework for memory research. *Journal of Verbal Learning and Verbal Behavior, 11,* 671–684. doi:10.1016/S0022-5371(72)80001-X

Dornisch, M., Sperling, R. A., & Zeruth, J. A. (2011). The effects of levels of elaboration on learners' strategic processing of text. *Instructional Science, 39,* 1–26. doi:10.1007/s11251-009-9111-z

Duckworth, A., & Gross, J. J. (2014). Self-control and grit: Related but separable determinant of success. *Current Directions in Psychological Science, 23,* 319–325. doi:10.1177/0963721414541462

Duckworth, A. L., & Seligman, M. E. P. (2005). Self-discipline outdoes IQ in predicting academic performance of adolescents. *Psychological Science, 16,* 939–944. doi:10.1111/j.1467-9280.2005.01641.x

Eagly, A. H., & Chaiken, S. (1993). *The psychology of attitudes.* Belmont, CA: Wadsworth.

Ericsson, K. A., Krampe, R. T., & Tesch-Romer, C. (1993). The role of deliberate practice in the acquisition of expert performance. *Psychological Review, 100,* 363–406. doi:10.1037/0033-295X.100.3.363

Fisher, C. D. (1993). Boredom at work: A neglected concept. *Human Relations, 46,* 395–417. doi:10.1177/001872679304600305

Gladwell, M. (2008). *Outliers: The story of success.* New York, NY: Little, Brown and Company.

Goetz, T., Frenzel, A. C., Pekrun, R., Hall, N. C., & Ludtke, O. (2007). Between- and within-domain relations of students' academic emotions. *Journal of Educational Psychology, 99,* 715–733. doi:10.1037/0022-0663.99.4.715

Goetz, T., & Hall, N. C. (2014). Academic boredom. In R. Pekrun, & L. Linnenbrink-Garcia (Eds.), *International handbook of emotions in education* (pp. 311–330). New York, NY: Routledge.

Keller, J. M. (1987). Development and use of the ARCS model of instructional design. *Journal of Instructional Development, 10,* 2–10. doi:10.1007/BF02905780

King, A. (1992). Facilitating elaborative learning through guided student-generated questioning. *Educational Psychologist, 27,* 111–126. doi:10.1207/s15326985ep2701_8

Kochanska, G., & Knaack, A. (2003). Effortful control as a personality characteristic of young children: Antecedents, correlates, and consequences. *Journal of Personality, 71,* 1087–1112. doi:10.1111/1467-6494.7106008

Kool, W., McGuire, J. T., Wang, G. J., & Botvinick, M. M. (2013). Neural and behavioral evidence for an intrinsic cost of self-control. *PLos ONE, 8,* e72626. doi:10.1371/journal.pone.0072626

Larson, R. W., & Richards, M. H. (1991). Boredom in the middle school years: Blaming schools versus blaming students. *American Journal of Education, 99,* 418–433. doi:10.1086/443992

Levin, J. R. (1988). Elaboration-based learning strategies: Powerful theory = powerful application. *Contemporary Educational Psychology, 13,* 191–205. doi:10.1016/0361-476X(88)90020-3

Ma, J., Han, X., Yang, J., & Cheng, J. (2015). Examining the necessary condition for engagement in an online learning environment based on learning analytics approach: The role of the instructor. *Internet and Higher Education, 24,* 26–34. doi:10.1016/j.iheduc.2014.09.005

Macnamara, B. N., Hambrick, D. Z., & Oswald, F. L. (2014). Deliberate practice and performance in music, games, sports, education, and professions: A meta-analysis. *Psychological Science, 25,* 1608–1618. doi:10.1177/0956797614535810

Mann, S., & Robinson, A. (2009). Boredom in the lecture theatre: An investigation into the contributors, moderators and outcomes of boredom amongst university students. *British Educational Research Journal, 35,* 243–258. doi:10.1080/01411920802042911

Means, B., Toyoma, Y., Murphy, R., & Bakia, M. (2013). The effectiveness of online and blended learning: A meta-analysis of the empirical literature. *Teachers College Record, 115,* 1–47.

Moffitt, T. E., Arseneault, L., Belsky, D., Dickson, N., Hancox, R. J., Harrington, H., Caspi, A. (2011). A gradient of childhood self-control predicts health, wealth, and public safety. *Proceedings of the National Academy of Sciences of the United States of America, 108,* 2693–2698. doi:10.1073/pnas.1010076108

Nett, U. E., Goetz, T., & Hall, N. C. (2011). Coping with boredom in school: An experience sampling perspective. *Contemporary Educational Psychology, 36,* 49–59. doi:10.1016/j.cedpsych.2010.10.003

Noftle, E. E., & Robins, R. W. (2007). Personality predictors of academic outcomes: Big five correlates of GPA and SAT scores. *Personality Processes and Individual Differences, 93,* 116–130. doi:10.1037/0022-3514.93.1.116

Pekrun, R., Goetz, T., Daniels, L. M., & Stupinsky, R. H. (2010). Boredom in achievement settings: Exploring control-value antecedents and performance outcomes of a neglected emotion. *Journal of Educational Psychology, 102,* 531–549. doi:10.1037/a0019243

Petty, R. E., & Cacioppo, J. T. (1986). The elaboration likelihood model of persuasion. In L. Berkowitz (Ed.), *Advances in experimental social psychology* (pp. 123–205). San Diego, CA: Academic Press.

Pressley, M., McDaniel, M. A., Turnure, J. E., Wood, E., & Ahmad, M. (1987). Generation and precision of elaboration: Effects on intentional and incidental learning. *Journal of Experimental Psychology, 13,* 291–300. doi:10.1037/0278-7393.13.2.291

Robbins, S. B., Allen, J., Casillas, A. Peterson, C. H., & Le, H. (2006). Unraveling the differential effects of motivational and skills, social, and self-management measures from traditional predictors of college outcomes. *Journal of Educational Psychology, 98,* 598–616. doi:10.1037/0022-0663.98.3.598

Tangney, J. P., Baumeister, R. F., & Boone, A. L. (2004). High self-control predicts good adjustment, less pathology, better grades, and interpersonal success. *Journal of Personality, 72,* 271–324. doi:10.1111/j.0022-3506.2004.00263.x

Additional References

Portions of this chapter have appeared in some of my journal articles including:

Bolkan, S., Goodboy, A. K., & Kelsey, D. (2016). Instructor clarity and student motivation: Academic performance as a product of students' ability and motivation to process instructional material. *Communication Education, 65,* 129–148. doi:10.1080/03634523.2015.1079329

Bolkan, S., & Griffin, D. J. (in press). Students' use of cell phones in class for off-task behaviors: The indirect impact of instructors' teaching behaviors through boredom and students' attitudes. Manuscript in press in *Communication Education.*

SECTION I

Capacity

This is it! You have reached the first section of the book, and it is dedicated to students' capacities to do well in school. In this section we will talk about three ideas: students' self-control, their achievement goal orientations, and what you might want to avoid as a teacher so that you do not inhibit student learning. Self-control represents students' capacities to engage in desirable behaviors (and to avoid undesirable behaviors), and achievement goals reflect students' beliefs about their ability to do well in school. We will cover each idea in turn and then discuss what you can do as a teacher to make sure you do not behave in ways that reduce students' capacities to do well in your classrooms.

TWO

Self-Control

OBJECTIVES

By the end of this chapter, you should be a changed person in the following ways:

1. You should be able to define self-control
2. You should know why people do not exert self-control at all times
3. You should be able to articulate how self-control contributes to students' academic success
4. You should be able to explain various methods for enhancing students' self-control
5. You should be able to do at least five pull-ups (Let's get fit and smart at the same time!)

Self-Control

In this chapter, I am going to talk about self-control in an attempt to help you understand what it is, how it works to influence students' educational outcomes, and what we can do as teachers to help facilitate its development in our students. Hopefully, by the end of this chapter you will have a better understanding of how self-control manifests itself in our lives and just how important it is to students' academic experiences. However, before we get into too much detail about self-control and its impact on students' academic achievement, I want to ask you a question about riding bicycles to help you understand the importance of control in our everyday lives. Are you ready to do it? Let's do it . . .

Imagine I gave you a bicycle and asked you to ride it on one condition. The condition is that you will not be able to control the bicycle as you pedal down the street. Instead of the bicycle being under your personal control, imagine I told you that it will be under the control of the environmental conditions under which you ride it. That is, the bike is going to ride differently (and perhaps even crash) depending on the weather, the road conditions, the people around you, the time of day, your emotions, and the emotions of others. Imagine I told you that there may be other factors in play as well—but at this point, we can't be sure which ones will matter. If you want to ride this bicycle, you have to agree to the idea that you have no say in the way it gets ridden, where it goes, and even if it stays upright or not. With all of these factors weighing in your decision, would you decide to ride my bike?

If you are like most people, you would probably decline my offer. Riding a bike is hard enough as it is without the added problems that come with not being able to dictate how it behaves. In fact, a bike like the one I just described would be downright dangerous and bad for your well-being. Most of us would never consent to such an unpredictable experience. Instead, when we get onto a bike, I am sure that the majority of us prefer to have its control squarely in our own hands. I know I do.

If controlling your experience on a bicycle is important to your well-being, then how much more important would you consider your ability to control your life's outcomes? Maybe controlling your life's outcomes is too strong a notion, but how much more important is it to be able to control your behaviors in pursuit of the outcomes you desire? I bet most of you would answer "very important." The majority of us want to be in charge of our own destinies, and being able to control our personal experiences is a lot better than being at the whims of outside forces. In fact, being free from the imposition of external forces is considered to be one of our fundamental human needs (Deci & Ryan, 2000).

Okay, so being in control is important. That said, who controls you? If you said you do, then the next question I have to ask is whether or not you do a good job controlling yourself. Ask yourself these questions: Do you floss every day? What about exercising, do you exercise at least 30 minutes a day? Have you ever spent money on something you didn't need when you knew you should have saved it instead? Have you ever cheated on a diet or perhaps even a lover? Ever eaten junk food or indulged in one too many alcoholic beverages? Hmmm . . . if you are in control, and if you know you should behave in a certain manner, then why do you avoid doing the things you know you should be doing and indulge in the things you know you should not? Even if the foregoing examples are not ones you can relate to, I am sure there have been times in your life when you acted in a manner that directly contradicted a long-term goal you had for yourself. So, why did you do that?

Depending on your answers to the questions just posed, you might start to realize that sometimes we behave in ways that are not necessarily in line with our long-term best interests. How can that be? Why is it that your current self might have reason to be upset with your past self? Why can't you simply do the things that are good for you and avoid the things that are not? The answer to these questions may be due, at least in part, to a lack of self-control. When tempted to behave in ways that you know are not aligned with your long-term personal goals, it is self-control that allows you to pursue the most appropriate alternative. Self-control allows you to take a step back from the forces of your temporary, rudimentary desires and make decisions that are in line with what a successful life looks like for a human being living in a modern world.

In case you think I am overstating the point, let me back up the importance of self-control with results from a study conducted by Terrie Moffitt and her colleagues (2011). These researchers followed more than 1,000 children from birth for approximately 32 years to trace the impact of self-control on their lives. Moffitt's goal was to examine how self-control influenced people's health, wealth, and criminal history over and above important variables such as intelligence and social class. To make a long story short, results from this research project showed that levels of childhood self-control ultimately predicted people's well-being as adults. Specifically, individuals who scored higher in measures of self-control as children enjoyed better health as adults including better respiratory, cardiovascular, dental, and sexual health. Moreover, individuals who had low self-control as children had a higher risk of developing substance dependence as adults. In addition, children's levels of self-control predicted whether or not they would raise their own children in one- or two-parent homes. Self-control was found to predict financial difficulties and credit problems into adulthood as well. As if that were not enough, Moffitt and colleagues also reported that compared to children with high self-control, when grown up, "children with poor self-control were more likely to be convicted of a criminal offense, even after accounting for social class origins and IQ" (p. 2696).

These results seem pretty convincing to me. The more self-control you have, the better your life's outcomes. And it is not just that people with high self-control do better in a few arenas of life compared with people who have low self-control. No, people with high self-control seem to enjoy benefits across a broad range of life's outcomes. The research team of Tangney, Baumeister, and Boone (2004) agree about the importance of self-control and claim that "the human capacity to exert self-control is arguably one of the most powerful and beneficial adaptations of the human psyche" (p. 272). In support of this assertion, Tangney et al. demonstrated that self-control is an important predictor of outcomes ranging from self-esteem, to alcohol abuse, to successful interpersonal relationships. In fact, self-control is so pervasive that Denise de Ridder's research team (2012) argues it influences behaviors in all aspects of our lives from consuming potato chips to sexual infidelity. Who knew self-control was so important?! Turns out researchers Baumeister, Gailliot, DeWall, and Oaten (2006) did; these researchers claim that the capacity for self-control is "one of the most important elements of personality" if not "the single most important aspect" (p. 1796). Wow.

Okay, hopefully by now you agree that self-control is an important component of living a successful life. But, this is a book about teaching students. That said, considering the extensiveness of the benefits linked to self-control, it should be no surprise to learn that it is also an important predictor of academic performance. Thus, the more we know about self-control and how we might influence it in our classrooms, the more we will be able to facilitate our students' success.

What is Self-Control?

What is self-control? Depending on whom you ask, you are likely to get a different answer; self-control is described in a variety of ways by various scholars. For example, an examination of the literature referencing the concept reveals that descriptions of self-control can include terms such as self-discipline, self-regulation, volition, and the delay of gratification (Duckworth & Seligman, 2006). However, it is important to note that these terms are often used interchangeably and likely refer to a general underlying temperament (Duckworth & Seligman, 2006) related to a person's level of conscientiousness (Costa & McCrae, 1995; Costa, McCrae, & Dye, 1991) stemming from the executive function of the brain located in the dorsolateral prefrontal cortex (Kool, McGuire, Wang, & Botvinick, 2013). In English? Self-control stems from your genetic makeup (this is why this chapter is housed under the category of "capacity" in our COWs framework) and is often called by different names in different areas of research. Despite the variety of names often given to the idea, I use the terms self-control or self-discipline in this chapter to maintain consistency.

Okay, so again, what is self-control? Self-control is a person's "capacity to alter or override dominant response tendencies and to regulate behavior, thoughts and emotions" (de Ridder et al., 2012, p. 77). This definition is similar to the one Tangney et al. (2004) proposed, which is "the ability to override or change one's inner responses, as well as to interrupt undesired behavioral tendencies and refrain from acting on them" (p. 275). According to Duckworth and Gross (2014), self-control "entails aligning actions with any valued goal despite momentarily more-alluring alternatives" (p. 319). If you understand these complementary definitions, you understand what self-control looks like in your life. It looks like you working out when you would rather sit and watch TV. It looks like you saying "no" to the second helping of cookies instead of indulging yourself with just one more. And it looks like you saving your money in the short term so you can have it for important purchases that might need to be made in the future. According to researchers, the ability to do what you should and avoid everything else is at the heart of what it means to be self-controlled.

There are at least two places from which self-control might stem. The first place self-control can stem from is your genetic makeup, and the second includes your personal goals. We'll tackle each of these in turn. However, to explain these ideas I first have to break some bad news to you. Are you ready for it? Here it is: When it comes to using our minds, you (and I) are inherently lazy. Shocker, right?

I know it sounds cynical, but plenty of smart scientists believe that you and I and everyone else on this planet are cognitive misers or lazy thinkers (for example, see Kahneman, 2011; Stanovich, 2009). Maybe I am being too harsh with my choice of the word "lazy" when I describe our unwillingness to engage in cognitive processing. Maybe a better way to frame our inherent mental laziness is to say that we tend to be conservative with our mental energy. As Kool and his colleagues (2010) put it, when it comes to thinking, people tend to follow what is called *the law of less work* where "actions are taken so as to minimize demands for exertion" (Kool, McGuire, Rosen, & Botvinick, 2010, p. 665). This is because expending mental effort leads to experiences of subjective costs (Kool et al., 2010) and, as a result, people try to minimize their labor if at all possible.

Why is cognitive demand costly? Wouldn't it be beneficial for us to be thinking deeply about all of life's experiences? Wouldn't we be better off if we found cognitive labor to be easy and used our mental resources at full capacity at all times? Not really. In fact, some researchers claim that experiencing cognitive labor as costly is, ultimately, adaptive. This might be the case for two reasons. First, our mental capacity is highly limited, which means that cognitive demands in one arena restrict our ability to simultaneously think deeply about other activities (Kool & Botvinick, 2014). Consequently, if we engage in leisure during one endeavor, we can reserve our mental abilities for other situations that may be more important. Second, detaching from deep thinking may be beneficial because of its ability to redirect our attention. According to researchers Kool and Botvinick, avoiding deep thinking may result in a wandering mind that is likely to be exploratory and creative which may allow individuals to prevent a narrow-minded focus on potentially suboptimal behaviors.

Interestingly, not all people experience the costs of mental effort in the same manner. According to Kool and colleagues (2013), because of their genetic makeup, some individuals happen to be less sensitive to the costs of employing their brains' executive function. And who are these lucky individuals? These individuals are people who score high on self-control. Essentially, compared with people who score low, people who score high on measures of self-control are more likely to choose to engage in tasks that require cognitive effort because they do not experience these activities being as costly as people with low self-control. That said, the conclusion we might come to from the foregoing information is that the first "source" of self-control stems from individual differences in people's experiences of mental costs, which are ultimately based on differences in their genetic makeup.

I just made the case that people are cognitive misers, and then I mentioned that some people may be less miserly than others. I also mentioned that these individuals may be more likely to engage in self-control because it is not experienced as negatively as it may be for other individuals. Good for the lucky ones, right? But, what about the rest of us? Are we doomed to be cognitive misers at all times? Do most people really avoid thinking deeply throughout the entirety of their life's experiences? Of course not. Although most of us have a strong predilection for being cognitive misers, people do not choose mental relaxation at all times. Instead, people often choose to relax their minds when the incentives are not large enough to offset the costs (Kool & Botvinick, 2014; Kool et al., 2010; Kool et al., 2013). Stated differently, people can become motivated to use their brains to think deeply.

Having said the above, the second "source" of self-control is a focus on higher-order goals. That is to say, people can protect themselves from the allure of immediate environmental temptations if they can incentivize themselves with long-term goals to which they are dedicated (Duckworth & Gross, 2014). In their book, *Out of Character*, authors David DeSteno and Piercarlo Valdesolo (2011) reference this notion and argue that the "good" decisions we make on a daily basis are usually made by contrasting the short-term benefits of a behavior against the benefits we might experience in the long run if we behave differently. Michael Inzlicht, Lisa Legault, and Rimma Teper (2014) agree about the importance of setting goals for guiding behavior. In fact, their model of self-control *begins* with a person setting goals to which he or she is committed. As far as these scholars are concerned, people must have goals to strive toward if they are ever to be expected to marshal efforts to engage in self-control. This idea might sound familiar: If you have ever dieted in order to fit into a swimsuit for an upcoming trip, then you know the incentivizing power of long-term goals. Similarly, if you ever trained hard for an upcoming athletic event or worked hard for an upcoming professional deadline, then you have experienced the importance of goal setting for guiding behavior as well.

Okay, so what have we learned so far? Having read the information just presented, we know that self-control refers to making yourself do what you are supposed to do and avoiding doing what you are not supposed to do. We also know that we need self-control in order to live successful lives; those of us who are self-controlled tend to do better than those of us who are not. Finally, we learned that self-control can stem from our genetic makeup and from having long-term goals that incentivize our behavior. So, how does all of this relate to our students' learning? We'll cover that next. In the following sections, we will talk about how self-control operates in educational settings, and we'll discuss how students who marshal self-control may enjoy academic benefits that their less self-controlled classmates do not. Finally, we'll talk about what you can do as an instructor, if anything, to help improve your students' self-control in your classrooms.

Self-Control in Academic Settings

Of course, the focus of this book is on academic achievement. So one question we might ask is, does self-control lead to better academic results? As you might reasonably predict, self-control has indeed been shown to significantly influence students' academic success. Two researchers, Angela Duckworth and Martin Seligman (2005), have been champions of this idea and their research shows just how important self-control can be in academic settings. For example, in one investigation, these scholars studied eighth grade students to test how self-control predicted their academic outcomes. In this study, the authors measured students' self-control and looked for relationships between this variable and various academic outcomes including attendance, report card grades, achievement test scores, and high-school admissions. What were the results? Let's let Duckworth and Seligman tell you: compared with less self-controlled students, those who were more self-controlled "earned higher GPAs and achievement test scores, were more likely to gain admission to a selective high school, had fewer school absences, spent more time on their homework, watched less television, and started their homework earlier in the day" (p. 941).

Now, you might be thinking that at least some of these results actually reflect differences in students' levels of intelligence. In other words, perhaps the self-controlled students did better because they were simply smarter than the less self-controlled students, and it is really intelligence that drives better academic outcomes. If you were thinking that intelligence could be driving these effects then you will be happy to know that so were Duckworth and Seligman. In an effort to test this assumption, these researchers also measured students' IQs to control for its influence on their results. And what did they find? They found that self-discipline was more strongly associated with students' academic outcomes than was students' intelligence. As a result, the authors concluded that "self-discipline has a bigger effect on academic performance than does intellectual talent" (p. 943).

Importantly, Duckworth and Seligman are not the only ones to demonstrate that self-control influences students' academic performance above and beyond their intelligence; other researchers have come to the same conclusion. For example, researchers have shown that self-control is positively related to students' exam performance, scores on course papers, and homework grades even after accounting for the influence of students' cognitive abilities (i.e., ACT scores; Corker, Oswald, & Donnellan, 2012). Similarly, researchers have shown that, after controlling for students' academic abilities (i.e., ACT and SAT scores), self-control still has a positive influence on students' overall college grade point averages (Conard, 2006; Noftle & Robins, 2007; Robbins, Allen, Casillas, Peterson, & Le, 2006).

At this point, you might be wondering why self-controlled students are able to outperform their less-disciplined peers. Perhaps the best answer is that they can avoid distractions. In school, these are aplenty and include social pressures outside of class such as parents, friends, and organized activities. Because of these potential disruptions, Boekaerts and Corno (2005) argued that an important aspect of student success involves students' ability to direct their own learning and to "protect concentration and directed effort in the face of personal and/or environmental distractions" (Corno, 1993, p. 16). Thus, to be successful in school, students need to marshal the self-control necessary to persist toward academic pursuits in the face of situations that might otherwise tempt them to engage in less fruitful endeavors. These behaviors might include completing homework when students could be watching TV, going to class when students would rather go to the beach, and studying for tests early instead of putting it off until the last minute. These choices may add up over the course of an entire academic term and might combine to create favorable outcomes because of their cumulative effects. Therefore, students who are highly self-controlled are likely to engage in behaviors that, over the long run, result in their academic success.

In addition to the long-term benefits of self-control, another reason self-control may be beneficial for academic achievement is that it helps students avoid distractions inside of class on a short-term basis as well. In particular, students with high levels of self-control are able to focus their mental efforts on learning despite the lack of environmental incentives for doing so (Bolkan, Goodboy, & Myers, in press). This is important because, unfortunately, not all teachers deliver their course lessons in ways that incentivize their students to pay attention to, and think deeply about, their course lessons (e.g., they may be boring or unclear, etc.). That said, students who are self-controlled are likely to perform better under these undesirable learning circumstances because, compared with their less self-controlled peers, they don't need as much external motivation to engage their minds in their learning activities. Stated differently, self-controlled students are individuals who are likely to pay attention to course lessons regardless of whether or not their teachers create an atmosphere that attracts their attention (Bolkan et al., in press). Thus, because paying attention to instructional material is an important predictor of student learning (Wei, Wang, & Klausner, 2012), in addition to the long-term benefits they enjoy, self-controlled students are likely to experience an academic advantage on a short-term basis as well.

Can You Help Students Exercise Self-Control?

At this point, we need to tackle the question of whether or not you, as an instructor, can help students develop their self-control. In response to this question, some people might say "nope." And why not? Because, as de Ridder et al. (2012) put it, "dispositional self-control is assumed to be relatively stable across situations and over time" (p. 77). Other researchers agree and argue that self-control is related to people's genetic disposition, making it a trait-like personality characteristic (Kochanska & Knaack, 2003; Tangney et al., 2004). If this is the best explanation for the origin of self-control, then there might not be much we can do to about it: Changing someone's ability to engage in self-control may be akin to changing their intelligence or height . . . it is not going to happen.

Or is it? Despite the fact that many of our traits stem from inborn genetic characteristics, you might be surprised to learn that these personal qualities are still open to influence from the outside environment. In his book discussing various behavioral outcomes associated with human evolutionary psychology, Robert Wright (1994) likens this notion to genetic "knobs" that get tuned by the environment. Wright argues that although some of these knobs may be more fixed than others, most of us have some room for adjustment (up or down) within our genetic potential. Researchers who study human behavioral genetics agree and argue that although "all psychological traits are heritable" (Bouchard, 2004, p. 148), "no traits are 100% heritable" (Plomin, DeFries, Knopik, & Neiderhiser, 2016, p. 5). Therefore, even if self-control is an important part of a person's personality, like other aspects of a person's genetic potential, it likely waxes and wanes in relation to environmental constraints and opportunities (Baumeister et al., 2006). The good news for us is that we can be a part of that environment.

Alerting and self-consequating

So, what can we do to help students develop self-control? There might be several ways to do this. First, we might consider letting students know about the importance of self-control. If students are aware of the benefits associated with exercising self-control in academic settings, they may be more likely to behave in ways that lead to success. Stated differently, alerting students to the importance of self-control may be beneficial insofar as it might influence the attention they pay to their various alternatives when facing important decisions in academic contexts. Cleary and Zimmerman (2004) support this assertion and argue that an important part of helping students do well in academic settings involves teaching them to monitor their use of appropriate and inappropriate study strategies so they come to recognize the impact they have on the learning process.

After alerting students about the importance of self-control, we can move on to teach them strategies for improving this aspect of their educational experience. For example, according to Elstad (2008), one strategy for increasing self-control includes self-consequating. That is, students might be able to develop better self-control if they can learn to place rewards or punishments on themselves for enacting (or failing to enact) a behavior. If you have ever withheld a dessert from yourself at dinner as a consequence of not exercising that day, then you have self-consequated. Alternatively, if you have ever rewarded yourself with three margaritas for a day of hard work then you have also self-consequated. In academic settings, self-consequating might include making a night out with friends contingent upon getting an important assignment done on time. Similarly, self-consequating may involve allowing one's self to enjoy a television show if a course project is completed ahead of schedule. Simply stated, by teaching students about self-consequating, we might introduce them to a method of incentivizing positive academic choices and de-incentivizing less productive alternatives.

Self-binding

Another strategy we might teach students is self-binding. According to Elstad (2008), self-binding involves eliminating alternatives to avoid engaging with these regardless of your desire. Most of us self-bind on a regular basis. For example, this weekend while at the grocery store, I refused to buy tortilla chips. Did I refuse to buy tortilla chips because I dislike them? Quite the contrary—I refrained from buying tortilla chips because of how much I love them! Here's the problem: I know that if I buy chips they will be gone within hours. I literally cannot stop myself from binge-eating tortilla chips even though I know it is not a good idea to eat a whole bag of chips in one sitting. As a consequence, the only way to stop myself from demolishing an entire bag of chips in less than a day is to make sure I cannot put any chips into my mouth in the first place. It's sad, but it's true.

The same principle of self-binding can be taught to our students. For instance, we can tell our students that it is important for them to think twice about studying with a friend if they know they tend to have fun together instead of working. We might also advise our students to leave their cellular telephones out of reach when attempting to read or study for class. If students cannot check their phones, they cannot be distracted by these devices as they attempt to study.

Similarly, we might tell students about the problems associated with using computers in class. For example, in a study of students' on-task behaviors, James Kraushaar and David Novak (2010) discovered what most teachers have known for some time: individuals who attempt to take class notes on their computers often engage in off-task and distracting activities (e.g., surfing the Internet, communicating with friends, looking up pictures of cool toads and frogs, etc.). Perhaps not surprisingly, the researchers found that students who were the most distracted also tended to have the lowest academic performance. Interestingly, it is not just students using the computers who suffer. In addition to the personal detriments, researchers have found that students who engage in off-task behaviors on their computers also distract their peers (who can see their computer screens) and therefore disrupt others' learning as well (Sana, Weston, & Cepeda, 2013).

In addition to being off task, another problem associated with using computers in the classroom is that students who take notes on computers tend to get distracted from meaningful learning by concentrating on recording their teachers' words perfectly instead of engaging with their lessons (Mueller & Oppenheimer, 2014). This can be a problem because students who try to write their notes verbatim reduce their ability to paraphrase their course lessons and are less likely to record class information in ways that are personally meaningful. Stated differently, by taking notes verbatim, students are less likely to elaborate on, and think deeply about, course content. Thus, because of the problems associated with using computers in class, we might ask our students to consider taking class notes like their forefathers did: with good old-fashioned pencils and paper, or feather quills and papyrus. By teaching students about the benefits of self-binding in this fashion, we might help them avoid indulging in unproductive behaviors and ensure they are on track to reaching their goals.

Having said the above, we know that self-binding is a tactic we can teach students to help them exercise self-control. But what about forcing our students to self-bind? Although you might be happy knowing that you can recommend self-binding to students, can you make them self-bind in your courses? For example, can you force students to leave their computers and cell phones in their backpacks when they come to class? My response to you is this: You are the teacher, right? Do whatever you want. In fact, researchers Baker, Lusk, and Neuhauser (2012) found that students agree with this sentiment; when it comes to policies regarding the use of electronic devices in class, students think these should be determined solely by the instructor. Simply put, if you want students to put these devices away, you should make this a course policy. That said, you should know that if you have rules in your courses, students tend to prefer that these are not arbitrary (Kearney, Plax, Hays, & Ivey, 1991), are included in the syllabus, and are discussed in class (Baker et al., 2012). Thus, clearly stating your rules at the beginning of your course, acknowledging students' desire to engage in the preferred behaviors, and telling students the reasoning behind your decisions should help them accept the rules and see value in your course policies. Moreover, doing these things should also help students internalize their desire for self-control instead of making the decision to avoid distractions seem 100% teacher directed (Deci, Eghari, Patrick, & Leone, 1994). Ultimately, if students are able to see compassion and reasoning behind the policies you enact for their self-binding, they may be more likely to respect and follow the rules you set for them in your classrooms.

Cue avoidance

Cue avoidance is another strategy Elstad (2008) promotes to enhance self-control. Put simply, people who use this strategy do not get started with small distractions because they know these can lead to bigger ones. This phenomenon is one I used to experience all too often. In the past, when working on a lecture or writing up a study, I would see an e-mail notification pop up on my screen, and even though I was deep in thought and working on an important task, I would usually click on the e-mail to read its content. Despite intending to only read one e-mail and get back to work, I would often find myself surfing the Internet after reading a few messages and getting distracted.

The trick with cue avoidance is to not get started on small distractions in the first place. In the case of my example, I have learned to keep my e-mail software closed while concentrating on an important topic. Of course, we can teach the same tactic to our students. We can tell them about the importance of avoiding small distractions and other small commitments of time if they know these things are likely to lead to bigger distractions. For example, students may benefit from being told that turning a cell phone on silent when studying, not checking e-mail for a certain period of time when writing, and shutting the door while reading are all ways to avoid small distractions that are likely to lead to bigger issues.

Self-consequating, self-binding, and cue avoidance are only three of the many tactics we might use to help students enhance their ability to exercise self-control; other strategies exist as well. For instance, according to Elstad (2008), other strategies that we might teach to students to help bolster their self-control include goal-oriented self-talk (e.g., telling one's self "you can do this" or to "stay focused"), attention management (e.g., sitting in the front of the classroom to avoid distractions), and transcending (e.g., looking at the long-term value of a stimulus if the short-term value is lacking). It is the idea of transcending and looking to the long-term value of a stimulus that we turn to next.

Long-term goals

As I alluded to earlier in this chapter, students might be able to marshal self-control if they can focus on long-term academic goals. This is equivalent to your being able to diet in order to look good for the summer or being able to save money when you have a goal of buying a new car. If students can commit to goals that are aligned with their academic success, they might be able to power through short-term temptations by focusing on these desired long-term outcomes.

Just how important are goals for exercising self-control? They are so important that Inzlicht et al. (2014) argue they are "the first step in establishing and improving self-control" (p. 303). According to Inzlicht and his colleagues, setting goals basically involves committing to an idea of the future that is different from what you experience in the present. Setting goals is important because having them allows you to plan your behaviors in ways that lead to specific end results. In other words, goals are essential to guiding meaningful human behavior because they help you prioritize beneficial actions and decisions over those that are less beneficial (Locke & Latham, 2006). Stated differently, goals help you stay focused.

Most of us have had goals for our futures, and I think we understand that these goals ultimately drive our subsequent decisions and actions. Take me, for example: After I had finished my Ph.D., I wanted to teach at a good school on the West Coast. To do that, I worked hard in my first job to earn high teaching evaluations and to publish several studies to make my academic resume attractive. Going back a few steps, when I was in college, my goal was to earn a Ph.D. To make this happen, I worked hard to get the best grades I could as an undergraduate and applied to master's programs that would help me make the transition to a good Ph.D. program. Going back another step, when I was in high school, my goal was to attend a good college. This goal helped me to stay focused on earning a good GPA and helped me study to do my best on the SAT. I think you get the point, and hopefully these illustrations make sense because if we go back much farther than this my goals start to fall apart. It's not that I didn't have any goals prior to this, but the goals I had for myself at a young age seem strange when I reflect on them. For example, when I was a little boy and my mom asked me what I wanted to be when I grew up, I told her that I wanted to be a monkey. So far, my childhood dream has yet to come true. Anyway, the point I am trying to make here is that in order to get to where you are going, you first need to know where you are headed. The same is true for your students. If your students have long-term goals for success, you might find that they are able to marshal self-control to help them behave in ways that allow them to reach these goals.

Having said that, I must point out that although it would be nice for students to have long-term goals for academic success when they sign up for your courses, it is important that you help them develop these goals when they are with you in class. In essence, you need to know that you can be a big part of your students' goal-setting activities. And, importantly, the kinds of goals that students strive toward matter as well. Locke and Latham (2006) noted this when they mentioned that one of the factors differentiating people who make progress toward their goals from people who do not is the importance of these goals. As may seem obvious, people tend to work harder toward goals they find important compared with those they do not.

So what goals seem to be the most important to people? Well, compared with extrinsic goals, scholars argue that the most important goals are those that are considered intrinsic. Intrinsic goals are goals that are linked to personal growth and self-fulfillment, whereas extrinsic goals are those linked to some type of endorsement or approval from others (Kasser & Ryan, 1996). Examples of intrinsic goals include self-acceptance, good relationships with friends and family, goodwill toward one's community, and being in good health. Extrinsic goals include financial success, social recognition, and having an appealing appearance (Kasser & Ryan, 2001). So why does the pursuit of different goals matter? The content of people's goals matters because, compared with people who pursue extrinsic goals, people who pursue goals that are intrinsic are more likely to have meaningful experiences that satisfy their psychological needs (Kasser & Ryan, 2001) and lead to greater personal well-being, self-esteem, psychological adjustment, vitality, and lower personal distress (Kasser & Ryan, 1993, 1996, 2001). Moreover, as it pertains to classroom experiences, Maarten Vansteenkiste and colleagues have consistently found that compared with extrinsic goal framing (e.g., showing how learning will lead to financial benefits or approval from others), intrinsic goal framing (e.g., showing how learning might allow students to help others or contribute to their communities) leads to better outcomes for students including more autonomous motivation, enhanced conceptual learning, more task involvement, and increased persistence (e.g., Vansteenkiste, Simons, Lens, Sheldon, & Deci, 2004; Vansteenkiste, Simons, Lens, Soenens, & Matos, 2005; Vansteenkiste, Soenens, Verstuyf, & Lens, 2009; Vansteenkiste, Timmermans, Lens, Soenens, & Van den Broek, 2008). Importantly, these positive results occur for students regardless of their stated goal preferences. That is, linking learning tasks to intrinsic goals is beneficial even for those students who generally report extrinsic goals as being more important to them (Vansteenkiste et al., 2008).

Content relevance

In the previous section, we learned that the types of goals students strive toward matter. Knowing this, the next question you might ask is "how do we help our students develop goals in our courses?" One answer is through the provision of content relevance. If you have ever sat through a lecture or presentation that you felt had no bearing on your life, then you know just how important relevance can be. Relevance links information you are learning to your personal interests, and material that lacks this quality tends to be hard to engage with. In the classroom, relevance is defined as students' perceptions regarding whether or not course material satisfies personal goals or is linked to valued personal outcomes (Frymier & Houser, 1998). In other words, content relevance answers the question "why do we have to do/study this?" (Keller, 1987). Importantly, if students don't see how the information they are being asked to learn is relevant to their lives, it becomes harder for them to get motivated to study the content in their courses. On the other hand, when instructors demonstrate the relevance of their class lessons, they positively influence students' perceptions that their classes are interesting and valuable (Frymier & Shulman, 1995). In support of this contention, researchers have demonstrated that compared with students who do not, students who perceive their course material to be relevant tend to enjoy their academic endeavors more and experience more intrinsic motivation as well (Deci et al., 1994; Frymier & Shulman, 1995; Frymier, Shulman, & Houser, 1996; Kember et al., 2008).

Having said the above, you should know that one of your jobs as an instructor is to help students see the relevance of their course lessons by demonstrating how the information they are learning can be of value to their lives. There are a variety of ways to do this. Some strategies for enhancing relevance include relating information to students' experiences (e.g., relating course information to students' lives or interests), explicitly stating the value of learning the material, addressing the future usefulness of the material, and showing how other people have used the information to meet their own goals in the past (Keller, 1987; Muddiman & Frymier, 2009). In addition, relevance can be enhanced by showing students how to apply theory in a practical manner and by linking content to local and current events (Kember, Ho, & Hong, 2008). Whatever method you choose for communicating relevance, the idea is to help students see how the information they learn in class can be linked to goals that matter in their lives.

Remember what I mentioned earlier, however; when you make information relevant to students, the goals you use to make information relevant matter too. Specifically, you may experience better results in the classroom if you focus on intrinsic goal framing (e.g., personal growth) as opposed to extrinsic goal framing (e.g., financial success). Examples of intrinsic goals you might relate to your lessons include helping your students: develop a sense of self-fulfillment, explain the world around them, understand other people's perspectives, develop personal competence, gain control over their life's outcomes, become informed/knowledgeable citizens, develop successful career trajectories, and experience a sense of accomplishment/self-confidence. Examples of extrinsic goals you might want to avoid include: being admired by others, simply passing a test or the class, becoming financially successful, and getting good grades for the sake of impressing others. The takeaway from this section is that linking course content to students' goals matters, but linking your content to the right types of goals matters too.

Summary

We covered a lot in this chapter. First, we started with the importance of self-control, and we learned that people who have the ability to exercise self-control in their lives tend to experience superior outcomes compared with people who do not. We also learned that people tend not to exercise self-control all of the time because it is effortful to do so. However, we mentioned that, as a teacher, there are a variety of ways to help your students engage in self-control. These include helping students with self-consequating, self-binding, cue avoidance, and developing long-term goals that should direct their behavior. We mentioned that this can be done by helping students see the relevance of your course lessons and, in particular, by linking these lessons to students' intrinsic goals. As it pertains to educational outcomes, having intrinsic goals can help direct students' behaviors toward activities that lead to success as opposed to more tempting activities that do not (e.g., studying for a test instead of watching TV). Moreover, in the classroom, goals may incentivize effortful thinking and direct students' attention to learning course concepts instead of engaging in distracted behaviors such as daydreaming, talking to classmates, or looking at their phones.

Think back to the question I asked you at the beginning of this chapter about riding a bike that was out of your control. Most of you probably said that you would not ride a bike like that if given the choice. You probably wouldn't let your students ride a bike like that either. And why not? Because you understand that without being in control of the ride, being on a bicycle can be a threat to your students' physical well-being. Similar to the bicycle analogy then, it should be clear that helping your students take control of their educational outcomes is important if you are to help them protect their academic well-being.

Ultimately, the point of this chapter is that students' self-control is an important component of their educational achievement. This is so much the case that several scientists argue it can predict students' academic accomplishment over and above indicators of their intelligence. Crucially, although self-control is based, in part, on genetic factors, as teachers we have the ability to help students marshal this resource to increase their potential for success in our classrooms.

END-OF-CHAPTER QUESTIONS

1. As you learned in this chapter, there are a variety of ways to influence self-control. Which one of these methods do you think has the potential to be the most useful for you, personally? What about for your students?

2. You learned that self-control is an important predictor of student success. Can you think of various ways in which self-control (or perhaps a lack thereof) has influenced your academic outcomes? How has self-control influenced other outcomes in your life?

3. You learned that self-control is a function of a person's genetic makeup. How much of an impact do you think you can really make on students' self-control? Do you think your own self-control can be influenced by various environmental conditions?

KEY TERMS

Self-control: A person's capacity to alter or override dominant response tendencies and to regulate behavior, thoughts, and emotions

Cognitive miser: The idea that people tend not to want to exert mental energy without good reason

Law of less work: People tend to gravitate toward actions that minimize cognitive exertion

Alerting: Helping students understand the importance of self-control

Self-consequating: Placing rewards or punishments on one's self for enacting (or failing to enact) a behavior

Self-binding: Eliminating alternatives, making it impossible to engage with alternatives regardless of your desire

Cue avoidance: Avoiding small distractions so they do not lead to bigger ones

Content relevance: Helping students understand the answer to the question "what's in it for me?"

REFERENCES

Baker, W. M., Lusk, E. J., & Neuhauser, K. L. (2012). On the use of cell phones and other electronic devices in the classroom: Evidence from a survey of faculty and students. *Journal of Education for Business, 87,* 275–289. doi:10.1080/08832323.2011.622814

Baumeister, R. F., Gailliot, M., DeWall, N., & Oaten, M. (2006). Self-regulation and personality: How interventions increase regulatory success, and how depletion moderates the effects of traits on behavior. *Journal of Personality, 74,* 1773–1802. doi:10.1111/j.1467-6494.2006.00428.x

Boekaerts, M., & Corno, L. (2005). Self-regulation in the classroom: A perspective on assessment and intervention. *Applied Psychology: An International Review, 54,* 199–231. doi:10.1111/j.1464-0597.2005.00205.x

Bolkan, S., Goodboy, A. K., & Myers, S. A. (in press). Conditional processes of effective instructor communication and increases in students' cognitive learning. Manuscript in press in *Communication Education.*

Bouchard, T. J. Jr. (2004). Genetic influence on human psychological traits: A survey. *Current Directions in Psychological Science, 13,* 148–151. doi:10.1111/j.0963-7214.2004.00295.x

Cleary, T. J., & Zimmerman, B. J. (2004). Self-regulation empowerment program: A school-based program to enhance self-regulated and self-motivated cycles of student learning. *Psychology in the Schools, 41,* 537–550. doi:10.1002/pits.10177

Conard, M. A. (2006). Aptitude is not enough: How personality and behavior predict academic performance. *Journal of Research in Personality, 40,* 339–346. doi:10.1016/j.jrp.2004.10.003

Corker, K. S., Oswald, F. L., & Donnellan, M. B. (2012). Conscientiousness in the classroom: A process explanation. *Journal of Personality, 80,* 995–1028. doi:10.1111/j.1467-6494.2011.00750.x

Corno, L. (1993). The best-laid plans: Modern conceptions of volition and educational research. *Educational Researcher, 22,* 14–22. doi:10.3102/0013189X022002014

Costa, P. T., Jr., & McCrae, R. R. (1995). Domains and facets: Hierarchical personality assessment using the revised NEO personality inventory. *Journal of Personality Assessment, 64,* 21–50. doi:10.1207/s15327752jpa6401_2

Costa, P. T., Jr., McCrae, R. R., & Dye, D. A. (1991). Facet scales for agreeableness and conscientiousness: A revision of the NEO personality inventory. *Personality and Individual Differences, 12,* 887–898. doi:10.1016/0191-8869(91)90177-D

Deci, E. L., Eghari, H., Patrick, B. C., & Leone, D. R. (1994). Facilitating internalization: The self-determination theory perspective. *Journal of Personality, 62,* 119–142. doi:10.1111/j.1467-6494.1994.tb00797.x

Deci, E. L., & Ryan, R. M. (2000). The "what" and "why" of goal pursuits: Human needs and the self-determination of behavior. *Psychological Inquiry, 11,* 227–268. doi:10.1207=S15327965PLI1104_01

de Ridder, D. T. D., Lensvelt-Mulders, G., Finkenauer, C., Stok, F. M., & Baumeister, R. F. (2012). Taking stock of self-control: A meta-analysis of how trait self-control relates to a wide range of behaviors. *Personality and Social Psychology Review, 16,* 76–99. doi:10.1177/1088868311418749

DeSteno, D., & Valdesolo, P. (2011). *Out of character: Surprising truths about the liar, cheat, sinner (and saint) lurking in all of us.* New York, NY: Crown Archetype.

Duckworth, A. L., & Gross, J. J. (2014). Self-control and grit: Related but separable determinant of success. *Current Directions in Psychological Science, 23,* 319–325. doi:10.1177/0963721414541462

Duckworth, A. L., & Seligman, M. E. P. (2005). Self-discipline outdoes IQ in predicting academic performance of adolescents. *Psychological Science, 16,* 939–944. doi:10.1111/j.1467-9280.2005.01641.x

Duckworth, A. L., & Seligman, M. E. P. (2006). Self-discipline gives girls the edge: Gender in self-discipline, grades, and achievement test scores. *Journal of Educational Psychology, 98,* 198–208. doi:10.1037/0022-0663.98.1.198

Elstad, E. (2008). Building self-discipline to promote learning: Students' volitional strategies to navigate the demands of schooling. *Learning Inquiry, 2,* 53–71. doi:10.1007/s11519-008-0027-3

Frymier, A. B., & Houser, M. L. (1998). Does making content relevant make a difference in learning? *Communication Research Reports, 15,* 121–129. doi:10.1080/08824099809362106

Frymier, A. B., & Shulman, G. M. (1995). "What's in it for me?": Increasing content relevance to enhance students' motivation. *Communication Education, 44,* 40–50. doi:10.1080/03634529509378996

Frymier, A. B., Shulman, G. M., & Houser, M. (1996). The development of a learner empowerment measure. *Communication Education, 45,* 181–199. doi:10.1080/03634529609379048

Inzlicht, M., Legault, L., & Teper, R. (2014). Exploring the mechanisms of self-control improvement. *Current Directions in Psychological Science, 23,* 302–307. doi:10.1177/0963721414534256

Kahneman, D. (2011). *Thinking, fast and slow.* New York, NY: Farrar, Straus, and Giroux.

Kasser, T., & Ryan, R. M. (1993). A dark side of the American dream: Correlates of financial success as a central life aspiration. *Journal of Personality and Social Psychology, 65,* 410–422. doi:10.1037/0022-3514.65.2.410

Kasser, T., & Ryan, R. M. (1996). Further examining the American dream: Differential correlates of intrinsic and extrinsic goals. *Personality and Social Psychology Bulletin, 22,* 280–287. doi:10.1177/0146167296223006

Kasser, T., & Ryan, R. M. (2001). Be careful what you wish for: Optimal functioning and the relative attainment of intrinsic and extrinsic goals. In P. Schmuck & S. M. Kennon (Eds.), *Life goals and well-being: Towards a positive psychology of human striving* (pp. 116–131). Ashland, OH: Hogrefe & Huber.

Kearney, P., Plax, T. G., Hays, L. R., & Ivey, M. J. (1991). College teacher misbehaviors: What students don't like about what teachers say or do. *Communication Quarterly, 39,* 309–324. doi:10.1080/01463379109369808

Keller, J. M. (1987). Development and use of the ARCS model of instructional design. *Journal of Instructional Development, 10,* 2–10. doi:10.1007/BF02905780

Kember, D., Ho, A., & Hong, C. (2008). The importance of establishing relevance in motivating student learning. *Active Learning in Higher Education, 9,* 249–263. doi:10.1177/1469787408095849

Kochanska, G., & Knaack, A. (2003). Effortful control as a personality characteristic of young children: Antecedents, correlates, and consequences. *Journal of Personality, 71,* 1087–1112. doi:10.1111/1467-6494.7106008

Kool, W., & Botvinick, M. (2014). A labor/leisure tradeoff in cognitive control. *Journal of Experimental Psychology: General, 143,* 131–141. doi:10.1037/a0031048

Kool, W., McGuire, J. T., Rosen, Z. B., & Botvinick, M. M. (2010). Decision making and the avoidance of cognitive demand. *Journal of Experimental Psychology: General, 139,* 665–682. doi:10.1037/a0020198

Kool, W., McGuire, J. T., Wang, G. J., & Botvinick, M. M. (2013). Neural and behavioral evidence for an intrinsic cost of self-control. *PLos ONE, 8,* e72626. doi:10.1371/journal.pone.0072626

Kraushaar, J. M., & Novak, D. C. (2010). Examining the effects of student multitasking with laptops during the lecture. *Journal of Information Systems Education, 21,* 241–251.

Locke, E. A., & Latham, G. P. (2006). New directions in goal-setting theory. *Current Directions in Psychological Science, 15,* 265–268. doi:10.1111/j.1467-8721.2006.00449.x

Moffitt, T. E., Arseneault, L., Belsky, D., Dickson, N., Hancox, R. J., . . . Caspi, A. (2011). A gradient of childhood self-control predicts health, wealth, and public safety. *Proceedings of the National Academy of Sciences of the United States of America, 108,* 2693–2698. doi:10.1073/pnas.1010076108

Muddiman, A., & Frymier, A. B. (2009). What is relevant? Student perceptions of relevance strategies in college classrooms. *Communication Studies, 60,* 130–146. doi:10.1080/10510970902834866

Mueller, P. A., & Oppenheimer, D. M. (2014). The pen is mightier than the keyboard: Advantages of longhand over laptop note taking. *Psychological Science, 25,* 1159–1168. doi:10.1177/0956797614524581

Noftle, E. E., & Robins, R. W. (2007). Personality predictors of academic outcomes: Big five correlates of GPA and SAT scores. *Personality Processes and Individual Differences, 93,* 116–130. doi:10.1037/0022-3514.93.1.116

Plomin, R., DeFries, J. C., Knopik, V. S., & Neiderhiser, J. M. (2016). Top 10 replicated findings from behavioral genetics. *Perspectives on Psychological Science, 11,* 3–23. doi:10.1177/1745691615617439

Robbins, S. B., Allen, J., Casillas, A., Peterson, C. H., & Le, H. (2006). Unraveling the differential effects of motivational and skills, social, and self-management measures from traditional predictors of college outcomes. *Journal of Educational Psychology, 98,* 598–616. doi:10.1037/0022-0663.98.3.598

Sana, F., Weston, T., & Cepeda, N. J. (2013). Laptop multitasking hinders classroom learning for both users and nearby peers. *Computers & Education, 62,* 24–31. doi:10.1016/j.compedu.2012.10.003

Stanovich, K. E. (2009). *What intelligence tests miss: The psychology of rational thought.* New Haven, CT: Yale University Press.

Tangney, J. P., Baumeister, R. F., & Boone, A. L. (2004). High self-control predicts good adjustment, less pathology, better grades, and interpersonal success. *Journal of Personality, 72,* 271–324. doi:10.1111/j.0022-3506.2004.00263.x

Vansteenkiste, M., Simons, J., Lens, W., Sheldon, K. M., & Deci, E. L. (2004). Motivating learning, performance, and persistence: The synergistic effects of intrinsic goal contents and autonomy-supportive contexts. *Journal of Personality and Social Psychology, 87,* 246–260. doi:10.1037/0022-3514.87.2.246

Vansteenkiste, M., Simons, J., Lens, W., Soenens, B., & Matos, L. (2005). Examining the motivational impact of intrinsic versus extrinsic goal framing and autonomy-supportive versus internally controlling communication style on early adolescents' academic achievement. *Child Development, 76,* 483–501. doi:10.1111/j.1467-8624.2005.00858.x

Vansteenkiste, M., Soenens, B., Verstuyf, J., & Lens, W. (2009). 'What is the usefulness of your schoolwork?' The differential effects of intrinsic and extrinsic goal framing on optimal learning. *Theory and Research in Education, 7,* 155–163. doi:10.1177/1477878509104320

Vansteenkiste, M., Timmermans, T., Lens, W., Soenens, B., & Van den Broek, A. (2008). Does extrinsic goal framing enhance extrinsic goal-oriented individuals' learning and performance? An experimental test of the match perspective versus self-determination theory. *Journal of Educational Psychology, 100,* 387–397. doi:10.1037/0022-0663.100.2.387

Wei, F. F., Wang, Y. K., & Klausner, M. (2012). Rethinking college students' self-regulation and sustained attention: Does text messaging during class influence cognitive learning? *Communication Education, 61,* 185–204. doi:10.1080/03634523.2012.672755

Wright, R. (1994). *The moral animal: Why we are the way we are: The new science of evolutionary psychology.* New York, NY: Vintage Books.

THREE

Achievement Orientation

OBJECTIVES

By the end of this chapter, you should be a changed person in the following ways:

1. You should be able to articulate the difference between mastery and performance orientations
2. You should be able to articulate the difference between approach and avoidance orientations
3. You should be able to define self-efficacy and response efficacy and relate these to both mastery approach and normative performance approach orientations
4. You should be able to explain the difference between entity theories of intelligence and incremental theories of intelligence
5. You should be able to answer the following question: A bat and a ball cost $1.10 together. The bat costs $1 more than the ball. How much does the bat cost? (Hint: you might have to really think about this one!)

Achievement Orientation

Fall is one of my favorite seasons of the year. Perhaps surprisingly, I don't love fall because of the changing colors of the trees or because of the holidays that are fast approaching. Instead, the reason I love fall is because it is the start of college football season. As such, it always brings back good memories of my time at the University of Texas at Austin, and it also gives me an excuse to visit my friends, drink a few beers, and shout at strangers on the TV. The nice part about being an adult who grew up watching football is that, when I watch college games, I can usually follow along with the action without thinking too much about what's happening. Because I understand how football works, I can relax when watching the games instead of straining to figure out what's going on. For example, when I watch college football, I know who is on offense because I can see how the players are lined up and who has possession of the ball when the play starts. I also know why the quarterback might hand the ball off to a running back, and I understand why the offensive linemen try to push the defensive players backward while the defensive players try to push the offensive linemen the other way. Generally speaking, the game makes sense to me, and I can follow the individual plays as they relate to the overall offensive and defensive strategies of both teams.

Football is not the only sport where this works; knowing the point of soccer allows me to follow this game pretty easily as well. In fact, soccer is pretty much the same thing as football except you cannot use your hands. Moreover, there is less contact, and the play doesn't stop as frequently. Also, everyone plays both offense and defense. Okay, so soccer is a lot different from football. Still, because I am familiar with the sport, I know that the reason players pass the ball to their teammates is because they are usually trying to develop a play that will allow them to get near their opponent's goal for a chance at scoring. On the other hand, when players are on defense, I know that they usually try to stop the other team from getting near their goal. Much of what I am writing is probably pretty obvious to you if you are familiar with these sports. I bet many of you have played soccer or football at some point in your lives and, even if you have not, I am sure that almost all of you have watched at least part of one of these games at some point in the past. Because you are familiar with these sports, following along with the run of play is easy to do.

Having said the above, what happens when you watch sports you are unfamiliar with? Is it just as easy to follow along with what happens in these games? If you ask me, I would say that it is not. For instance, when I visited England a while ago I remember my buddy introduced me to the game of cricket. For whatever reason, I had a hard time grasping the individual rules and the goal of the game altogether. In fact, to this day I have no idea how the game works. The best I can figure out is that a guy launches a ball at another guy who proceeds to try to whack it in whatever direction he sees fit. After that, I have no idea what happens... I have no clue how teams score points, how teams figure out when to switch from offense to defense, and I don't know how anybody decides when the game is over or determines who has actually won the match—in fact, I have been told that cricket games can last (literally) for days on end. How can that be?!

So, what is the difference between my experiences watching football, soccer, and cricket? Why do the sports of football and soccer make sense to me, while cricket does not? Simply put, the difference is that I know what the point of the game is when it comes to football and soccer and when it comes to cricket, I do not. Ultimately, understanding the goal of the game being played is what allows me to follow the action. In fact, if you think about it, if you were asked to explain how *any* game works, you would probably start with describing its goal as a way of framing everything that follows, wouldn't you? For instance, what is the goal of football? Of course, the goal is to try to score points by getting the ball into your opponents' end zone or by kicking a field goal all the while stopping them from doing the same to you. Once you know this, it becomes easier to understand why the offensive players try to push the defensemen backward and why the defense tries to push the offense in the opposite direction. Why do players try to get the ball near their opponents' goal in soccer? They do this because the way you win in soccer is to get the ball to cross your opponents' goal line more often than the opposing team can do the same to you. What about cricket? What is the goal in cricket? Again, I have no idea. And because I do not know what the goal is, I cannot follow the action or understand why the people playing the game do the things they do.

Again, knowing the objective of a sport helps you understand what is going on in the field of play. This is because the overarching goals of each game end up influencing the way the play unfolds including the teams' general strategies and the players' individual behaviors. The reason I bring this all up in a book about teaching is because just as teams have goals that shape their subsequent strategies and behaviors, your students also have goals that drive their academic decisions. And, just as knowing what goals teams have for winning games might help you understand their decisions and behaviors, knowing your students' goals might help you understand a host of their academic choices.

In reality, just like people playing sports, the goals students adopt for their academic achievement end up influencing a variety of their behaviors in school ranging from their pursuit of challenging work to their willingness to exert extra effort in the face of failure or personal setbacks. Thus, knowing how goals work to influence students' educational outcomes is important for understanding why students do the things they do in your classrooms. Moreover, knowing the various goals toward which students strive will also provide you with some insight regarding which ones you should help them adopt. Understanding what goals students might embrace when it comes to pursuing academic achievement and knowing how to help students pursue the right ones will ultimately allow you to help your students change their behavioral, cognitive, and emotional patterns in ways that have been shown to lead to success.

The Achievement Orientations

When it comes to students' goals for learning, researcher Carole Ames (1992) suggests that students can, generally speaking, pursue their academic endeavors in one of two ways: with a mastery goal orientation or with a performance goal orientation. A mastery orientation is reflected in students' beliefs that their efforts can influence their academic outcomes, and mastery goal-oriented students tend to try their best to develop new skills, understand their course lessons, improve their competence, and achieve a level of expertise with respect to the material they are learning (Ames, 1992). For mastery–oriented individuals, effort leads to competence (Dweck & Leggett, 1988). Therefore, these students focus on making progress, seek challenges to enhance their learning, are willing to risk failure to master their tasks, and, when they fail, interpret setbacks as providing information for personal improvement (Dweck, 1986).

On the other hand, students who adopt performance goal orientations tend to concentrate on how schoolwork reflects on their abilities as individuals. These students concentrate on being recognized by others, doing better than their peers, and are most satisfied when they can achieve success without having to put forth much effort (Ames, 1992). For performance-oriented individuals, expending effort is a sign of incompetence (they believe that people who are smart should not have to work hard), and thus these students often seek easy tasks (as opposed to challenging ones) that allow them to show off their abilities. Moreover, performance-oriented students experience failure as a threat to their self-esteem and respond to these situations in maladaptive and helpless ways. Specifically, students who are motivated by performance goals tend to interpret failures as indicating a lack of ability and, as a result, tend to avoid or withdraw from challenge (to avoid further damaging their self-esteem) and give up in the face of setbacks (Dweck, 1986).

After reading the last two paragraphs you should be aware of the differences in students' goal orientations and how these differences manifest themselves in students' academic decisions. In summary, students who embrace performance goals are interested in looking smart, whereas students who pursue mastery goals are interested in becoming smart. Stated differently, performance-oriented students are interested in proving themselves, whereas mastery-oriented students are interested in improving themselves (Dweck & Leggett, 1988).

Although the mastery/performance dichotomy reflects the original framing of students' achievement goal orientations, there has been a call to study these ideas with more specificity by further splitting mastery and performance goals by students' desire to approach or avoid these outcomes. As a result, scholars consider there to be (at least) four achievement goal orientations that guide students' behaviors in their classes, these include: a mastery approach orientation, a mastery avoidance orientation, a performance approach orientation, and a performance avoidance orientation.

A *mastery approach* goal orientation reflects students' pursuit of understanding, learning, and challenge and is related to a high need for achievement and autonomous motivation/self-determination (Elliot & McGregor, 2001; Hulleman, Schrager, Bodmann, & Harackiewicz, 2010). A *mastery avoidance* goal orientation, on the other hand, refers to students whose goals are to avoid incompetence, mistakes, and misunderstanding, and is usually driven by worry and a fear of failure (Elliot & McGregor, 2001). A *performance approach* orientation reflects students whose goal in academic contexts is to try to either: (1) show off their abilities to others (i.e., wanting to appear competent to others), or (2) outperform others (i.e., performing better than others in class; Grant & Dweck, 2003; Hulleman et al., 2010). Performance approach goal orientations tend to be related to both a need for achievement and a fear of failure (Elliot & McGregor, 2001). Finally, *performance avoidance* goal orientations reflect students' efforts to avoid looking like they have limited ability or doing worse than others in class (e.g., failing; Elliot & McGregor, 2001). Like some of the other goals, performance avoidance is also driven by a fear of failure (Elliot & McGregor, 2001). Although we might also label students as *work-avoidant* (where people try to avoid work and effort) representing a fifth type of achievement goal orientation (Pintrich, 2000a), most researchers tend to focus on the four goal orientations characterized by the mastery/performance and approach/avoidance categories.

Now that you know about students' goal orientations, you might be wondering which ones are the most beneficial in your classrooms. Let me help make this clear: In general, students' academic outcomes tend to be enhanced when they adopt approach orientations and suffer when they adopt avoidance orientations (Hulleman et al., 2010; Van Yperen, Blaga, & Postmes, 2014). As a result, we might conclude that mastery and performance approach goals lead to beneficial academic outcomes, whereas mastery and performance avoidance goals do not. However, as noted earlier, performance approach orientations can be split into the two sub-goals of showing off and outperforming others. That said, researchers have shown that performance approach goals where students are concerned with creating the appearance of competence and showing off their abilities (i.e., an *ability* performance approach orientation) tend to be negatively associated with academic outcomes, whereas performance approach goals where students are concerned with outperforming others (i.e., a *normative* performance approach orientation) are positively associated with academic outcomes (Hulleman et al., 2010; Van Yperen et al., 2014). Consequently, based on the information presented above we may conclude that students tend to perform better in their academic environments when (1) they are mastery approach goal–oriented and when (2) they are performance approach–oriented to outperform others.

Now that you know what the various goal orientations are, and which two you want to promote, you might be wondering *how* and *why* the mastery approach and normative performance approach orientations are related positively to students' academic outcomes. As far as the how part is concerned, the benefits of these two types of goal orientations likely stem from their ability to get students autonomously motivated to perform well in their classes. Although I discuss this notion more fully in the chapter on self-determination (Chapter 8), for now I will just say that students who are mastery approach– and normative performance approach–oriented might ultimately be driven to success because they enjoy the learning process and/or because they link their performance to a desired personal outcome or value. This is in contrast to mastery avoidance, performance avoidance, and ability-focused performance approach goal orientations which have been linked to a fear of failure and approval from others (Elliot & McGregor, 2001; Hulleman et al., 2010). As you might have noticed, the difference between these goals is similar to the intrinsic/extrinsic dichotomy related to long-term goals and relevance that we went over in the chapter on self-control (Chapter 2). Thus, as researchers Richard Ryan and Edward Deci (2000) would predict, mastery avoidance, performance avoidance, and ability-focused performance approach goal orientations likely to lead to extrinsic or controlled/pressured motivation. Conversely, when students are focused on a drive toward mastery or performing better than others, they are likely to be intrinsically/autonomously motivated.

So, why is this important? It is important because researchers have shown that, compared with students who are motivated in a controlled fashion, students who are motivated in an autonomous manner are more likely to approach their studies in ways that result in increased academic achievement including, for example, thinking deeply about their course lessons and challenging themselves in the classroom (for a review, see Deci & Ryan, 2000; Guay, Ratelle, & Chanal, 2008). In other words, compared with students who are controlled, students who are autonomously motivated tend to be more likely to behave in ways that lead to academic success. Similarly, students who are mastery approach oriented and who are normative approach oriented tend to behave in ways that produce positive results in school as well.

Specifically, as it pertains to a mastery approach goal orientation, researchers have found that students who pursue this goal are likely to deeply process their course material, which leads to greater conceptual learning (Elliot & McGregor, 2001; Grant & Dweck, 2003). In addition, mastery approach goals are related positively to perceptions of higher task value and interest in course material (Pintrich, 2000b), which may influence students' motivation to study the information in their courses. Moreover, Carol Dweck and her colleagues argue that one of the most important benefits of a mastery orientation occurs when people experience failure. According to Dweck and Leggett (1988), people who are mastery-oriented enjoy challenges and are willing to sustain their efforts in the face of setbacks. In particular, these individuals see setbacks as opportunities to learn, engage in self-instruction, and redouble their efforts.

Results from Grant and Dweck's (2003) study support these conclusions insofar as mastery approach goal orientations were associated with active coping, planning, and the positive interpretation of setbacks following academic failures. In other words, following a failure, individuals with mastery approach orientations were less likely to behave in ways that reflected denial and behavioral or mental disengagement. Grant and Dweck argue that these positive reactions to academic setbacks occur because people with mastery approach orientations tend to blame a lack of effort for their negative outcomes and, as such, see the path to success as flowing through increased labor (e.g., "If I try harder, I can be more successful"). These authors argue that mastery approach goals are beneficial in academic contexts because they help students interpret failures as positive experiences that provide information regarding how to improve and therefore help preserve students' motivation in the face of various obstacles.

As it pertains to normative performance approach orientations, these goal orientations are related positively to students' academic outcomes as well. How does this work? Well, you already know that students who endorse these goals tend to be described as people who seek to outperform others. And, although this notion might conjure up images of uber-competitive students fighting each other for rank, Hulleman et al. (2010) note that a normative performance approach orientation might be better conceptualized as reflecting students' striving for performance that meets or exceeds some challenging objective standard. That said, because they strive for a high level of achievement that reflects doing well (not just looking good), these students might devote resources toward learning strategies that result in superior academic outcomes (Seaton, Parker, Marsh, Craven, & Yeung, 2014) and may be unlikely to give up when they experience academic setbacks (Grant & Dweck, 2003). If you have ever wanted to be the best at something and devoted extra energy to make sure you performed to your potential, then you know that the desire for superior performance can become a self-fulfilling prophesy.

Facilitating the "Good" Achievement Orientations

Based on the preceding information, we know that, as teachers, our efforts are best spent guiding students toward mastery approach goals or normative performance approach goals. That said, our next job should be to figure out the best way to do this. As I stated earlier, one of the reasons mastery-oriented students are able to achieve success is because they react to academic challenges in adaptive ways (Burnette, O'Boyle, VanEpps, Pollack, & Finkel, 2013; Grant & Dweck, 2003; Lou & Noels, 2016). This is because they see these as opportunities to develop their potential (Dweck, 1986). Similarly, students who are normative performance approach oriented and who set high standards for their success may also work hard to achieve their goals when faced with assorted academic challenges (Grant & Dweck, 2003). Thus, by focusing our efforts on helping students react adaptively in the face of academic obstacles, we might be able to get them to behave in ways that align with mastery approach and normative approach goal orientations.

Ultimately, we might think of academic challenges as opportunities for students to exhibit self-protective behaviors in the face of academically threatening situations. And, if we can agree that academic challenges in school represent potential threats to students' educational well-being, we can use the theory of *protection motivation* (Maddux & Rogers, 1983; Rogers, 1983) to help us predict and control whether or not students subsequently engage in adaptive or maladaptive behaviors. To put it differently, if we can agree to think of academic challenges as potential threats to students' scholastic success, we can use protection motivation theory to learn how we can help students overcome these obstacles (i.e., engaging in effortful persistence, Dweck, 1986) as opposed to giving up or withdrawing their efforts.

According to protection motivation theory, when people experience threats to their well-being they can either react adaptively by taking care of the threat, or maladaptively by avoiding the threat. Proponents of protection motivation theory argue that two variables known to influence the direction this reaction include individuals' perceptions of response efficacy and self-efficacy. Response efficacy refers to the effectiveness of a behavior for reducing a threat, and self-efficacy refers to a person's perception that he or she can engage in the behaviors necessary to reduce the threat. Essentially, when faced with a challenging decision, the more a person believes that he or she can engage in adaptive behaviors (i.e., self-efficacy) and the more he or she believes that adaptive behaviors will lead to desired results (i.e., response efficacy), the more likely he or she will be to engage in these behaviors.

Let me see if I can help make sense of these definitions by using an example. Imagine you and I are hiking in the woods and come across a grizzly bear. Imagine that, instead of being friendly and cuddly, it looks menacing, has its sights fixed on us, and is out for blood; if we do nothing, the bear is going to attack and possibly harm us. As we look at each other and see our lives flash before our eyes, I want you to imagine I told you that the best way to make sure the bear does not harm us is for *you* to stab it in the heart as it charges us. Imagine I hand you a two-foot long Bowie knife and tell you that when it charges, you should let me run away to safety and when the bear turns to you, you should let the bear fall on you and you should use its weight to sink the knife into its heart.

What do you think about that plan? Would you do it? Would you even try? I know I would not. And why not? Because I don't think that I could do what is being asked. You want me to patiently wait for the bear to charge me and jump on top of me with claws and fangs and hair and eyes while I hold the knife perfectly straight aimed at its heart? Not going to happen. As this example demonstrates, when a person does not believe that he or she can do what is being recommended to remove a threat, that person is not likely to engage in the recommended behavior: this is the idea of self-efficacy.

Okay, so what if instead of stabbing the bear, I told you that in order to fight this beast *you* need to pick up a small stick, point it at the bear, and sing Sisqo's *Thong Song* to the best of your vocal ability. Imagine I told you that this is the only way to save both of our lives. Is this plan any better? Based on what I just said, would you do what I recommended? My guess is that you would probably not. And why not? Because, although you *can* do what I am recommending, you know that pointing a stick at a bear and singing the *Thong Song* is not going to stop it from harming us. If you don't think that a plan will work, you are not likely to try it: this is the idea of response efficacy.

Generally speaking, the more a person believes that he or she can enact the plan (self-efficacy), and the more a person believes that a plan will work (response efficacy), the more likely he or she is to try to do what is being recommended. And the same thing is true for your students. That is, when faced with academic challenges, the more students believe they can affect their academic outcomes through effort and the more they believe they have the ability to be successful in school, the more likely they should be to behave in ways that align with mastery and normative performance approach goal orientations. If this is true, the next thing we need to do is figure out how to help our students come to believe these things. To begin this process, we'll first turn to a discussion of response efficacy.

Response efficacy: Incremental versus entity theorists

Recall from the beginning of this chapter that a mastery goal orientation is reflected in students' believing that their efforts can influence their academic outcomes (Ames, 1992). Thus, I argue that one way for us to bolster people's response efficacy in the face of academic challenges is to get them to endorse this point of view by making the connection between effort and academic success as strong as possible. One way to achieve this is to influence students' implicit theories of intelligence, or mindsets.

According to various scholars, one factor that can influence students' achievement goal orientations is their implicit theories of intelligence (Burnette et al., 2013; Dweck, Chiu, & Hong, 1995; Dweck & Leggett, 1988; Lou & Noels, 2016). Specifically, students can adopt either an entity theory of intelligence or an incremental theory of intelligence. Entity theorists believe that intelligence is fixed, whereas incremental theorists believe that intelligence can be increased through effort and persistence (Blackwell, Trzesniewski, & Dweck, 2007; Dweck, 2010). As these theories pertain to students' goal orientations, Nussbaum and Dweck (2008) note that if people believe intellectual improvement is possible (incremental mindset), they are likely to try to improve upon their failures. On the other hand, if people do not believe that intellectual improvement is possible (entity mindset), they might give up in the face of failures. Essentially, having an incremental theory of intelligence boils down to believing that academic challenges can be overcome with hard work (e.g., studying more will lead to higher achievement). Crucially, researchers have shown that students' beliefs in the modifiability of their deficits are related to their effort expenditure (Ziegler & Stoeger, 2010) and, as I am arguing in this chapter, their adoption of a mastery goal orientation (Burnette et al., 2013).

If we can agree that adopting an incremental theory of intelligence can help students pursue a mastery orientation in their academic endeavors, the next thing we might try to do is determine what we can do as teachers to help students develop this type of mindset. Luckily for us, various researchers have offered some compelling advice. First, according to Dweck (2010), one way to help students develop an incremental mindset is to help them appreciate deep learning as opposed to success that is easily won. Stated differently, Dweck argues that if teachers want to help students develop an incremental mindset, they should emphasize that getting the right answer quickly is not as important as developing a genuine understanding of a topic.

In my classes, I try to do this by telling students that the grades they earn are not nearly as important as the knowledge they take with them into the future. I try to emphasize to my students that their grades and a deep understanding of our course topics are not perfectly correlated and that if they want to feel proud of something, it should be their personal development and not the score they earn on a test. To help students understand my point, I tell them that when they graduate, most people are going to give more weight to what they actually learned in class and know about a subject than to what they scored on their exams. I tell my students that most employers will be more impressed with a student who knows a lot about communication theory, for example, but received a B in my class than a student who simply memorized the terms and forgot them but earned an A in the course. By emphasizing the importance of self-growth over performance and grades, Dweck (2010) would argue that my teaching style helps build students' incremental theories of intelligence.

Second, scholars argue that a simple way to help students develop an incremental mindset is to tell them that they can improve their intelligence, or at least improve upon their learning deficits, if they only put forth the effort to learn. In fact, several experimental manipulations of the phenomenon pretty much do just that (e.g., Lou & Noels, 2016; Nussbaum & Dweck, 2008). Essentially, these experimental manipulations simply explain to students that their intelligence can be increased through hard work and focused effort. Thus, if you can reinforce the idea that students' intelligence is modifiable and not fixed, instead of blaming their abilities for failures, students might come to experience academic setbacks as being amendable through the provision of more effort (Dweck, 1986). With regard to this point, Lou and Noels (2016) argue that it is equally important that *teachers* believe in an incremental theory of intelligence so they can interact with students in a manner that communicates this possibility to their pupils. If they give up on students because they think improvement is impossible, teachers run the risk of communicating this sentiment to students, which might ultimately result in students giving up on themselves (Rattan, Good, & Dweck, 2012).

Third, teachers can also help students develop an incremental theory of intelligence to the extent that they provide feedback that focuses on growth, effort, and persistence in addition to simply providing correct answers (Dweck, 2010). There are several ways for teachers to do this. For example, according to Ames (1992), teachers can reward the process of learning as much as they evaluate the product. One way to do this is to provide grades with an opportunity for improvement (Ames, 1992). For instance, as a student, I have personally had teachers who allowed me to correct my exam mistakes to earn a certain percentage back on my tests. Similarly, I have known teachers who help students develop term papers by grading various writing portions (that are rewritten for future drafts) as students develop toward a final paper.

Moreover, teachers might be able to facilitate incremental theories of intelligence to the extent that they promote individual effort, not just students' ability to perform well on their tests and assignments (Linnenbrink & Pintrich, 2002). That is, instead of taking an absolute measure of excellence, we can help students develop incremental theories of intelligence to the extent that we also recognize their attempts at improvement in our classes. One way teachers can help students understand the importance of effort is by requiring that they demonstrate the steps of their performance, not just the final product. For example, I know that teachers often mandate that students "show their work" as a way of evaluating (and giving credit for) the effort that went into completing an assignment or solving a problem.

The point of each of the tactics noted here is to communicate to students that improvement and development in academia are the result of effort and persistence that stem from the decision students make to work hard in their classes. If students can come to appreciate effortful studying and understand the link between hard work and their academic success, instead of giving up because they do not believe they have the ability to influence their outcomes, they may be more likely to adopt a mastery orientation where they expend extra effort, appreciate challenge, and perceive failures as opportunities for improvement (Romero, Master, Paunesku, Dweck, & Gross, 2014). Research supports this conclusion insofar as scholars have found that after doing poorly, students who hold an incremental theory of intelligence are more likely than those who hold an entity theory to be willing to take a remedial course to shore up their performance (Hong, Chiu, Dweck, Lin, & Wan, 1999), to pay attention to corrective feedback (Mangels, Butterfield, Lamb, Good, & Dweck, 2006; Moser, Schroder, Heeter, Moran, & Lee, 2011), and to try to learn about why they performed poorly (presumably in an attempt to improve) as opposed to attempting to bolster their self-esteem (Nussbaum & Dweck, 2008).

Ultimately, then, one of our jobs as teachers is to help students see that their efforts in class are linked to their outcomes. By helping students develop a sense of response efficacy with respect to their efforts in challenging educational situations, they may be more likely to engage in adaptive behaviors that help them develop their academic potential.

Self-efficacy

In various contexts, people will sometimes say that they have "saved the best for last." In the case of self-efficacy, Albert Bandura might say that this is exactly what I have done here. Bandura is perhaps the scholar most well-known for promoting the importance of self-efficacy in human behavior, and he is so adamant about its importance that he created a theory (social cognitive theory) and wrote a book (*Self-efficacy: The Exercise of Control*) to explain how the concept influences various aspects of our lives. According to Bandura, self-efficacy is one of the most important determinants of human behavior, and for this reason, he might say that focusing on improving students' self-efficacy is one of the best ways for teachers to help build students' academic potential.

So what is self-efficacy? According to Bandura (1997), self-efficacy is the "belief in one's ability to produce desired effects" (p. 32) and is at the heart of what it takes to foster accomplishment in human endeavors. Having self-efficacy essentially equates to believing that you can do something and, as you have probably experienced in your lifetime, the more that you believe you can do something, the more likely you are to try it (depending, of course, on your desire to do the thing in the first place). As Bandura (1998) states, "efficacy belief is a major basis of action. Unless people believe they can produce desired effects by their actions, they have little incentive to act." (p. 624). The same idea is true in academic settings: the more students believe they can do well, the more likely they are to exert effort toward this end (Multon, Brown, & Lent, 1991; Zimmerman, 2000).

The point of discussing self-efficacy here is that, as I argued earlier in the chapter, the more you believe you can do what it takes to succeed in academia, the more likely you are to adopt an achievement goal orientation that aligns with success. In support of this assertion, researchers have shown that students who are high in self-efficacy are more likely than students who are low in self-efficacy to adopt both mastery goals and normative performance approach goals (Diseth, 2011; Hsieh, Sullivan, & Guerra, 2007; Komarraju & Nadler, 2013). Of course, as you recall, these goals are the two we have discussed as being important for academic success. Thus, supporting students' perceptions of their self-efficacy, or their belief that they can be successful in their classes, is likely to lead to goal orientations that prove to be adaptive.

What can we do to help students develop their self-efficacy? According to Bandura (1997), people can build self-efficacy in four ways. Specifically, self-efficacy can be built through *mastery experiences* (i.e., when people experience success), *vicarious experiences* (i.e., when people see others experiencing success), *verbal persuasion* (i.e., when people are told that they can be successful), and *people's interpretations of their physiological states* (i.e., when people feel confident as opposed to anxious when completing a task). That said, if you want to help your students experience a sense of self-efficacy in your classrooms, you might consider adopting any one of these four approaches. Now that you know about the four ways to influence self-efficacy, let's examine some specific things you can do in the classroom to enhance these beliefs.

It is no mistake that students' sense of self-efficacy is related to their prior academic achievement (Middleton & Midgley, 1997); the more people have experienced success in a specific domain in the past, the more likely they should be to expect success in the future. Thus, if you want them to develop their self-efficacy in an academic context, it is important that your students experience success, especially at tasks that are difficult or demanding (Bandura, 1997). Of course, one question that might arise when you read about helping students experience success in challenging situations is how you can make this happen without overwhelming students' capabilities. The answer I have for you is to teach students in steps, or, as Siegle and McCoach (2007) state, you can break up larger goals into smaller, more attainable goals. People do this sort of thing all the time. For example, I did this the other day while running. Although I was on an eight-mile run, I felt exhausted at five miles and wanted to quit—thinking about running another three miles on top of the already grueling five seemed impossible. That said, instead of thinking of the rest of the run in totality, I started thinking about the remainder of the run in half-mile increments. In other words, I told myself to just keep running until I got to mile five and a half to see how I felt then. At mile five and a half, I did the same thing for mile six. After doing this several times, I eventually made it back home. In essence, by breaking up the large task of running an extra three miles into smaller half-mile increments, I was able to focus on smaller, achievable goals that eventually helped me finish my run.

You can do the same thing I did on my run for students who are learning new concepts. That is, by teaching your students one step at a time, they are likely to better understand the lessons they are learning and, as a result, build confidence toward their abilities in your classrooms. For example, this might include asking students to complete and turn in long assignments one section at a time, showing students how to solve multifaceted problems step by step, and explaining to students how various theories work by breaking complex material into specific, manageable content blocks. Of course, in addition to breaking large projects into smaller tasks, there are other ways you can help students experience a sense of mastery as well. These include helping students set periodic goals to document their progress, providing feedback regarding students' growth and accomplishments, and asking students to reflect on what they have learned at various points in your classes (Siegle & McCoach, 2007).

In addition to mastery experiences, you can also help students develop a sense of self-efficacy if they see someone similar to themselves accomplish a desired goal. This is the idea of building self-efficacy through vicarious experience, and it happens all the time with commercials touting self-help. For example, if you have ever seen a "before" and "after" image of a person who lost weight because of a specific diet or workout plan, you have experienced advertisers trying to influence your perception of self-efficacy. The idea in these commercials is both that the plan works (response efficacy) and also that people just like *you* can be successful in enacting the plan (self-efficacy). Similarly, one of the ways to help students increase their self-efficacy is by having models, especially those who are similar to your students, demonstrate the successful enactment of various academic behaviors. For example, you might consider having a student demonstrate how to solve a problem or perform a desired action for his or her classmates. According to Bandura (1997), the successful modeling of desired behaviors helps students gain insight into how something can be done and also builds their self-confidence regarding their ability to do that thing themselves.

The third way to influence students' self-efficacy is through verbal persuasion. According to Bandura (1997), "people who are persuaded verbally that they possess the capabilities to master given tasks are likely to mobilize greater effort and sustain it than if they harbor self-doubts" (p. 101). Thus, teachers can enhance students' self-efficacy beliefs if they provide positive feedback to students regarding their abilities and efforts. As long as it is perceived to be sincere, this type of feedback can ultimately be helpful to students. This might be manifested in class by the framing of constructive feedback. For example, imagine a student scores an 80 on an assignment out of a possible 100 points. As Bandura (1997) argues, the same informative feedback can be delivered to this student while highlighting their progress to date (i.e., their learning associated with an 80%) or the deficits the student still needs to overcome to score a higher grade. According to Bandura, the framework within which the feedback students are given matters insofar as focusing on the student's accomplishment is likely to lead to enhanced perceptions of self-efficacy whereas focusing on the student's deficiencies is not.

The fourth way to help students experience a sense of self-efficacy is through the reduction of negative emotional feedback. This is because, as Bandura (1998) notes, people "interpret their stress reactions and tension as signs of inefficacy" (p. 626). That said, you can help people reinterpret their stress, or you can help them reduce it as methods for helping build students' beliefs in their self-efficacy. For example, to help students build their self-efficacy, you might teach them techniques to help them relax when experiencing anxiety, or you might help them come to understand that experiences of anxiety are normal and to be expected. For instance, when I teach classes on public speaking, I try to help students understand that even people with extensive experience speaking in public feel nervous when they deliver their presentations. I try to help students interpret these feelings as natural, and I try to help them learn how to relax when they speak to their classmates. By helping students reinterpret their emotional reactions to public speaking, my goal is to get them to experience their anxiousness as a natural byproduct of the event instead of a sign of incompetence.

In the end, self-efficacy is an important construct for academic achievement because the more they believe in themselves, the more students should be willing to expend the effort necessary to be successful in school. That said, if we want our students to pursue goal orientations where they work hard to be their best, master the material, and put forth effort to overcome difficulties and setbacks, we should help students develop a positive sense of their personal ability to achieve the goals they set out to accomplish.

Summary

In this chapter, we learned that the goal orientations students adopt in the classroom have important implications for their learning behaviors. Specifically, we learned that students who tend to be the most successful in school are those who adopt mastery goal orientations and normative performance approach orientations. We also learned that two ways to help change students' goal orientations include facilitating their beliefs that effort and academic outcomes are related, and building students' confidence in their abilities to be successful in the first place. These ideas were discussed in reference to students' response efficacy and self-efficacy beliefs and relate to students' willingness to work hard in the face of academic challenges.

As a quick review, you can help build students' response efficacy beliefs if you help them develop an incremental theory of intelligence by emphasizing growth and personal development, by telling them about how intelligence can be modified through hard work, and by changing your evaluation policies to include rewards for effort, persistence, and improvement. When it comes to self-efficacy, you can help students develop a sense of self-confidence to the extent that you help them experience success, see others who are like them experience success, provide positive feedback about their growth, and reinterpret stressful situations in beneficial ways.

In the beginning of this chapter, we discussed how understanding the goals of various sports can help viewers understand the strategies and behaviors of the teams and individuals engaged in sporting contests. The reason I mentioned this idea was to orient you to the notion that students' academic goals also influence a variety of their learning strategies and behaviors. Although it is not possible to change the goals of the sports you watch on TV to change the way the players approach the game, after reading this chapter you should feel confident knowing that it *is* possible for you to change the goals your students adopt in the classroom. And, by doing so, you should feel good knowing that you can help change the way your students approach their studies for the better.

END-OF-CHAPTER QUESTIONS

1. What type of achievement orientation best describes your approach to school? Why do you think you approach your studies in this manner? Do you think your achievement orientation has influenced your academic outcomes in any way?

2. Do you think it is possible for a person to have different achievement orientations for different aspects of their education? For example, do you think it is possible to have completely different orientations for two different classes?

3. Based on what you learned in this chapter, what are some ways you can influence your students' perceptions of self-efficacy in your courses?

KEY TERMS

Mastery approach orientation: A goal orientation that reflects students' pursuit of understanding, learning, and challenge

Mastery avoidance orientation: A goal orientation aimed at avoiding mistakes, the appearance of incompetence, and misunderstanding

Performance approach orientation: A goal students might adopt in academic contexts to try to either (1) create the appearance of competence by showing off their abilities (i.e., an ability performance approach orientation) or (2) outperform others (i.e., a normative performance approach orientation)

Performance avoidance orientation: Students' goal to avoid looking like they have limited ability or doing worse than others in class

Work-avoidant orientation: A student's goal to try to avoid work and effort

Self-efficacy: The belief in one's ability to produce desired effects

Response efficacy: The perceived effectiveness of a behavior for producing desired effects

Entity theory of intelligence: The belief that intelligence is largely fixed

Incremental theory of intelligence: The belief that intelligence can be increased through effort and persistence

REFERENCES

Ames, C. (1992). Classrooms: Goals, structures, and student motivation. *Journal of Educational Psychology, 84,* 261–271. doi:10.1037/0022-0663.84.3.261

Bandura, A. (1997). *Self-efficacy: The exercise of control.* New York, NY: W. H. Freeman and Company.

Bandura, A. (1998). Health promotion from the perspective of social cognitive theory. *Psychology and Health, 13,* 623–649. doi:10.1080/08870449808407422

Blackwell, L. S., Trzesniewski, K. H., & Dweck, C. S. (2007). Implicit theories of intelligence predict achievement across an adolescent transition: A longitudinal study and an intervention. *Child Development, 78,* 246–263. doi:10.1111/j.1467-8624.2007.00995.x

Burnette, J. L., O'Boyle, E. H., VanEpps, E. M., Pollack, J. M., & Finkel, E. J. (2013). Mind-sets matter: A meta-analytic review of implicit theories and self-regulation. *Psychological Bulletin, 139,* 655–701. doi:10.1037/a0029531

Deci, E. L., & Ryan, R. M. (2000). The "what" and "why" of goal pursuits: Human needs and the self-determination of behavior. *Psychological Inquiry: An International Journal for the Advancement of Psychological Theory, 11,* 227–268. doi:10.1207/S15327965PLI1104_01

Diseth, A. (2011). Self-efficacy, goal orientations and learning strategies as mediators between preceding and subsequent academic achievement. *Learning and Individual Differences, 21,* 191–195. doi:10.1016/j.lindif.2011.01.003

Dweck, C. S. (1986). Motivational processes affecting learning. *American Psychologist, 41,* 1040–1048. doi:10.1037/0003-066X.41.10.1040

Dweck, C. S. (2010). Even geniuses work hard. *Educational Leadership, 68,* 16–20.

Dweck C. S., Chiu, C., & Hong, Y. (1995). Implicit theories: Elaboration and extension of the model. *Psychological Inquiry, 6,* 322–333. doi:10.1207/s15327965pli0604_12

Dweck, C. S., & Leggett, E. L. (1988). A social-cognitive approach to motivation and personality. *Psychological Review, 95,* 256–273. doi:10.1037/0033-295X.95.2.256

Elliot, A. J., & McGregor, H. A. (2001). A 2 × 2 achievement goal framework. *Journal of Personality and Social Psychology, 80,* 501–519. doi:10.1O37//OO22-3514.80.3.501

Grant, H., & Dweck, C. S. (2003). Clarifying achievement goals and their impact. *Journal of Personality and Social Psychology, 85,* 541–553. doi:10.1037/0022-3514.85.3.541

Guay, F., Ratelle, C. F., & Chanal, J. (2008). Optimal learning in optimal contexts: The role of self-determination in education. *Canadian Psychology, 49,* 233–240. doi:10.1037/a0012758

Hong, Y., Chiu, C., Dweck, C. S., Lin, D. M. S., & Wan, W. (1999). Implicit theories, attributions, and coping: A meaning system approach. *Journal of Personality and Social Psychology, 77,* 588–599. doi:10.1037//0022-3514.77.3.588

Hsieh, P., Sullivan, J. R., & Guerra, N. S. (2007). A closer look at college students: Self-efficacy and goal orientation. *Journal of Advanced Academics, 18,* 454–476. doi:10.4219/jaa-2007-500

Hulleman, C. S., Schrager, S. M., Bodmann, S. M., & Harackiewicz, J. M. (2010). A meta-analytic review of achievement goal measures: Different labels for the same constructs or different constructs with similar labels? *Psychological Bulletin, 136,* 422–449. doi:10.1037/a0018947

Komarraju, M., & Nadler, D. (2013). Self-efficacy and academic achievement: Why do implicit beliefs, goals, and effort regulation matter? *Learning and Individual Differences, 25,* 67–72. doi:10.1016/j.lindif.2013.01.005

Linnenbrink, E. A., & Pintrich, P. R. (2002). Motivation as an enabler for academic success. *School Psychology Review, 31,* 313–327.

Lou, N. M., & Noels, K. A. (2016). Changing language mindsets: Implications for goal orientations and responses to failure in and outside the second language classroom. *Contemporary Educational Psychology, 46,* 22–33. doi:10.1016/j.cedpsych.2016.03.004

Maddux, J. E., & Rogers, R. W. (1983). Protection motivation and self-efficacy: A revised theory of fear appeals and attitude change. *Journal of Experimental Social Psychology, 19*, 469–479. doi:10.1016/0022-1031(83)90023-9

Mangels, J. A., Butterfield, B., Lamb, J., Good, C., & Dweck, C. S. (2006). Why do beliefs about intelligence influence learning success? A social cognitive neuroscience model. *Social Cognitive and Affective Neuroscience, 1,* 75–86. doi:10.1093/scan/nsl013

Middleton, M. J., & Midgley, C. (1997). Avoiding the demonstration of lack of ability: An underexplored aspect of goal theory. *Journal of Educational Psychology, 89,* 710–718. doi:10.1037/0022-0663.89.4.710

Moser, J. S., Schroder, H. S., Heeter, C., Moran, T. P., & Lee, Y-H. (2011). Mind your errors: Evidence for a neural mechanism linking growth mind-set to adaptive posterror adjustments. *Psychological Science, 22,* 1484–1489. doi:10.1177/0956797611419520

Multon, K. D., Brown, S. D., & Lent, R. W. (1991). Relation of self-efficacy beliefs to academic outcomes: A meta-analytic investigation. *Journal of Counseling Psychology, 38,* 30–38. doi:10.1037/0022-0167.38.1.30

Nussbaum, A. D., & Dweck, C. S. (2008). Defensiveness versus remediation: Self-theories and modes of self-esteem maintenance. *Personality and Social Psychology Bulletin, 34,* 599–612. doi:10.1177/0146167207312960

Pintrich, P. R. (2000a). An achievement goal theory perspective on issues in motivation terminology, theory, and research. *Contemporary Educational Psychology, 25,* 92–104. doi:10.1006/ceps.1999.1017

Pintrich, P. R. (2000b). Multiple goals, multiple pathways: The role of goal orientation in learning and achievement. *Journal of Educational Psychology, 92,* 544–555. doi:10.I037//0022-O663.92.3.544

Rattan, A., Good, C., & Dweck, C. S. (2012). "It's ok—not everyone can be good at math": Instructors with an entity theory comfort (and demotivate) students. *Journal of Experimental Social Psychology, 48,* 731–737. doi:10.1016/j.jesp.2011.12.012

Rogers, R. W. (1983). Cognitive and physiological processes in fear appeals and attitude change: A revised theory of protection motivation. In J. T. Cacioppo, & R. Petty (Eds.), *Social psychophysiology: A sourcebook* (pp. 153–177). New York, NY: The Guilford Press.

Romero, C., Master, A., Paunesku, D., Dweck, C. S., & Gross, J. J. (2014). Academic and emotional functioning in middle school: The role of implicit theories. *Emotion, 14,* 227–234. doi:10.1037/a0035490

Ryan, R. M., & Deci, E. L. (2000). Self-determination theory and the facilitation of intrinsic motivation, social development, and well-being. *American Psychologist, 5,* 68–78. doi:10.1037110003-066X.55.1.68

Seaton, M., Parker, P., Marsh, H. W., Craven, R. G., & Yeung, A. S. (2014). The reciprocal relations between self-concept, motivation and achievement: Juxtaposing academic self-concept and achievement goal orientations for mathematics success. *Educational Psychology, 34,* 49–72. doi:10.1080/01443410.2013.825232

Siegle, D., & McCoach, D. B. (2007). Increasing student mathematics self-efficacy through teacher training. *Journal of Advanced Academics, 18,* 278–312. doi:10.4219/jaa-2007-353

Van Yperen, N. W., Blaga, M., & Postmes, T. (2014). A meta-analysis of self-reported achievement goals and nonself-report performance across three achievement domains (work, sports, and education). *PLoS ONE, 9*, e93594. doi:10.1371/journal.pone.0093594

Ziegler, A., & Stoeger, H. (2010). Research on a modified framework of implicit personality theories. *Learning and Individual differences, 20,* 318–326. doi:10.1016/j.lindif.2010.01.007

Zimmerman, B. J. (2000). Self-efficacy: An essential motive to learn. *Contemporary Educational Psychology, 25,* 82–91. doi:10.1006/ceps.1999.1016

FOUR

Teacher Misbehaviors

OBJECTIVES

By the end of this chapter, you should be a changed person in the following ways:

1. You should be able to explain what teacher misbehaviors are
2. You should be able to articulate six categories of teacher misbehaviors
3. You should be able to articulate the benefits of student feedback
4. You should be able to explain how to use protection motivation theory to enhance student feedback
5. You should be able to name five U.S. presidents and something special they did for the country (Why not? History is important too!)

Teachers Misbehaviors

When you think about the tools you have at your disposal, I bet you mostly think about the positive things you can do with those objects. A car, for example, helps you get from one place to another without having to use your feet and your legs to cover great distances. Cars are, indeed, a positive presence in your life because they allow you to show up to work, class, or even social events by simply sitting in a seat and pressing your foot on a gas pedal. This is truly amazing—if there were no cars and we all had to walk everywhere, the world would certainly seem like a much bigger, and sweatier, place. What about knives? We all have those tools in our kitchens, right? Knives are great because they help you slice objects that are hard to otherwise split open, and they allow you to use minimal force to achieve a desired outcome like having pieces of tomatoes, instead of whole tomatoes, on a turkey sandwich. Hammers are tools with positive uses too. If you happen to own a hammer, you know that it is a very useful tool for achieving the goal of getting one thing to stick into something else. Can you imagine using your hand to try to punch a nail into the wall just so you can hang your favorite picture of Justin Bieber in your bedroom? For all but the most accomplished karate masters, this would be an impossible feat to accomplish.

Although the way I wrote about cars, knives, and hammers is obviously positive, the thing about tools is that, in reality, they are neither inherently positive nor negative. In other words, despite the fact that most of us tend to see the objects I wrote about as being beneficial in our lives, if they are put to use in a manner that leads to destruction, the things we perceive as being helpful can turn out to be downright dangerous. As I am sure you are aware, hammers, knives, and cars can harm people in a variety of ways, and in some cases they can even be deadly objects. Of course, the same is true for just about any tool you can think of. The reason I bring all this up is because it is important to point out that the things we have at our disposal are really only good or bad to the extent that we use them for good or bad purposes. Knives, for example, are neither good nor bad: It is how we decide to use those knives that make the outcomes we experience with them as either good or bad.

If you understand the idea that tools have the potential to be good and bad, then you will realize that, as a tool for student instruction, the same thing goes for you as a teacher. That said, although many of the things we do as teachers are beneficial for students' development, the fact of the matter is that instructors do not always teach their classes in ways that help students learn. Even worse, teachers often conduct themselves in a manner that is counterproductive to students' academic success (Bolkan & Goodboy, 2016). Thus, although teachers have the potential to help students in important ways, if we engage in behaviors that are counterproductive to student learning, then we have the potential to harm them as well.

At this point, you may be thinking that teachers rarely do things to disrupt student learning. In reality, research on the subject suggests the opposite: According to Goodboy (2011a), students are frequently dissatisfied with their instructors. Other researchers support this claim and note that only a small portion of students report never having experienced conflict with their instructors (Harrison, 2007; Tantleff-Dunn, Dunn, & Gokee, 2002). What does this mean? Quite simply, it means we can *all* do something to improve our instruction. Never heard a complaint from your students? That doesn't mean much to me. Just because you don't hear from your students doesn't mean they are satisfied with their educational experiences. In fact, an important idea to keep in mind when it comes to student satisfaction is that no news is *not* necessarily good news; most students who experience dissatisfaction in their classes never complain to their instructors (Bolkan & Goodboy, 2013).

In this section of the book, we are interested in students' capacity to learn the material we present in the classroom. But, instead of seeing students as the sole owners of their educational capacities, this chapter was designed to help you understand *your* role as it pertains to making learning possible, or impossible. Just as the tools we own can be linked to negative outcomes if used incorrectly, this chapter was written to help you realize that the things you do as a teacher can be detrimental to student learning if you behave inappropriately (Kearney, Plax, Hays, & Ivey, 1991).

Specifically, this chapter was written to articulate what we can do as instructors to make sure that our behaviors do not negatively affect student learning. To do this, we will look at the variety of ways students report that teachers can misbehave. After we cover the various ways that you can inhibit student achievement, we will discuss an important method for gathering information regarding your teaching practices that might help you avoid some of these detrimental behaviors. After all, if you never learn about how your students perceive the effectiveness of your instruction, you might never know if you are doing what it takes to promote their learning.

Teacher Misbehaviors

Teacher misbehaviors can stem from a variety of instructional activities and are defined simply as behaviors that "interfere with instruction and thus, learning" (Kearney et al., 1991, p. 310). When you first read this definition, you might wonder if these types of behaviors even happen in the classroom at all. This mindset is normal. Researchers mostly focus on the constructive impact teachers have on students and often fail to think about the ineffective or destructive things teachers do in their classrooms (Kearney et al., 1991; Zhang, 2007). I think the same thing is true for us as instructors: Most of the time we see ourselves as instrumental to student learning and we often fail to acknowledge the possibility that our behaviors can be detrimental to students' academic success. In fact, data gathered by Joan Gorham and Diane Millette (1997) indicates that this way of thinking is pervasive. According to these researchers, teachers seem to underestimate the extent to which their misbehaviors can be demotivating. But, what do students think? Compare teachers' ways of thinking to students' interpretations of their classroom experiences. When asked to report reasons for being demotivated in class, the majority of students state that these reasons stem largely from their instructors' misbehaviors including doing things like presenting course material unenthusiastically, failing to demonstrate an interest in students, and failing to structure class in a meaningful fashion (Christophel & Gorham, 1995). Of course, these are just a few of the things teachers can do to interfere with student learning.

So what? Teachers misbehave. Why should you care? The reason you should care is because the way instructors interact with their students can affect how students think and behave in the classroom. Thus, it should be no surprise to learn that misbehaviors are linked to a variety of undesirable outcomes and student problems (Kearney et al., 1991). For example, teacher misbehaviors are associated with a reduction in students' motivation to learn (Goodboy & Bolkan, 2009; Zhang, 2007), reduced student interest in class (Broeckelman-Post et al., 2016), lower positive affect, lower levels of perceived teacher credibility including teachers' competence, trustworthiness and caring (Banfield, Richmond, & McCroskey, 2006), and lower participation and communication satisfaction (Goodboy & Bolkan, 2009). In a nutshell, teachers who misbehave decimate student motivation in the classroom and reduce the potential for developing a sense of relatedness with their students. Both of these factors are important contributors to student success. Thus, by misbehaving, instructors ultimately reduce students' capacity to do well in their academic pursuits.

At this point, you might be thinking that perhaps instructors' misbehaviors are unintentional and that students are likely to forgive teaching problems in class. Maybe. But, the research I have read points more toward the conclusion of "maybe not." According to Kelsey, Kearney, Plax, Allen, and Ritter (2004), students tend to perceive teacher misbehaviors as stemming from internal causes (i.e., misbehaviors are typically seen as intentional) as opposed to external causes such as accidents or mistakes, there being good reasons to misbehave, or circumstances beyond the teacher's control. In other words, students tend not to think of teachers' (potentially valid) reasons for misbehaving. Instead, they are more likely to interpret misbehaviors as a function of teachers' inability to teach well. As a result, students often become disenfranchised with their learning experiences in classes where teachers misbehave. But, you don't have to take my word for it; take a look at some of the sentiments collected from students by Kelsey et al.'s (2004, p. 53) study on the subject:

- "How can she expect me to learn when she's not motivated to teach me?"
- "He conveys the material in a pointless, boring manner that the students can't understand."
- "She has her own views and is not willing to be open minded to what her students think. There's no way for me to communicate my opinion without her saying that it is wrong."

Poor students! We have all had teachers who made us feel the way these unfortunate students felt, and I am sure you will agree that these were terrible experiences. Based on what we have just seen then, it is important that we, as instructors, work hard to make sure that we do not engage in behaviors that students perceive to be harmful to their learning.

So, what are the behaviors we can potentially engage in that lead to detriments in student learning? Perhaps we should ask the people who are in the best position to tell us—our students. In fact, this is exactly what Pat Kearney and her colleagues (Kearney et al., 1991) did in their seminal study on the subject. This is the same thing that Alan Goodboy and Scott Myers (Goodboy & Myers, 2015) did more than two decades later. Essentially, in these studies students were asked to "think back over their college career and to recall specific instances where teachers had said or done something that had irritated, demotivated, or substantially distracted them in an aversive way during a course" (Kearney et al., 1991, p. 313). Despite the list of potential problems being almost limitless (indeed, in their original study, Kearney and her colleagues catalogued a total of 1,762 descriptions of teacher misbehaviors), researchers studying the topic have condensed potential misbehaviors to a core set of categories. Although various researchers label and organize misbehaviors in a variety of ways, below I report a concise definition of 31 potential misbehaviors based on my interpretation of Kearney et al.'s original classification and more recent studies of teacher misbehaviors (e.g., Goodboy & Myers, 2015; Thweatt & McCroskey, 1996).

The first category of teacher misbehaviors refers to the ability to manage time appropriately and reflects teachers' *punctuality and absenteeism*. The specific misbehaviors in this category include:

- Being absent (e.g., canceling class without notifying students)
- Being tardy (e.g., showing up late without a good reason)
- Keeping students over time (e.g., keeping class late or starting before class is supposed to begin)
- Early dismissal (e.g., dismissing class early or rushing through the material in an attempt to finish quickly)

The second category of misbehaviors refers to how teachers manage their class resources and reflects the ways instructors *organize and structure course material.* Specific misbehaviors in this category include:

- Straying from the subject matter (e.g., wasting class time with tangential personal opinions)
- Confusing and unclear lectures/course policies (e.g., having unclear classroom expectations, providing unclear assignments, presenting poorly organized lectures)
- Being unprepared and disorganized (e.g., failing to adequately prepare for class, forgetting important course dates)
- Deviating from the syllabus (e.g., getting behind schedule, changing course requirements, failing to use assigned books, requiring unnecessary expenses)
- Pointless assignments (e.g., asking students to complete work irrelevant to course objectives)
- Poor feedback habits (e.g., taking an extraordinary amount of time to provide feedback on exams and papers, failing to provide meaningful feedback on exams and assignments)

The third category of misbehaviors refers to the way teachers treat their students and reflects the extent to which instructors are *insensitive to students as individuals.* Misbehaviors in this category include:

- Being sarcastic and using putdowns (e.g., being willing to embarrass or insult students)
- Being verbally abusive (e.g., intimidating students, yelling at students)
- Having unreasonable/arbitrary rules (e.g., being inflexible, failing to see student perspectives for late work or the need for breaks during 3-hour classes, for example)
- Engaging in sexual harassment (e.g., flirting with individuals or making sexual comments in class)
- Displaying a negative personality (e.g., acting selfish, showing up to class moody, looking down on students, telling students their opinions are wrong while the instructor's are right)
- Having double standards (e.g., doing things in class like checking text messages that he/she asks students not to do)

The fourth category of misbehaviors reflects teachers' willingness to help students both inside and outside of class. This category relates to *unavailability* and includes misbehaviors like:

- Being unresponsive to student questions (e.g., becoming annoyed when students ask for more information or for information to be repeated)
- Being apathetic to students (e.g., failing to learn students' names, failing to acknowledge students' perspectives)
- Being inaccessible outside of class (e.g., being difficult to access outside of regular class time, failing to respond to student e-mails)

The fifth category of misbehaviors refers to the way teachers evaluate students and reflects ambiguous, temperamental, or inconsistent grading. This category is referred to as *unfair student evaluation* and includes misbehaviors such as:

- Unfair testing (e.g., using ambiguous exam questions, failing to review for exams)
- Unfair grading (e.g., refusing to assign 'A's, not having a predetermined grading rubric)
- Showing favoritism or prejudice (e.g., demonstrating preferential treatment to certain individuals)

Finally, the sixth category of misbehaviors refers to the way information is presented in class and is labeled *poor presentation*. This category includes misbehaviors such as:

- Presenting boring lectures (e.g., lacking enthusiasm and variety when delivering information, presenting information without nonverbal immediacy)
- Information overload (e.g., assigning too much work, failing to pace lectures appropriately, having unrealistic expectations, asking too much of students)
- Information underload (e.g., making the course too easy, failing to teach by showing movies instead of lecturing, for example)

- Not knowing the subject matter (e.g., providing outdated material, not being able to answer student questions)
- Having a foreign or regional accent (e.g., speaking in a manner that makes understanding difficult)
- Speaking with inappropriate volume (e.g., speaking in a manner that makes it difficult to listen)
- Using bad grammar/spelling (e.g., having poor handwriting, poor English skills)
- Having a negative personal appearance (e.g., having a sloppy demeanor, behaving in an unprofessional manner like acting crude or too familiar)
- Failing to use technology (e.g., using outdated delivery methods)

As I noted, the classification system and the six categories reported here are my own interpretation of Kearney et al.'s (1991) original taxonomy (from their Study 1) together with my reading of some of the more recent studies of teacher misbehaviors. That said, there are other ways to classify these behaviors as well (see Kearney et al., 1991, Study 2) including breaking misbehaviors into three categories of: incompetence (e.g., confusing lectures, boring lectures, information overload), offensiveness (e.g., sarcasm, sexual harassment), and indolence (e.g., being absent, deviating from the syllabus). Another classification system (see Goodboy & Myers, 2015) also includes three categories including: antagonism (e.g., yelling at students, discriminating against students), lectures (e.g., lectures in a dry manner, speaks too quickly), and articulation (e.g., has an accent, does not speak English well). The reason I chose to use the categorization system I did is because doing so preserves the full range of misbehaviors for your perusal; the other categorization systems reduce the number of misbehaviors to 21 (Kearney et al., 1991) or to just 16 (Goodboy & Myers, 2015). In my opinion, it is important to be aware of all the ways you might potentially upset your students throughout the course of your time together.

As you have almost certainly concluded, the list of potential teacher misbehaviors is long. That said, it is important to be able to recognize all the ways we can work against our goal of helping students. Still, there are some behaviors that students report as occurring more often than others, and these may be particularly important to keep an eye out for. For example, Kearney and her colleagues (1991) report that the top five most frequently cited misbehaviors include: boring lectures, straying from the subject matter, unfair testing, unclear lectures, and returning students' work back late. Similarly, some two decades later, Alan Goodboy and Scott Myers (2015) report that the five most frequently cited instructor misbehaviors include: having boring lectures, deviating from the syllabus, unfair grading, lack of technology, and information overload. These behaviors are comparable to the top five most frequently reported misbehaviors articulated by students across American, German, Japanese, and Chinese classrooms including: information overload, boring lectures, straying from the subject, keeping students overtime, and early dismissal (Zhang, 2007).

After reading this section, you now know what instructor misbehaviors are, why they are bad, and you have an idea of the specific things you can do that are interpreted by students as being demotivating, distracting, and detrimental to learning. Having learned all of this, the next step is to try to avoid engaging in these behaviors in class. And how do you do that? If you ask me, the best thing to do is to understand how your students experience your teaching. Only by understanding students' perspectives can we hope to know whether or not we are engaging in behaviors that are known to be harmful to their educational experiences. To learn about how we can gather this information, let's turn to a discussion of student feedback.

Student Feedback

I recently read a book by Adam Grant (2016) titled *Originals* where the author explains how people can work to strategically make a difference in the lives and experiences of other individuals. In one chapter of this book, Grant writes about an organization, Bridgewater Associates, that has been consistently ranked as having an outstanding company culture. This organization is in the business of handling financial investments and, according to Grant, is an exemplar of outstanding company principles. Chief among these principles, Grant notes, is Bridgewater's dedication to the promotion and expression of what the author calls original ideas. Essentially, expressing original ideas in this context refers to airing concerns about the way the company is run and communicating about practices that employees find to be counterproductive to the mission of the organization. Put succinctly, Grant writes that one of the reasons Bridgewater is so successful is because it promotes a culture where ideas, both complimentary and antagonistic, are discussed openly and where people use these ideas to change the organization into a more productive unit. In essence, the folks at Bridgewater see employee feedback as an important source of information with the potential to help correct mistakes and make operations more efficient.

When I read about the people at Bridgewater, I remember thinking to myself that it makes sense for an organization to promote the sharing of information, even—and especially—information that might reflect complaints or problems with the way things are run. This is because information, both the good and perhaps more importantly the bad, can help the people in charge determine what is working and what is not. Instead of crossing their fingers and hoping that their actions lead to organizational success, the people at Bridgewater Associates value both positive and negative feedback because they realize it can help them determine how their behaviors are being translated into results.

From an organizational perspective, gathering information about how to improve makes sense. Specifically, by determining what a company is doing wrong, the people in charge can better position themselves to streamline their business practices to facilitate success. This may explain why researchers examining employee-employer interactions typically interpret the provision of critical feedback from employees to employers as constructive attempts to communicate the need for change (Kassing & Avtgis, 1999; Sprague & Ruud, 1988). Similarly, in the consumer literature, customer complaining is considered beneficial because the information contained in these messages provides retailers with the opportunity to address and repair various problems (Blodgett & Anderson, 2000; Bolkan, 2015). Of course, the same is true in college classrooms. Although asking students for feedback regarding problematic teaching practices may seem like something instructors would want to avoid as a way of protecting their face (e.g., Brown & Levinson, 1987; Sidelinger, Bolen, Frisby, & McMullen, 2012), similar to organizational settings, student feedback should be considered an important source of information with the potential to help instructors determine what they can do to best facilitate learning (e.g., Bolkan & Goodoby, 2013). After all, if we want to reduce our ineffective teaching behaviors it seems reasonable to seek help from the people who are in the best position to report on these activities.

In the instructional communication literature, students' provision of feedback regarding problematic teaching practices is called rhetorical dissent and is defined by Goodboy (2011a) as communication for the purposes of correcting a perceived wrongdoing. Because these messages provide teachers with the opportunity to fix various classroom problems, communicating rhetorical dissent to instructors should be thought of as a constructive process of information sharing (Bolkan & Goodboy, 2013). Why? Because the more students are willing to speak up about the problems they experience in class, the better we should be able to rectify these issues for (1) the students articulating their problems and for (2) future students who might also experience dissatisfaction as a result of the same ineffective teaching behaviors (Bolkan & Goodboy, 2016).

Unfortunately, most people do not think of rhetorical dissent in such a positive manner. For example, in my experience, many teachers don't want to know about what their students think regarding their instruction and they often report that student complaints are unjustified or reflect the sentiments of students who are only interested in their grades. These conclusions are simply not true. First, researchers note that when it comes to dissent, the principle drivers for this type of communication stem from students' perceptions of ineffective teaching (Goodboy & Martin, 2014). That said, this type of communication seems pretty justified to me. Second, as opposed to being interested in their grades, students who express rhetorical dissent have been found to be particularly interested in their learning (Goodboy & Frisby, 2014). In my opinion, teachers who resist student feedback have adopted a performance avoidance mindset and are unwilling to struggle with the process of getting better at teaching because they are afraid of getting their feelings hurt. Try not to think like this. As teachers, our job is to help students learn to the best of their abilities and, although their feedback regarding our attempts at achieving this goal may be critical, this information is crucial to our development as successful educators.

Okay, having read the foregoing, we might be on the same page regarding the importance of soliciting candid feedback from students. This is good news. The bad news, however, is that most students who experience dissatisfaction in class do not complain to their instructors (Bolkan & Goodboy, 2013). In other words, the people who have the best information regarding what you can do to improve your instruction are usually not very likely to share it with you. And for good reason; according to some of the research I conducted, students tend to be strategic with their complaints and will not provide critical feedback to instructors if (1) they do not see problems as egregious enough to warrant speaking up, (2) they do not perceive classroom problems as fixable, or (3) they perceive that there will be costs associated with articulating their concerns (Bolkan & Goodboy, 2016).

So what do these students do instead? Instead of speaking up to their teachers, students who are dissatisfied with their instruction tend to engage in a variety of alternative responses including doing nothing (Bolkan & Goodboy, 2013; Horan, Chory, & Goodboy, 2010), airing their grievances to friends or classmates (Bolkan & Goodboy, 2013; Goodboy, 2011a, 2011b), talking to their advisors, addressing the issue with the chair of the department or dean of the college, venting on course evaluations, or dropping the class (Bolkan & Goodboy, 2013; Goodboy, 2011a). Although some of these responses may be beneficial insofar as they help lead to catharsis (e.g., venting to others) or alert supervising individuals to problems in their subordinates' classrooms (e.g., speaking with the chair), others may prove to be maladaptive if they do not lead to positive outcomes.

So where does this leave us? In this section, we learned that it is important for students to voice their discontent in order to help us identify our potential misbehaviors. However, we also learned that students are not likely to speak up because of a variety of concerns. That said, it makes sense that if we want our students to come to us with information regarding what we can do to improve our instruction, we should focus on these concerns in an attempt to alleviate them. In order to learn how to do that, we'll turn to a discussion of protection motivation theory.

Protection motivation

Protection motivation theory was created as a way to help explain the relationship between fear appeals and changes in people's attitudes and behaviors (Maddux & Rogers, 1983; Rogers 1975, 1983; Rogers & Mewborn, 1976). In the last chapter (Chapter 3), we learned about two components of this theory—self-efficacy and response efficacy—and how they relate to students' achievement goal orientations. In this chapter, we will discuss the idea of protection motivation a bit more fully and relate this notion to helping students provide feedback in our classrooms.

Proponents of protection motivation theory suggest that for fear appeals to lead to adaptive behavior, messages need to address five essential ideas. Put in the context of smoking cessation, this means that there are five things communicators need to be concerned with to ensure that others actually stop smoking as opposed to simply ignoring the message. Two of these ideas include the severity of the problem and a person's perceived vulnerability to the problem. Severity refers to the perceived seriousness of the threat, and vulnerability refers to how much the threat is perceived to affect someone personally (Norman, Boer, & Seydel, 2005). Severity and vulnerability combine to create what scholars call *threat appraisal.* The third and fourth ideas in protection motivation theory include self-efficacy and response efficacy. You already know about these, but to recap, self-efficacy refers to a person's perceptions of their ability to perform a protective behavior and response efficacy is concerned with the perceived effectiveness of a behavior for addressing a threat (Norman et al., 2005). Self-efficacy and response efficacy combine to create a person's *coping appraisal.* Finally, the fifth idea to consider regarding fear appeals refers to the *costs* associated with enacting protective behaviors.

Using the smoking example that we started, researchers conclude that when listening to a persuasive message, people are likely to be motivated to stop smoking (as opposed to simply ignoring the message) to the extent that they believe smoking is a threat because it is harmful (i.e., severity) and because the harms of smoking will actually happen to them (i.e., vulnerability). Next, if the threat related to smoking can be made salient for individuals, people are likely to change their behavior in a positive manner (i.e., stopping smoking) to the extent that they believe they can cope by actually quitting smoking (i.e., self-efficacy) and to the extent that they believe stopping smoking will, in fact, lead to better health (i.e., response efficacy). Of course, all of this happens in the context of the perceived costs related to stopping smoking. The more it costs people to stop smoking (e.g., withdrawal pains, loss of friendships, etc.), the less likely they are to do so.

At this point, you might be wondering why we are talking about smoking cessation and fear appeals in a book about effective instruction. The reason I brought up protection motivation theory is because the components that have been found to influence people's decisions to engage in healthy behaviors have also been found to predict a variety of other behaviors as well; importantly, one of these behaviors includes speaking with instructors when students experience dissatisfaction in class (Bolkan & Goodboy, 2016). Specifically, as it pertains to the components of protection motivation theory, we know that students are more likely to communicate their discontent to teachers with the hopes of promoting positive change to the extent that the problems they experience are highly threatening, they believe they can cope with the problems, and the costs of communicating about the issues are low.

In reality, the relationships between the these variables are a little more complicated (see Bolkan & Goodboy, 2016). In particular, under conditions of low costs, we know that students are more likely to voice their discontent when the perceived threat related to classroom problems is high (i.e., the severity of the problem and the impact it has on students is perceived to be high). When costs are low, students' perceptions of their ability to cope (i.e., their perceptions regarding whether or not they can communicate the feedback and if it would make a difference in their situations) seem not to affect their decisions. On the other hand, under conditions of relatively high perceived costs (e.g., discomfort associated with providing feedback to an instructor, threat of punishment for speaking up about negative classroom experiences), students are most likely to speak up when both the perceived threat of classroom problems is high *and* when they believe that speaking up will lead to positive change. Put simply, when the costs of speaking up are perceived to be low, students are likely to communicate feedback to their instructors to the extent that they perceive problems to be a big deal.

However, when the costs of speaking up are perceived to be high, students are likely to voice their concerns only if their issues are perceived to be a big deal and if they think that a solution will be forthcoming.

Although the foregoing information has several working components, the conclusion we should draw from it all is quite simple: If you want to gather information regarding whether or not your students think you are doing a good job teaching, you need to work on reducing the costs of providing feedback, increasing the perceived effectiveness of providing feedback, and helping students to see that no problem is too small to bring to your attention. These three aspects of students' experiences have been shown to be important predictors of students' decisions to voice their discontent and therefore they should be the focus of your efforts to solicit meaningful feedback. That said, let's talk about what you can do to influence each of these ideas.

Reducing costs

Bang for your buck, I think the best thing you can do to help facilitate students' honest feedback regarding your teaching behaviors is to reduce the costs associated with their providing it. These costs typically include perceptions that (1) providing feedback to instructors would be perceived as rude, stressful, uncomfortable, or nerve-racking. These costs also include perceptions that (2) it will take unnecessary time or effort to make a complaint. In addition, these costs include perceptions that (3) communicating feedback to instructors would make teachers mad, hold a grudge, or otherwise think negatively of the student. In my opinion, these costs represent legitimate concerns—especially that last one! Although some teachers might scoff at the idea of retaliating against students in such a way, some of my own research points to the conclusion that instructors may think of, and potentially treat, students differently depending on how they feel toward specific individuals (e.g., Bolkan & Holmgren, 2012). Yikes!

Now that you know some of the costs associated with communicating feedback in an academic environment, what can you do to eliminate these? I think the best way to do this is to ask for anonymous feedback and to do so in class. Asking for information in this manner serves two purposes. First, by keeping the feedback anonymous, students might feel more comfortable being honest about their experiences because the threat of individual retaliation is diminished. Moreover, there is no need for an awkward or uncomfortable meeting where students must communicate their discontent directly to an instructor's face.

Second, asking for feedback in class makes it easy for students to complete the assessment. Instead of asking them to complete a survey at home, on their own time, students can simply use their time in class to provide the feedback you seek. Making it easy to offer feedback eliminates the cost of preparing comments on their own and, importantly, this should increase the likelihood that students provide the information you desire. Not to mention, making the provision of feedback easy is linked to the notion of *procedural justice* (Tax, Brown, & Chandrashekaran, 1998), which, in rhetorical dissent episodes, has been associated with students' communication satisfaction and motivation in class (Holmgren & Bolkan, 2014).

Having said the above, one way to help reduce the costs of providing feedback is to solicit quantitative feedback from your students. This is because asking for quantitative feedback only requires that students circle (or underline) a number to indicate their sentiments which makes the provision of feedback easier and might also eliminate students' fears of your recognizing their handwriting. Knowing this, one way to collect quantitative data from your students is to make an informal version of your institution's teacher evaluation form and to ask students to rate you just as they will at the end of the semester. Doing this will help you get a handle on classroom problems during the semester and may allow you to correct for any teaching misbehaviors before they become a part of your permanent record. Alternatively, why not list the specific misbehaviors noted in this chapter and ask students to rate, on say a scale of 1 to 7, the extent to which they perceive you engaging in these behaviors in class? Obviously, if you are behaving in ways that students perceive to be problematic, asking students for this type of information will make your engagement in negative teaching practices readily apparent.

In addition to asking for feedback in a manner that reduces the costs associated with its provision, it is critical that you demonstrate your openness to student comments so your pupils perceive you as someone who is not threatened by, and who will not react negatively to, constructive criticism. To do this, it is important that you create an atmosphere of politeness and open-mindedness in class. One way to achieve this goal may lie in the way you handle classroom discussions; if students ask questions in class or provide opinions that differ from yours, it may be wise to react in a manner that demonstrates respect for others' viewpoints. Why? Well, there are a variety of reasons to react in the fashion just described. But, as it pertains to soliciting feedback, if students perceive you as being open to alternative beliefs, they may be more likely to provide you with information regarding their perceptions of your teaching effectiveness. What I am promoting here is the notion of demonstrating *interpersonal justice,* which refers to showing respect, empathy, and politeness in the face of alternative viewpoints and, in response to constructive criticism, has been associated with positive outcomes such as commitment and trust in organizational settings (e.g., Tax et al., 1998).

Ultimately, the point I am trying to make in this section is that your students' thoughts about your instruction do not have to be a mystery. If you give students an opportunity to safely and easily share their opinions, they may be more likely to do so. More specifically, you now know that getting rid of the potential for students to experience costs linked to awkward interactions, unnecessary effort, and the potential for retaliation is important if you want to ensure the provision of meaningful feedback.

Increasing the perceived effectiveness of feedback

If you want students to speak up regarding potential teaching misbehaviors, it is also important for students to see that you are willing to change the way things are done in class. One way to achieve this goal is to use the feedback gathered from the evaluations mentioned earlier and to communicate to students what you plan to do to address their complaints. Stated differently, instead of simply collecting the data for your own edification, you should share the results of the evaluation and then demonstrate your commitment to change by outlining the steps you plan to take to address your students' concerns. What does this look like in real life? This looks like you walking into class the next day and articulating (1) the concerns expressed by your students and

(2) the actions you plan to take to alleviate these. Crucially, being willing to change your teaching behaviors based on your students' requests reflects the provision of *distributive justice,* which has been linked to important classroom outcomes such as student motivation and positive affect for both the class and the instructor (Holmgren & Bolkan, 2014). Not to mention, your students might have some great ideas regarding the ways in which you can improve your instruction!

Of course, it is impossible to meet all students' demands. That said, you might find that students appreciate even having the chance to be heard. As such, addressing the issues they brought up and noting why you cannot make specific changes may help students at least understand why things are the way they are in your class. Significantly, providing adequate explanations regarding decision-making policies is linked to the notion of *informational justice,* and this type of behavior has been associated with a variety of positive organizational outcomes such as increased task performance and an enhanced likelihood of engaging in organizational citizenship behaviors (e.g., Colquitt et al., 2013).

If you really want to get empirical when it comes to assessing your students' perceptions of your being open to input, you might choose to use the feedback mechanism suggested earlier to ask your students about their perceptions of your openness as well. To do so, you can simply borrow three items used in a recent study of organizational feedback (Lebel, 2016) and ask your students to rate the extent to which they agree or disagree with the following statements (I have already adapted them for a classroom context for you):

1. My teacher uses my suggestions
2. My teacher considers ideas from students
3. My teacher rejects new ideas

Ultimately, understanding how students view your openness to feedback might help you determine the extent to which they think sharing their perceptions will make a difference in class. The more your students believe that you are willing to change, the more they may be willing to offer information regarding their experiences with your teaching practices.

No problem too small

Finally, it is important to note that people tend to communicate feedback to the extent that they see problems as being worth fixing. That said, we might encourage students to communicate their perceptions of classroom problems by letting them know that we are interested in hearing about these—both big and small. Though we certainly don't want to increase the severity of the problems our students experience in class, we can communicate that even small problems are serious to us. In my experience, some students simply need the encouragement to come to us with feedback. Thus, perhaps by letting them know just how important their feedback is to our teaching, students might be more willing to offer us this type of information.

The way I promote the provision of feedback in my classes is to tell my students that I see myself as the owner of a company that is in the business of educating my clients. I tell them that, just as the owner of a burrito restaurant might want to know what he or she could do to have the best burrito product, I want to know what I can do to best facilitate student learning. Essentially, I try to tell my students that I consider feedback to be a sign of loyalty and that I consider suggestions for improvement as information that will ultimately make me a better teacher. By communicating the importance of feedback and by helping students see how their suggestions can help me improve, I hope to influence my students to provide feedback even if they don't think their suggestions are all that consequential.

Importantly, when I tell my students all of this, I really mean it. And, so should you. Of course, you don't always have to follow your students' advice, and you don't have to adjust your teaching for every piece of feedback you receive. However, having the information will at least give you the option to react to it. Just remember, when students communicate their feedback you should try to keep in mind that they are essentially trying to articulate what you can do to teach them more effectively. As far as I am concerned, the most appropriate way to respond to someone who is trying to help you is with a simple "thank you" and a smile.

Summary

We started this chapter with a discussion about tools and how these have the potential to be either good or bad depending on how they are utilized. We used this idea to discuss our role as teachers and how, as facilitators of student learning, we act as tools in the classroom to help our students achieve academic success. Of course, we mentioned that just like hammers, or knives, or cars, teachers can be capable of both great and not-so-great things. The point for us as teachers then is to do the things that facilitate student success while avoiding behaviors that might be detrimental to student learning.

In this chapter, we learned what some of these detrimental behaviors are and we defined them as teacher misbehaviors. These include 31 specific misbehaviors organized into six categories including punctuality and absenteeism, the organization and structure of course material, insensitivity to students, being unavailable, unfair evaluation, and poor presentation. Next, we learned that the best way to figure out whether or not you are engaging in misbehaviors is to ask the people who experience your teaching themselves. However, we learned that students tend to be hesitant about providing this information, and therefore to help them do so we learned that we should focus on reducing the costs associated with providing feedback, increasing students' perceptions of your openness to feedback, and helping students see that no problem is too small to rectify.

In summary, your job as a teacher is to help students learn as best you can. Thus, if you want to be a great teacher, you should not settle on doing what makes you comfortable. Instead of avoiding problems in the classroom, you should focus on a mastery approach goal orientation and try to use constructive feedback to help you be your best. Consider challenging yourself to uncover your weaknesses so you can work on eliminating these behaviors from your teaching repertoire, and instead of seeing students who offer feedback as nagging or problematic, try to see them as loyal customers—these are people who are willing to speak up to help you do your job to the best of your ability.

END-OF-CHAPTER QUESTIONS

1. Why do you think teachers engage in misbehaviors in the first place? In other words, what is it that causes teachers to misbehave in their classrooms?

2. Do you think the misbehaviors listed in this chapter are, in fact, misbehaviors? Or might some of these behaviors be better labeled as violations of student preferences? Is there a difference? Would this difference matter for student learning?

3. What can you do in your classroom to facilitate more student feedback?

KEY TERMS

Teacher misbehaviors: Behaviors that interfere with instruction and learning

Punctuality and absenteeism: Misbehaviors relating to instructors' ability to manage time appropriately

Organization and structure of course material: Misbehaviors relating to the way teachers manage class resources

Insensitivity to students: Misbehaviors relating to the way teachers interact with students

Unavailability: Misbehaviors relating to teachers' willingness to help students both inside and outside of class

Unfair student evaluation: Misbehaviors relating to the way teachers evaluate students

Poor presentation: Misbehaviors relating to the way information is presented in class

Threat: The combination of the severity (the perceived seriousness of a threat) of a problem and a person's vulnerability (how much the threat is perceived to affect someone personally) to a problem

Coping: The combination of self-efficacy (a person's perceptions of their ability to perform a behavior) and response efficacy (the effectiveness of a behavior for addressing a threat) as it relates to a problem

Costs: The perceived costs of engaging in behaviors to address a problem

Distributive justice: Providing responses that address concerns raised during feedback

Procedural justice: Making the process of providing feedback easy and consistent

Interpersonal justice: Responding to feedback politely and with respect

Informational justice: Providing adequate explanations regarding decision-making policies

REFERENCES

Banfield, S. R., Richmond, V. P., & McCroskey, J. C. (2006). The effect of teacher misbehaviors on teacher credibility and affect for the teacher. *Communication Education, 55*, 63–72. doi:10.1080/03634520500343400

Blodgett, J. G., & Anderson, R. D. (2000). A bayesian network model of the consumer complaint process. *Journal of Services Research, 2,* 321–338. doi:10.1177/109467050024002

Bolkan, S. (2015). Threat, coping, and cost: Protection motivation in the context of consumer complaining. *Communication Research.* Advance online publication. doi:10.1177/0093650215600492

Bolkan, S., & Goodboy, A. K. (2013). No complain, no gain: Students' organizational, relational, and personal reasons for withholding rhetorical dissent from their college instructors. *Communication Education, 62,* 278–300. doi:10.1080/03634523.2013.788198

Bolkan, S., & Goodboy, A. K. (2016). Rhetorical dissent as an adaptive response to classroom problems: A test of protection motivation theory. *Communication Education, 65,* 24–43. doi:10.1080/03634523.2015.1039557

Bolkan, S., & Holmgren, J. L. (2012). "You are such a great teacher and I hate to bother you but…": Instructors' perceptions of students and their use of email messages with varying politeness strategies. *Communication Education, 61,* 253–270. doi:10.1080/03634523.2012.667135

Broeckelman-Post, M. A., Tacconelli, A., Guzman, J., Rios, M., Calero, B., & Latif, F. (2016). Teacher misbehavior and its effect on student interest and engagement. *Communication Education, 65*, 204–212. doi:10.1080/03634523.2015.1058962

Brown, P., & Levinson, S. C. (1987). *Politeness: Some universals in language usage.* Cambridge, MA: Cambridge University Press.

Christophel, D. M., & Gorham, J. (1995). A test-retest analysis of student motivation, teacher immediacy, and perceived sources of motivation and demotivation in college classes. *Communication Education, 44*, 292–306. doi:10.1080/03634529509379020

Colquitt, J. A., Scott, B. A., Rodell, J. B., Long, D. M., Zapata, C. P., Conlon, D. E., . . . Wesson, J. (2013). Justice at the millennium, a decade later: A meta-analytic test of social exchange and affect-based perspectives. *Journal of Applied Psychology, 98,* 199–236. doi:10.1037/a0031757

Goodboy, A. K. (2011a). Instructional dissent in the college classroom. *Communication Education, 60,* 296–313. doi:10.1080/03634523.2010.537756

Goodboy, A. K. (2011b). The development and validation of the instructional dissent scale. *Communication Education, 60,* 422–440. doi:10.1080/03634523.2011.569894

Goodboy, A. K., & Bolkan, S. (2009). College teacher misbehaviors: Direct and indirect effects on student communication behavior and traditional learning outcomes. *Western Journal of Communication, 73,* 204–219. doi:10.1080/10570310902856089

Goodboy, A. K., & Frisby, B. (2014). Instructional dissent as an expression of students' academic orientations and beliefs about education. *Communication Studies, 65,* 96-111. doi:10.1080/10510974.2013.785013

Goodboy, A. K., & Martin, M. M. (2014). Student temperament and motives as predictors of instructional dissent. *Learning and Individual Differences, 32,* 266-272. doi:10.1016/j.lindif.2014.03.024

Goodboy, A. K., & Myers, S. A. (2015). Revisiting instructor misbehaviors: A revised typology and development of a measure. *Communication Education, 64,* 133–153. doi:10.1080/03634523.2014.978798

Gorham, J., & Millette, D. M. (1997). A comparative analysis of teacher and student perceptions of sources of motivation and demotivation in college classes. *Communication Education, 46,* 245–261. doi:10.1080/03634529709379099

Grant, A. (2016). *Originals: How non-conformists move the world.* New York, NY: Viking.

Harrison, T. R. (2007). My professor is so unfair: Student attitudes and experiences of conflict with faculty. *Conflict Resolution Quarterly, 24,* 349–368. doi:10.1002/crq.178

Holmgren, J. L., & Bolkan, S. (2014). Instructor responses to rhetorical dissent: Student perceptions of justice and classroom outcomes. *Communication Education, 63,* 17–40. doi:10.1080/03634523.2013.833644

Horan, S. M., Chory, R. M., & Goodboy, A. K. (2010). Understanding students' classroom justice experiences and responses. *Communication Education, 59,* 453–474. doi:10.1080/03634523.2010.487282

Kassing, J. W., & Avtgis, T. A. (1999). Examining the relationship between organizational dissent and aggressive communication. *Management Communication Quarterly, 13,* 100–115. doi:10.1177/0893318999131004

Kearney, P., Plax, T. G., Hays, E. R., & Ivey, M. J. (1991). College teacher misbehaviors: What students don't like about what teachers say and do. *Communication Quarterly, 39,* 309–324. doi:10.1080/01463379109369808

Kelsey, D. M., Kearney, P., Plax, T. G., Allen, T. H., & Ritter, K. L. (2004). College students' attributions of teacher misbehaviors. *Communication Education, 53*, 40–55. doi:10.10/0363452032000135760

Lebel, R. D. (2016). Overcoming the fear factor: How perceptions of supervisor openness lead employees to speak up when fearing external threat. *Organizational Behavior and Human Decision Processes, 135*, 10–21. doi:10.1016/j.obhdp.2016.05.001

Maddux, J. E., & Rogers, R. W. (1983). Protection motivation and self-efficacy: A revised theory of fear appeals and attitude change. *Journal of Experimental Social Psychology, 19*, 469–479. doi:10.1016/0022-1031(83)90023-9

Norman, P., Boer, H., & Seydel, E. R. (2005). Protection motivation theory. In M. Conner & P. Norman (Eds.), *Predicting health behaviour: Research and practice with social cognition models* (pp. 81–126). Maidenhead, England: Open University Press.

Rogers, R. W. (1975). A protection motivation theory of fear appeals and attitude change. *The Journal of Psychology, 91*, 93–114. doi:10.1080/00223980.1975.9915803

Rogers, R. W. (1983). Cognitive and physiological processes in fear appeals and attitude change: A revised theory of protection motivation. In J. T. Cacioppo, & R. Petty (Eds.), *Social Psychophysiology: A sourcebook* (pp. 153–177). New York, NY: The Guilford Press.

Rogers, R. W., & Mewborn, C. R. (1976). Fear appeals and attitude change: Effects of a threat's noxiousness, probability of occurrence, and the efficacy of coping responses. *Journal of Personality and Social Psychology, 34*, 54–61. doi:10.1037/0022-3514.34.1.54

Sidelinger, R. J., Bolen, D. M., Frisby, B. N., & McMullen, A. L. (2012). Instructor compliance to student requests: An examination of student-to-student connectedness as power in the classroom. *Communication Education, 61*, 290–308. doi:10.1080/03634523.2012.666557

Sprague, J., & Ruud, G. L. (1988). Boat-rocking in the high-technology culture. *American Behavioral Scientist, 32*, 169–193. doi:10.1177/0002764288032002009

Tantleff-Dunn, S. T., Dunn, M. E., & Gokee, J. L. (2002). Understanding faculty–student conflict: Student perceptions of precipitating events and faculty responses. *Teaching of Psychology, 29*, 197–202. doi:10.1207/S15328023TOP2903_03

Tax, S. S., Brown, S. W., & Chandrashekaran, M. (1998). Customer evaluations of service complaint experiences: Implications for relationship marketing. *Journal of Marketing, 62,* 60–76. doi:10.2307/1252161

Thweatt, K. S., & McCroskey, J. C. (1996). Teacher nonimmediacy and misbehavior: Unintentional negative communication. *Communication Research Reports, 13,* 198–204. doi:10.1080/08824099609362087

Zhang, Q. (2007). Teacher misbehaviors and learning demotivators in college classrooms: A cross-cultural investigation in China, Germany, Japan, and the United States. *Communication Education, 56,* 209–227. doi:10.1080/03634520601110104

Additional References

Portions of this chapter have appeared in some of my journal articles including:

Bolkan, S., & Goodboy, A. K. (2013). No complain, no gain: Students' organizational, relational, and personal reasons for withholding rhetorical dissent from their college instructors. *Communication Education, 62,* 278–300. doi:10.1080/03634523.2013.788198

Bolkan, S., & Goodboy, A. K. (2016). Rhetorical dissent as an adaptive response to classroom problems: A test of protection motivation theory. *Communication Education, 65,* 24–43. doi:10.1080/03634523.2015.1039557

SECTION II

Opportunity

Here it is, the section on opportunity. In the following pages we are going to cover some important ideas related to how you can create an environment that allows students to thrive. If you recall, the element of opportunity refers to external forces that inhibit or facilitate human performance. In the case of students' academic achievement, that external force is often you. In this section of the book we will cover three ideas related to your creating opportunities for student learning including retention and transfer, cognitive load, and clarity. Are you ready to do it? Let's do it.

FIVE

Retention and Transfer

OBJECTIVES

By the end of this chapter, you should be a changed person in the following ways:

1. You should be able to describe why remembering facts is important to learning
2. You should be able to articulate various methods you can use to help students remember their course lessons
3. You should have an understanding of the difference between retention and transfer
4. You should know how to increase students' ability to transfer their lessons to new contexts
5. You should be able to explain the difference between hair and fur (This might come in handy during a trivia game at some point in your life)

Retention and Transfer

Recall from Chapter 1 that I mentioned you can help your students learn their course material by getting them to think deeply about their class lessons. That said, this section of the book was written to give you a bit more detail regarding the specifics of this process. In order to do that, however, we are going to use this chapter to first figure out what our goals are for student learning. This is crucial because we can only behave in ways to facilitate students' academic success if we have a definition of what it means for students to be successful in the first place. So, to get the process started, let me ask you this question: what are your goals for student learning in your classrooms?

Now, when you think about your goals I don't mean that you should ask yourself about the content of the material you teach. Instead, when you think about your goals I want you to think about what you want your students to be able to do with the material they learn in your classes. For example, if you are teaching persuasion, will you be happy if, at the end of the term, your students have memorized the different components of various persuasive theories? Is that good enough for you? Or, would it be better if your students walked away from your class able to use the components of these theories to design a persuasive campaign on their own? Maybe that is too much. Perhaps creating a campaign is unrealistic. Maybe you would be happy if, instead, your students left your class able to analyze advertisements and political rhetoric using the theories you taught them. Whatever the case, being clear about what you want from your students is an important step in teaching; knowing this information will help you determine the types of thinking processes your students should engage in to reach this outcome.

Having said the above, this chapter was written to help you determine the goals you might adopt for student learning and to help you understand how the types of educational opportunities you provide to your students might influence their attainment of these goals. Specifically, in the section on retention, we will first learn about the importance of helping students remember their course material. Although some people might ridicule the simple goal of helping students remember what they learned, we will talk about why it is important to help students make changes to their long-term memories and we will discuss how accumulating information can eventually lead to their expertise. After retention, we will cover the idea of transfer. In this section we will learn what it takes to get students to apply the information they learn in a variety of situations that fall outside their immediate learning environment.

How Do Students Learn?

According to researchers Lorin Anderson and David Krathwohl (2001), teachers might concentrate on helping their students learn in one of two general ways. These include rote learning (i.e., giving students the ability to remember course concepts) and meaningful learning (i.e., giving students the ability to transfer the knowledge they gain in class to new problems or situations). To be fair, I am not so sure that rote learning is any less meaningful than "meaningful learning," so it might be better to think of these two outcomes by the other names they are typically referred to: retention and transfer.

As teachers, it is important to know that retention and transfer can be facilitated by a variety of cognitive processes related to what is often called "Bloom's Taxonomy" of learning including: *remembering, understanding, applying, analyzing, evaluating,* and *creating* (Anderson & Krathwohl, 2001; Krathwohl, 2002). According to Anderson and Krathwohl (2001), each of the cognitive processes listed here differ in regards to the depth and complexity of learning; and, anything beyond remembering (i.e., understanding, applying, analyzing, evaluating, and creating) is usually associated with the idea of transfer. We'll take a look at each of these ideas in turn to determine what it means to help students retain and transfer what they learn in our classes.

Retention

As a teacher, I am sure you give your students tests. But, when was the last time you took a test? I took a test about a month ago, but it was a blood test so it doesn't count. Besides that, I can't remember the last time I took an exam. Can you? Whether or not you can remember the last time you took a test, I want you to take one now. Specifically, I want you to take a look at a few questions posted below to see how well your previous teachers helped you learn. These questions aren't too hard, they're something like what you might expect to see on the television show *Are You Smarter than a Fifth Grader.*

Okay... So let's see if you are, in fact, smarter than a fifth grader. See if you can get these questions right...

1. What is the capital of Georgia?
2. In what year did the Second World War begin?
3. What is the tallest mountain on the planet?

How did you do? The answers to the questions above are: (1) Atlanta, (2) 1939, and (3) either Mt. Everest (if you are measuring from land) or Mauna Kea (if you are measuring from the sea floor). Did you get all of them correct? Do we need to re-enroll you in the fifth grade?

In this part of the chapter we are learning about retention, and at this point I should mention that retention is usually associated with either recognition or recall (Krathwohl, 2002). In the case of the three questions listed above, I asked you to recall information because you had to search your brain, and then retrieve the correct answers from your long-term memory (Anderson & Krathwohl, 2001). This is different from recognition where you only have to identify the correct answers in order to pick them. The following questions are recognition questions, take a look at these and see how you do:

1. What state has the nickname "the Golden State?"
   a. Hawaii
   b. Florida
   c. California
   d. Alaska

2. In what years did the American Civil War take place?
   a. 1673–1681
   b. 1781–1893
   c. 1861–1865
   d. 1902–1904

3. What is the capital of New Jersey?
    a. Newark
    b. Atlantic City
    c. Trenton
    d. Jersey City

So, how did you do with these questions? Here are the answers: c, c, and c. After seeing the questions posed here, you know that remembering involves recall and recognition. These are the basic building blocks of knowledge and, as they compare to transfer, they represent what Anderson and Krathwohl consider to be less sophisticated learning outcomes. Knowing this, I want you to ask yourself: Is this how you want your students to learn? Do you really want them to simply memorize facts? My reaction to these questions is usually, "why not?" Let me explain . . .

Some educators might interpret the goal of retention as being inferior to transfer. If pressed, these people might make it seem like remembering information is a simple exercise for the students of teachers who do not ask them to apply themselves in a more thoughtful fashion. But, I am not so sure. Fundamentally, even if you have been exposed to information, if you cannot retrieve what you have studied then some people might argue that you never really learned anything in the first place. Not to mention, although some teachers might think memorizing facts is an unworthy goal to pursue, the reality is that remembering information is essential to higher levels of learning—such as transfer (Anderson & Krathwohl, 2001). Specifically, some researchers argue that having a large store of information in one's memory helps lead to the formation of more advanced knowledge and claim that this store is one of the things that differentiates experts from non-experts (see Chase & Simon, 1973; Lane & Gobet, 2011).

In support of the arguments made above, researchers John Sweller, Paul Ayres, and Slava Kalyuga (2011) argue that helping students remember is at the heart of what it means to provide competent instruction. Essentially, helping students remember is crucial in education because, as the researchers claim, the reason humans are able to successfully navigate a complex world in the first place is because we have built up large stores of information that can be recalled when the situation asks for it. As Sweller et al. (2011) put it, "the extent to which we are able to go outside and pick a flower or carry out mathematical operations are both determined by the amount of knowledge held in long-term memory" (p. 19). According to Sweller and his colleagues, experiences that seem easy to us (e.g., picking a flower) are only simple after we have stored enough information about these situations to make them seem routine.

In reality then, remembering is important because knowing what to do and recognizing when to do it are crucial determinants of our ability to function as operative adults. Thus, as Sweller et al. argue, one of the main purposes of teaching is to move information into the long-term memory stores of our students in order to help them behave in ways that are appropriate for their environments. So, what does this all mean? It means that helping students retain the information they are learning *is* important to their academic success. And, the same is true for you. If you want to be considered learned, you must first create a large store of information in your tiny head if you are to ever draw on this knowledge when the circumstances call for it. Let me see if I can make this point clearer with a few examples.

The authors who write about human memory and its role in expertise often use the example of chess to make their point. According to these researchers (e.g., Sweller, 2010; Sweller et al., 2011), what makes chess experts, well experts, is that they have superior memories for chess. To be clear, expert chess players do not have superior memories compared to you or me, it is just that they have better memories regarding chess moves compared to you or me (Chase & Simon, 1973). Essentially, based on their vast experience with the game, researchers claim that expert chess players have memorized thousands of configurations of various chess pieces and understand how the placement of these might lead to different outcomes. Put differently, expert chess players are better than beginners because they have memorized thousands of potential chess moves (and counter-moves) so no matter what decision you make as a novice, experts are likely to react in a way to defeat you because they have seen your move before and know the most appropriate way to respond.

Similar conclusions might be drawn from the study of sports contests. According to some researchers, elite athletes are the ones who use their brains the least. Yes, you read that correctly. Although it may sound counterintuitive, it's true. A recent study demonstrated this fact by conducting research on the brain of Neymar Junior, a Brazilian soccer star who plays for the esteemed club team Barcelona in Spain. In this study, scientists found that when moving his foot, the soccer player expends less mental effort compared with other individuals who are not at his level of soccer badassness (Naito & Hirose, 2014). Essentially, findings from this study point toward the conclusion that when Neymar plays a game of soccer, he only needs to use small amounts of mental energy to get his body to do what he wants.

Similar to what we learned about chess masters, the researchers who undertook this study concluded that by practicing a behavior many times (i.e., building up the knowledge of what to do and in what circumstances to do it), elite athletes cause long-term changes in their brains that allow them to perform intended behaviors without having to think about them very much. In Neymar's case, the authors noted that his extensive training as a kid allowed him to automate (memorize) much of the process of moving his feet to play soccer as an adult. As a result, the authors contend that he spends fewer mental resources focusing on the details of what he is doing and therefore has more resources to devote to higher-order needs such as game strategy.

Although all of this might sound complex, it really is not. What Neymar did is essentially the same thing you and I did when we learned how to drive. At first, I am sure you had to think about everything you did when you drove (e.g., hands at a specific spot on the wheel, check the mirrors, check the speedometer, cover the brake when you see red lights ahead, etc.). Now, you can probably drive without really thinking about it at all. Admittedly, when it comes to driving this might sound kind of scary, but the work of William Smiley Howell (1982) might help us make sense of what's going on.

According to Howell, people move through various stages of competence to reach proficiency. And, the people who are the most proficient are the ones who have memorized the skills they need to be successful. The bulk of Howell's stages include: *unconscious incompetence, conscious incompetence, conscious competence, and unconscious competence*. Here's how they work . . . Imagine you are interested in going surfing. Before you learn to surf, you might be under the mistaken impression that surfing is easy. Do you think surfing looks easy? I bet your answer depends on whether or not you have ever tried to surf. I know that when I was in high school, before I ever tried the sport, I thought it would be simple: Just catch a wave, stand up, look cool, and do it all over again—piece of cake! I figured that, if given the chance, I would take a board into the water, ride a massive wave, and then go on to live the life of a cool surfer dude. My misperception of surfing is best described by the first stage of Howell's ladder of proficiency: *unconscious incompetence*—I was terrible at the sport, and I had no clue how terrible I was.

I completed my undergraduate degree at the University of San Diego. And, in my first semester, I was excited about my proximity to the Pacific Ocean so I decided to make the most of it by taking a surfing class for some physical education credits. On the first day of class, I went to the Mission Bay Aquatic Center and learned about the mechanics of surfing for a few hours before being handed a wetsuit and a massive 10-foot foam board. I was a bit upset at having to learn with a lame foam board (as opposed to a cool fiberglass board), but I took it anyway and walked to the beach. As I walked into the water and made my first attempt to get past the breaking waves, I realized that perhaps I had oversold myself on my ability to actually surf. Wave after wave pounded my fragile body and there was nothing I could do to make progress beyond the whitewash. When a particularly large wave crashed in front of me and slammed the surfboard onto my head, I just about quit (I also realized why they had given me a soft foam board instead of one made out of hard fiberglass).

Although I probably looked like a drowning cat out there, I kept trying, and I was finally able to catch a tiny "wave" of whitewater as it swept past me. However, my excitement was short-lived as my board went nose-first into the sea, flipping me into the churning foam and leaving me with water in my ears, nose, and throat. At that point, I gave up and I walked up the beach to take a seat on the sand and watch my classmates engage in their own struggles with the ocean. Looking back on it now, I know that as I walked out of the water, defeated, I was in Howell's second stage of proficiency: *conscious incompetence*—I was bad at surfing, and now I knew exactly how terrible I was.

It is said the first step toward recovery is admitting you have a problem, and we might use that saying as a colloquial definition of conscious incompetence. Essentially, conscious incompetence is the stage where you know you are bad at something and use this realization to do the things you need to do to get better. That said, knowing how bad I was at the sport, I took several more surf lessons and tried hard to learn how to do it the best I could. After several experiences like the first one, I finally got past the whitewater and into the open sea. From there, I eventually learned how to catch an actual breaking wave. Success!

Still, even though I can finally surf, to this day I have to think about what is happening to perform adequately. That is to say, when I am in the water, I have to talk to myself about my position on the board, when to paddle, and when to stand up. I literally have to think about all of these steps as I attempt to catch a wave. Although I can do it, I have to think about the process to coach myself to success each time. This is the third step in Howells' ladder of proficiency: *conscious competence*—I can perform a behavior, but I have to think about it as I go.

Although I am not the worst surfer in the lineup anymore, I still envy the people who sit on top of their boards enjoying the sunshine and who, at the first sight of a wave, are able to paddle toward it, flip around to meet it, and then take off without any real effort. When I see these people, it is apparent that they are not experiencing the activity like I am and talking themselves through their success—they are just doing it. Put succinctly, they have practiced for so long and have learned how to surf to such a degree that they no longer have to think about what they are doing when they catch a wave.

As it relates to what we have been discussing, these individuals have reached the fourth step of Howell's ladder of proficiency: *unconscious competence*. Athletes who are able to get to this stage do not have to use their mental resources to think about what they are doing. Instead, they use their knowledge of their bodies and the situation to simply behave appropriately. They have encountered experiences like this in the past and these individuals simply select the appropriate response from their store of information. Athletes like this do not have to think about their actions; they have memorized what they need to do to be successful and, as such, they just act.

Importantly, the information related to athletic ability also pertains to learning in general. As you already know, one of the differences between beginners and experts lies in experts' ability to marshal the appropriate information from long-term memory when faced with environments that demand it (Sweller et al., 2011). In the case of athletic performance, this difference may occur in the form of what scientists call procedural or implicit memory. In the case of educational attainment, this difference occurs in the form of semantic or declarative memory. Either way, beginners have to use limited mental resources to think through problems. Experts, on the other hand, simply use knowledge (i.e., the ability to recognize and respond to problems based on experience) to solve them. In other words, while novices have to try to figure out and think through what they are doing, experts just know what to do.

One of the conclusions we might reach from the information outlined above is that helping students memorize and perhaps even automate information is crucial to their becoming experts in a particular field. This may explain why Sweller and his colleagues are so adamant that one of the most important purposes of teaching should be to help our students develop a store of information that they have access to from their long-term memories. As Sweller (2011) and his colleagues argue, "If nothing has changed in long-term memory, nothing has been learned" (p. 24).

How to promote retention

At this point, you might be wondering how you can help your students remember their course lessons. This is a good question, and it is one that Peter Brown, Henry Roediger, and Mark McDaniel (2014) answer comprehensively in their book titled *Make It Stick: The Science of Successful Learning*. In this book, the authors note that there are several techniques teachers can use to help enhance students' memories for class material. Based on my reading of their work, one of the most important things teachers can do to achieve this goal is to ask students to retrieve their memories after they have already been formed.

But, how do we get students to retrieve their memories? Simply put, we can get students to do this by asking them to remember (and think about) the things they have learned previously. One of the easiest ways to do this is to quiz students when we teach. For example, the authors note that instead of simply reviewing the information students were supposed to read from their textbooks for class, teachers might consider having a short quiz at the beginning of their lessons to get students to remember the things they learned from their readings. Similarly, instead of reviewing the core components of a lecture at the end of class, the authors argue that teachers can enhance students' memories by providing a short quiz that allows students to test themselves. In both cases, students have to remember the information they learned and are forced to engage their minds to search for the answers to the questions being posed. As Brown and his colleagues argue, the process of remembering is active and the thinking that takes place when student do this makes their memories stronger than they would be if students sat and passively listened to you review their lessons.

Importantly, to maximize the positive effects of memory retrieval, Brown and his colleagues go on to argue that teachers should provide multiple, cumulative quizzes throughout the learning term. Essentially, the idea being promoted by Brown and his colleagues with this advice is that students are more likely to remember what they have been taught when they are provided with multiple opportunities to retrieve information at spaced intervals throughout a course. So, for example, this may mean that instead of having one or two tests in a semester, teachers might consider providing a variety of quizzes throughout the length of the term.

As Brown et al. note, quizzing students at multiple points in the semester, with information accruing cumulatively, provides students with the chance to think about and learn their course information on several occasions: Doing so benefits students in at least two ways. First, students benefit because they are exposed to, and responsible for, information more than once. Instead of simply studying course material on one occasion because it is only tested on one midterm, having multiple, cumulative quizzes requires that students revisit what they learned throughout a course to keep the information fresh in their minds. Second, students benefit from multiple quizzes over an extended period of time because they are exposed to information at spaced intervals, which allows their memories to consolidate. Consolidation refers to the idea that, as Brown et al. explain, after we learn something, our memories take time to stabilize in our heads—similar to how Jello takes time to stabilize in your refrigerator. Thus, by providing spaced exposure to course information, we can ensure that students are learning in a manner that allows for the creation of stable, long-term memories.

In summary, the point of this section was to teach you that memorizing information is an important aspect of student learning. This is so much the case that some scholars argue it is at the heart of what it means to learn. Knowing this, we should work hard to help our students retain what we teach them, and we can achieve this goal by asking students to remember their course material over several spaced intervals to help make sure their memories become both strong and durable.

Transfer

Now that we have learned about the importance of retention, it should be clear that remembering information is a crucial aspect of student learning. Still, we have to keep in mind that for many of us, helping students learn is not just about providing factual information they can store in their long-term memories. In addition to helping them learn facts, another purpose of instruction is to help students "recognize large numbers of problem states and situations and what actions [they] should take with those" (Sweller et al., 2011, p. 24). In other words, learning is not *just* about remembering; it is also about being able to apply newly acquired information under a variety of circumstances. Although teaching factual information is crucial, it is also important to help students develop enough experience to recognize when using that information might be considered appropriate or inappropriate.

Consider me for example. I teach a class on bargaining and negotiation, and in that class there are several rules, techniques, and procedures students need to remember if they are to become proficient. That said, do you think I would be happy if my students only learned the material to the point where they could recognize it on a multiple choice test? Of course not. What's the point of learning to negotiate if students can't transfer that knowledge to new scenarios where they engage with others outside the classroom? If all my students earned 'A's on my tests and yet failed as negotiators in their business or personal negotiations, I am not certain I would be too proud of my instruction. Thus, as I am sure most of you would agree, helping students use the information they learn in our classes in novel situations is an important second step after we help them remember what they have been taught. To get to this second step, we have to focus on helping students transfer what they learn.

To transfer information, students must be able to make sense out of the connections between facts and figure out how to apply course lessons in new settings. That's where cognitive processes like understanding, applying, analyzing, evaluating, and creating come in. The difference between each of these ideas and remembering is that, as Anderson and Krathwohl (2001) put it, students who engage in these processes think of information in new contexts instead of simply relying on what has been taught to them in the past. Students who are able to transfer their knowledge don't just memorize facts, they also learn the meaning of the ideas behind the information they are taught so they can apply their knowledge under a variety of circumstances.

For example, in the class I lead on bargaining and negotiation, I teach students a rule for making concessions that we call the "baby rule." This rule is based on negotiator Jim Thomas' (2005) assertion that when you get below your target price in negotiation, each concession should be made to seem increasingly difficult to give. In his own words, Thomas notes that when you get below your target price and are forced to make concessions, you should do so while "kicking and screaming" (p. 83). I call this the baby rule to help students remember that when they get below a predetermined point in their bargaining plan, they should act like babies and only give tiny concessions while simultaneously making a big deal out of each one. When I teach students this rule, I want them to understand the underlying principle—not just memorize the terms "kicking and screaming." That said, if students learn the underlying idea of what it means to offer concessions while kicking and screaming, they should get the following test question right.

> What should your concession plan be if you get below your target?
>
> a. Rule of halves
> b. Steeply tapered concession
> c. Small concessions made reluctantly
> d. Do not go below your target
> e. Both A and B

Unfortunately, as you might imagine, some students don't get this question right. When I ask them why not, these individuals often tell me that they did not see the answer "kicking and screaming" and therefore had to guess when choosing their response. Although my students obviously remembered what I taught them, when I hear my students say this, I know that I failed to help them transfer the idea to a new situation.

In the case of this example, students who only memorized the terms kicking and screaming can only get one question right—if I phrase the response option exactly as they learned it, they will be able to answer correctly. However, students who learn information for transfer ultimately comprehend the underlying principle related to the baby rule and, as such, are able to select the right response regardless of the phrasing of the answer or the circumstances of the question. Because these students are able to recognize the shared characteristics between "kicking and screaming" and "concessions made reluctantly," they are more likely to pick the correct answer, "c."

As should be clear from this example, one of our jobs as teachers is to help students learn information in such a way that they can apply it appropriately under varying conditions. So, how do we help students transfer information and who are the students who end up learning to transfer their knowledge to new situations? The answer to both of these questions is simple: Students who learn to transfer information are those individuals whose teachers ask them to practice transferring the information they learn. I want you to notice something particular about the answer I gave so I am going to repeat it. The students who are able to transfer their knowledge are those people *whose teachers ask them to practice transferring the information they learn.* As Levin (1988) noted, students' ideas about "what are and what are not effective learning strategies are not very accurate" (p. 197), and because this is the case, if you want students to be able to transfer the information they learn, you need to help them do it. There are several ways to help students transfer information including understanding, applying, analyzing, evaluating, and creating. We'll cover these ideas next.

Understanding

Despite the fact that many of us use the word regularly, do you really know what it means to understand something? Do your students? Maybe we should turn to the experts for help. According to Anderson and Krathwohl (2001), people understand something "when they build connections between the new knowledge to be gained and their prior knowledge" (p. 70). Essentially, people are said to understand an idea when they can provide examples, or otherwise explain a topic by paraphrasing it. To put it simply, if you can't explain something in your own words, it is impossible to say that you understand it. For instance, can you tell me how fear appeals work to gain influence? Can you explain why a magnetic compass made on Earth won't work on the moon? Can you tell me why you are able to fire a bullet from a gun when you are under water (even though there is a lack of oxygen)? If you can explain these ideas, put them in your own words, and come up with new examples that illustrate the same concepts under different circumstances, then you can say that you understand the topics. If not, then it would be difficult to convince me that you do, in fact, understand them.

That said, if we want to ensure that students understand the concepts we teach in our classes we should think about doing two things. First, we should ask them to demonstrate that they comprehend the concepts being taught in our classes. Engaging students in the process of forming a deep understanding of class lessons is crucial if they are to develop their knowledge to this level. Second, we should present our course concepts in a manner that allows students to develop a deep understanding of what we are teaching. By helping students recognize the underlying principles in our course lessons, we can help them form a better understanding of the topics we are trying to teach. Let's go over each of these ideas in the order they were introduced . . .

Okay, so first things first, to get students to learn information in ways that help them transfer their knowledge to new situations you should ask them to demonstrate their understanding. How can you do this? You can do this by asking students to explain ideas in their own words and to come up with examples that illustrate the concepts they are learning. In addition, you can ask them to: compare and contrast different ideas, look for patterns in various lessons, summarize course material, and extrapolate beyond what they have learned to new situations (Anderson & Krathwohl, 2001).

Whatever you do, you need to remember that you are a huge part of the process: You have to ask your students to do these things. Simply lecturing to students and then crossing your fingers and hoping that they engage in thoughtful processing is not going to cut it. Instead, if you want students to think about their course lessons in ways that demonstrate and enhance their understanding, *you have to ask them to think about the course material in this manner.* This is because without being prompted to think deeply about course concepts, most students will not engage in this behavior (King, 1992). The problem we are trying to overcome by asking students to demonstrate their knowledge is the "illusion of knowing," where being confident about knowing the ideas presented during class gets confounded with actually mastering the ideas presented in that lesson (Brown et al., 2014). Thus, by asking students to demonstrate their understanding using the techniques reported in the previous paragraph, we can help students think through their course lessons in a meaningful fashion and we can guide them to deeper levels of understanding if necessary.

The second idea to keep in mind when it comes to promoting understanding is the notion of helping students move beyond surface level observations to deeper levels of abstraction. In their chapter on how experts differ from novices, writers for the National Research Council (2000) note that this is one of the differences between these two groups of people. Essentially, while novices tend to focus on the specifics of various scenarios, experts are able to move beyond the surface level traits of examples to extract the meaning that underlies each. Thus, to help students transfer what they learn, you might try to get them to think like experts by helping them move beyond the surface structure of their lessons to focus on the meaning of what each lesson represents. One way to achieve this outcome is to use multiple examples when you explain course concepts. I'll give you an illustration of how to do this below . . .

Imagine you want your students to learn the idea that knowledge is power. To explain this concept, pretend you tell your students that when a person takes their car to get fixed, a mechanic who knows more about cars than the car owner can force this person to pay for unnecessary work. You tell your students that if the victim does not know any better, he or she might have to do what the mechanic says. Now imagine that after you give this example, you ask your students to paraphrase its meaning. In doing so, you learn that your students understand the meaning of the example to be that people in positions of power can force others to do what they want. Is that what you wanted students to learn? Not really. In this case, students came close to the answer you were looking for but might not have gotten it completely right.

So, after hearing from them, you might give a few more examples of the concept. For instance, you could tell your students how informed shoppers can protect themselves from high prices if they do their research before attempting to purchase a service or a product. In addition, you could give the example of police interrogations to let students know that, unless they are under arrest or suspected for a crime, the police do not have the right to detain them for an extended period of time. And you can tell your students that, even if they are detained or arrested, they do not have to talk to the police unless they feel like doing so. Thus, you might tell your students that knowing their rights as American citizens gives them the ability to interact with others in a manner that protects their best interests.

Do you think your students would get it now? Would they understand the idea that knowledge is power if you taught it with all of these examples? I bet they would. And, why would they? Because by giving multiple examples, you can help students think about the concept in a variety of ways. And, importantly, by helping students think about a concept in different ways you can help them move beyond thinking about the surface elements present in a single example to detecting the patterns and underlying principles (i.e., the similarities and differences) being explained in the various illustrations you provide.

To sum up, this section was written to teach you that by having students explain a topic (e.g., asking students to paraphrase the lesson or come up with examples of their own) and by taking the time to use a variety of methods to explain a topic yourself (e.g., giving multiple examples), you can help students develop a better understanding of their course lessons. This, in turn, should help students transfer the information they have learned to novel situations (National Research Council, 2000). Just remember, it is important for you to promote students' understanding of course concepts at a deep level of abstraction . . . they need your help to make this a reality.

Applying

The next idea related to transfer refers to promoting students' ability to apply what they have learned in class to solve problems. In many cases, this idea might be best expressed when students engage in active learning exercises. Having students engage in active learning exercises is important because these experiences provide tangible benefits to student learning. I'll discuss some of these benefits below.

In the class I mentioned I teach on bargaining and negotiation, I have my students perform no fewer than eight in-class negotiation exercises, each with a different person. Those are just the exercises I have in class; there are several others students must complete outside of class as well. The reason I have my students engage in so many negotiations is because asking students to participate in these exercises operates as a test of their knowledge. And, as such, these activities force students to remember what they have been taught. This is important because, as you know, students can only really be expected to transfer the skills and knowledge they have retained somewhere their memories.

The second reason I have students engage in these exercises is because doing so provides them with opportunities to receive an objective measure of their learning; asking students to participate in various negotiation interactions allows them to realistically experience and reflect on their strengths and weaknesses as negotiators. Instead of thinking that they know how to correctly structure a plan for their movement from one price to another, for example, my students are forced to actually put what they learned into practice. Because this is the case, these students receive tangible feedback on their progress and are less likely to fall prey to experiencing the illusion of knowing we learned about earlier.

In addition, a third benefit related to the provision of so many negotiation exercises is that my students get to experience multiple opportunities to negotiate across a variety of situations. This is beneficial because students who are able to think about how their lessons apply under several circumstances are more likely to envision their use in multiple settings. For example, by participating in the exercises with several other students, pupils in my class are forced to recall the information they learned and apply it appropriately across a variety of social interactions. By providing my students with opportunities like this, they get to practice what they have learned and apply this knowledge in dynamic environments that more closely align with the experiences they are likely to have outside the classroom. If, on the other hand, I only asked my students to apply the information they learned in one specific negotiation context, they may be less likely to see the connections between what they have learned and how this information might be applicable in a variety of unique situations (National Research Council, 2000).

The process of application is especially important when teaching any type of skill. For example, a few years ago while I was in Bangkok, Thailand, I took a cooking class at one of their famous cooking schools (the Blue Elephant!). The class was set up so that we first learned about the ingredients of a dish and then watched a professional cook it up. After learning about how to make the dish, we were asked to apply our new knowledge. Specifically, the next step in the class was for us to go to a kitchen and try to replicate the steps we had just learned. Now, was it necessary for us to actually go to the kitchen and cook the dish for ourselves? You bet it was. Letting me practice cooking for myself allowed me to focus on what I had been taught and use the information I learned to solve a problem. Although I thought I knew how to follow the directions of our instructor when I saw him prepare the meal, I realized that I only really learned how to make the dishes we were taught when I had the chance to make them on my own. By cooking the dishes myself, I was forced to remember the steps of the recipe to figure out what I was doing right and what needed work, and by cooking several dishes I was able to practice my new skills under varying circumstances.

Of course, the same process could be used for theoretical instruction as well. For example, teachers can ask students to apply a theory of student need satisfaction or relational stability to help solve issues of student dropout rates on campus or to devise a plan for addressing student complaints about instructors. Essentially, by asking students to apply what they know to a variety of actual or hypothetical scenarios, you provide them with opportunities to transfer their knowledge in the moment. And, having them engage in this type of activity is good training for future instances that will require the same set of skills or knowledge. The more students are asked to apply course lessons under different circumstances, the more they should be able to apply their lessons to situations other than ones where the information was first learned.

Analyzing

In addition to understanding and applying, to help students transfer information you can also ask them to analyze the concepts they are learning. Generally speaking, analyzing refers to the processes of differentiating, organizing, and attributing when learning. In practice this might include, for example, determining how various parts of a theory or business plan work together in a coherent manner to reach a desired goal (Anderson & Krathwohl, 2001). The fundamental ideas related to analyzing involve distinguishing various parts of a class lesson from one another, deciding which aspects are relevant and which are not, and organizing the information in ways that lead to appropriate conclusions.

Because I loved the Thai cooking school so much, let me explain how this works with an example from this context. Though they did not have us complete this step in the actual class (the class was only 3 hours long, after all), analyzing at the cooking school might involve taking students to a market, giving us 20 dollars (or 700 Baht), and asking us to gather the ingredients necessary for a specific plate. Doing so would necessitate that we use what we learned in class to distinguish what ingredients we need from those we do not, and use that information in a manner that could be organized toward the development of a specific dish. To complete this task successfully, we would have to demonstrate an understanding of what the necessary ingredients are, we would have to explain why we chose to leave others out, and we should be able to articulate how these decisions relate to the underlying purpose and flavor of the dish we are trying to create.

Evaluating

According to Anderson and Krathwohl (2001), evaluating is the act of making a judgment based on perceptions of quality, effectiveness, or some other criteria. For example, evaluating might involve asking students to use what they know to check the effectiveness of a solution in a hypothetical scenario, asking students to critique the behaviors of others, asking students to critique their own performance, or asking students to improve the outcomes that result from a case study. Basically, the process of evaluating involves asking students to thoughtfully reflect on how the lessons they learned can be used, or have been used, in an effort to reach some desired goal.

At its core, the ability to promote transfer through evaluation might come from the "reflection principle" articulated by Roxana Moreno and

Richard Mayer (2010). This principle is associated with the idea that asking students to reflect on the correct methods for executing some behavior forces them to think deeply about the concepts being learned in their classes. The reason this is important is because students can, and often do, mindlessly engage in their course lessons. That said, asking students to evaluate their lessons in novel ways will help them become more reflective in the learning process. Stated differently, evaluating allows you to help students think about their course lessons in deep and meaningful ways—ways of thinking they might not engage in on their own. Thus, when paired with understanding, application, and analysis, students might be able to use evaluation to more fully comprehend the material they are exposed to in class.

Creating

Finally, creating refers to the idea that teachers ask students to use what they learn in class to generate solutions to new problems or to think about scenarios in ways that lead to new conclusions. Again, using my experience at the cooking school as an example, the notion of creating might include me producing a new recipe for a new Thai dish based on my knowledge of the tastes and textures of various traditional ingredients. Similarly, creating might include planning a Thai dinner that combines diverse and complementary dishes to craft a meal with a variety of balanced flavors. In addition, creating might include my ability to generate substitutions in an original recipe if the requisite ingredients were not available at my local grocery store. In each of these cases, the notion of creating showcases my ability to put together the concepts I learned regarding Thai cuisine in a manner that allows me to produce a novel outcome.

Feedback

In the previous sections I noted that you should help your students transfer the information they learn in your classes through the processes of understanding, applying, analyzing, evaluating, and creating. It must be said, however, that you should not leave your students to their own devices when asking them to participate in these activities. Instead, it is important that you, as the expert, provide feedback to help ensure that students are learning the information they are studying correctly. This is what Moreno and Mayer (2010) meant when they suggested the "guided activity principle." The idea underlying this principle is that students tend to learn better when asked to engage in guided activities compared with when they are asked to engage in activities on their own. This is the case for two reasons. It turns out that students learn better with guided activities because when activities are guided, you can ensure that students stay on task and you can provide immediate feedback as they encounter various issues related to their experiences.

A guided activity is exactly what I experienced when I took the cooking class in Bangkok. As I mentioned earlier, when our teachers trained us how to cook various dishes, they took us through several stages of instruction. The first stage included written directions regarding how to cook a dish and the second included a visual demonstration of what we were going to do. The third stage of the process was to actually prepare the meals we were learning to cook. As I noted, this part of the lesson involved us traveling to a small cooking station where we tried to replicate the recipes we had just been taught. However, as it pertains to providing feedback, the cooking school did something that I thought was impressive. You see, we were not left to our own devices when cooking the meal. Instead, the school had experienced chefs walking around to help the class along the way. So, for example, instead of letting me unsuccessfully cook Pad Thai on my own, the chefs observed me and provided corrective feedback that helped me avoid mistakes that would be detrimental to my final product. Instead of letting me fail at cooking the meal by myself, the cooking school ensured that I was given help through the provision of pointers so that I could practice in such a way as to learn how to cook correctly.

Okay, now you know that providing feedback during transfer activities is important. But, let me ask you this: Do you know what kind of feedback is best? You don't have to actually answer that question, Moreno and Mayer (2010) have already done it for you. According to these researchers, the best kind of feedback is that which is both corrective *and* explanatory. In other words, the best feedback you can provide to your students is feedback that (1) helps them understand what they are doing incorrectly *and* (2) explains why the behaviors might be considered erroneous in the first place. For example, when I first arrived at my cooking station in the cooking class, I remember turning the gas burner all the way on high as I put oil and crushed garlic into my skillet. My goal was to heat the ingredients up quickly so that I could get to the appropriate cooking temperature as fast as possible. When my instructor saw what I did, however, he asked me to turn the burner down *and* explained that by keeping the burner on high I would likely scorch my garlic before I added any other ingredients. Doing so, he told me, would change the flavor of my dish from delicious to not-so-delicious. As this example illustrates, the provision of feedback that included a correction and an explanation helped me adjust my behavior and allowed me to understand the importance of doing so.

Summary

Retention and transfer—those are the two major goals you might have for your students when it comes to their learning. So, as a teacher you have to ask yourself: what do you want your students to do. Do you want them to memorize facts and discipline-related terms? Or, would you prefer it if your students were able to use those facts to understand events they have not yet encountered?

Maybe thinking about what you want for your students doesn't actually make a difference. What I mean is that, perhaps based on the way you interact with your students, it doesn't matter what your goals are. This is because, whether or not you want your students to retain or transfer information, the tests and assignments you ask students to complete might communicate what you want your students to learn. For example, if you tend to use tests that ask students to fill in the blanks or respond to matching items, you might be simply asking your students to remember their course information. Similarly, if you tend to lecture to students exclusively and if students are only tested using multiple choice exams, you might be surprised to learn that many of them end up simply studying to recognize the terms you put on your tests.

On the other hand, if you ask students to apply the things they have learned in more thoughtful ways, such as through open-answered exam questions, you may be happy to know that your students might, in fact, move beyond the goal of just retaining information. Research supports this conclusion insofar as students who perceive that they will be assessed at a deep level of comprehension tend to study their course materials to understand them as opposed to simply memorizing them to pass their classes (see Baeten, Kyndt, Struyven, & Dochy, 2010 for a review). The reason I bring all of this up is because I want you to recognize that despite your intentions for student learning, the types of teaching tasks, learning assignments, and tests you ask your students to engage with might influence their cognitive processing in ways you do not anticipate. Consider your students like little economists—they react to the external incentives present in their environment in a logical manner.

Perhaps the simplest way to assess what you are asking your students to learn is to take a look at your class lessons to determine what students are doing for most of their time. If you want students to remember information, then lecturing, providing opportunities to drill what has been learned, and asking for responses to multiple choice tests might be a good idea. On the other hand, if your goal is to promote transfer, you should look into how much time your students spend explaining concepts on their own, applying the ideas they have learned in various exercises, analyzing their class lessons, evaluating the performance or presence of some behavior as it relates to the concepts you have taught, or creating new outcomes from the lessons they have been exposed to. Whatever your goal is for learning, you should understand that the way you teach your students ultimately helps to create opportunities that either facilitate or impede this outcome.

END-OF-CHAPTER QUESTIONS

1. Why do you think the act of remembering information gets a bad rap compared to transfer?

2. Based on what you learned in this chapter, what's one thing you can start doing to help students transfer the information they have learned in your courses?

3. What is the structure of your classroom like? In other words, based on the way you teach and evaluate your students, do you think you are most likely promoting retention or transfer?

KEY TERMS

Retention: The process of remembering information including recalling and recognizing

Unconscious incompetence: Being bad at something and not knowing it

Conscious incompetence: Being bad at something and knowing it

Conscious competence: Being good at something, but having to think about your performance to do it well

Unconscious competence: Being good at something without having to think about it

Consolidation: After we learn something, our memories take time to stabilize

Illusion of knowing: Thinking that you understand information because it was easy to process

Transfer: The ability to apply information under a variety of circumstances

REFERENCES

Anderson, L. W., & Krathwohl, D. R. (Eds.). (2001). *A taxonomy for learning, teaching, and assessing: A revision of Bloom's taxonomy of educational objectives: Abridged edition*. New York, NY: Addison Wesley Longman.

Baeten, M., Kyndt, E., Struyven, K., & Dochy, F. (2010). Using student-centered learning environments to stimulate deep approaches to learning: Factors encouraging or discouraging their effectiveness. *Educational Research Review, 5,* 243–260. doi:10.1016/j.edurev.2010.06.001

Brown, P. C., Roediger, H. L. III, & McDaniel, M. A. (2014). *Make it stick: The science of successful learning.* Cambridge, MA: Harvard University Press.

Chase, W. G., & Simon, H. A. (1973). Perception in chess. *Cognitive Psychology, 4,* 55–81. doi:10.1016/0010-0285(73)90004-2

Howell, W. S. (1982). *The empathic communicator*. Prospect Heights, IL: Waveland Press.

King, A. (1992). Facilitating elaborative learning through guided student-generated questioning. *Educational Psychologist, 27,* 111–126. doi:10.1207/s15326985ep2701_8

Krathwohl, D. R. (2002). A revision of Bloom's taxonomy: An overview. *Theory Into Practice, 41,* 212–218. doi:10.1207/s15430421tip4104_2

Lane, P. C. R., & Gobet, F. (2011). Perception in chess and beyond: Commentary on Linhares and Freitas (2010). *New Ideas in Psychology, 29,* 156–161. doi:10.1016/j.newideapsych.2010.08.002

Levin, J. R. (1988). Elaboration-based learning strategies: Powerful theory = powerful application. *Contemporary Educational Psychology, 13,* 191–205. doi:10.1016/0361-476X(88)90020-3

Moreno, R., & Mayer, R. E. (2010). Techniques that increase generative processing in multimedia learning: Open questions for cognitive load research. In J. L. Plass, R. Moreno, & R. Brunken (Eds.), *Cognitive load theory* (pp. 153–177). New York, NY: Cambridge University Press.

Naito, E., & Hirose, S. (2014). Efficient foot motor control by Neymar's brain. *Frontiers in Human Neuroscience, 8,* 1–7. doi:10.3389/fnhum.2014.00594

National Research Council. (2000). *How people learn: Brain, mind, experience, and school.* Washington, DC: National Academy Press.

Sweller, J. (2010). Cognitive load theory: Recent theoretical advances. In J. L. Plass, R. Moreno, & R. Brunken (Eds.), *Cognitive load theory* (pp. 29–47). New York, NY: Cambridge University Press.

Sweller, J., Ayres, P., & Kalyuga, S. (2011). *Cognitive load theory.* New York, NY: Springer Publishing.

Thomas, J. T. (2005). *Negotiate to win: How to get the best deals every time!* New York, NY: HarperCollins.

SIX

Cognitive Load

OBJECTIVES

By the end of this chapter, you should be a changed person in the following ways:

1. You should be able to explain the barriers associated with learning due to our working memories
2. You should be able to articulate the three categories of cognitive load
3. You should be able to articulate how to increase students' germane load
4. You should be able to explain how to reduce students' extraneous load
5. You should be able to understand the meaning behind this quote (sometimes attributed to the Buddha): "a jug fills drop by drop"

Cognitive Load

In Chapter 5, we went over how teachers can ask their students to engage in a variety of processes that ultimately help them retain and transfer the information they learn in their classes. But, one question you might ask is, where did this information come from in the first place? Well, when it comes to most academic subjects, the answer is as follows: Although you might be able to learn something on your own, most of us gather information about our world from other people. As it pertains to teaching your students, these other people might include you, your teachers, or researchers in your field of study who wrote the book you assigned for the course. That said, the goal of instruction is to get information to your students from these sources, and this is what scholars mean when they argue that, at its heart, teaching is really just the transfer of information from the brains of one set of people to the brains of others (Sweller, Ayres, & Kalyuga, 2011).

That said, because information is stored in the heads of other people, it must be communicated to be learned. And, although as a professor of Communication Studies it pains me to say it: There are some major problems when it comes to communication and our cognitive ability to acquire information. Ultimately, this means that teaching others is inherently constrained by our system of transferring information. Let me see if I can make the point by contrasting an ideal method of communication with the method we actually use . . .

If you could design a perfect system of communication it would, at its core, have to be one that allows you to transfer your intended meaning to others with no loss of information. That means, when communicating, you would have to be able to send all the requisite details and information associated with your message without any loss in fidelity. Essentially, a perfect system of communication would allow you to, literally, transfer information from your head to somebody else's head in a manner that perfectly replicated the meaning of the data that originated from your noggin. It might be something like sending an attachment in an e-mail to a friend over the Internet; when you send a word document to your buddy through Gmail, the information arrives exactly as it was sent—the substance and the details remain exactly the same.

So, think about it . . . is that how you communicate? When you speak to others, are you able to communicate your intended meaning perfectly, with no loss in data? I doubt it. For instance, when you tell someone that you love him or her, does this person know exactly how you feel? I mean this literally; does the person you communicated your love to know *exactly* what you feel inside? Probably not. And, why not? Because when you communicate you do not throw thoughts or feelings from your head into the heads of other people. Don't believe me? Let's try it. Take a moment to think of a beautiful woman. Do it. Close your eyes and try to determine who this person is and think about what she looks like. Got it? Okay good. Did you happen to think of the 1980's supermodel Kathy Ireland? That's who I had in mind. Wait, you didn't think of the person I thought of? Why not?

The reason you did not think of Kathy Ireland is because I was unable to throw my thoughts into your head. Instead, you probably thought of a beautiful woman based on your personal experiences with one in your life or in the media. And, that's the point. Unfortunately, with our current methods of human communication, all we can do is tell others what's inside our brains and hope that our experiences overlap enough so that they interpret our messages the way we intended. Thus, because human communication is an imperfect system of information transfer, you can never really be sure that when you tell someone that you love him or her, this person understands exactly what you mean when you articulate your feelings. Of course, the same thing is true for other words and, really, the rest of your communication as well.

Okay, so what? Human communication is imperfect. Is there any living thing that can communicate perfectly? Maybe. A few years ago, I remember watching a television show about aliens, and in the particular program I was watching there was the story of a spacecraft that crashed in Roswell, New Mexico. In that show, a man recalled being at the crash site when he was a boy. He said that when he encountered the site, he saw a little alien laying in the wreckage and when he approached it, the alien looked at him with its huge alien eyes. When their eyes locked, the alien reached out his little alien hand and rubbed the boy's shoulder with its alien skin. When this happened, the boy remembered experiencing the feeling of falling from a great height and missing home. In other words, the alien was able to communicate its exact feelings to the boy without having to use any words.

Okay, this might not be the exact story the boy told, but it was something like that. Regardless of the important details, the point is that the little alien was able to touch the boy with its hand and its skin and in doing so, it was able to throw its thoughts into the head of the boy it was touching. To me, that sounds like the perfect transfer of information—like sending an e-mail attachment to someone else's brain. What a great way to communicate! If only humans could throw their thoughts into the minds of other humans. Can you imagine what that would mean for us as teachers? Instead of having to teach our students their lessons for the day, we could just walk into class, touch each one on the shoulder, and go along our merry way. I could perfectly transfer my lessons to students without any loss of information . . . what an ideal way to teach!

Though the method of communication described above might be the ideal toward which we strive, this process is not likely to be made possible in our lifetimes. However, despite this setback, we are not altogether deficient in our ability to transfer information because we *can* throw sounds and light into other people's heads by talking and sharing images. And, although we already learned that this method of communication is not perfect, we can still use it to teach others in our role as educators. That said, when it comes to instruction there is another hugely problematic issue with our form of communication; transferring words and pictures by sending sound and light into other people's heads necessitates that information gets stored in the brains of others only after it passes through their visual and auditory processing systems. Unfortunately, as we will learn in this chapter, the problem with this process is that these systems are not all that great at passing along information.

So, what should we do? I suggest that instead of waiting around for Google to develop a thought-throwing device that allows us to communicate with others by simply rubbing their shoulders with the skin from our hands, we should learn to teach within the limits of our methods of communication. In this chapter, we are going to cover cognitive load theory which will help us outline some of these limits. Specifically, we will cover how researchers slice up learners' different processing capacities to better understand how students' working memories are used during instruction. By taking into consideration the limits of students' mental capabilities, you should have a better understanding of how various instructional practices might improve the opportunities you provide to students for learning your course material.

Cognitive Load

I once read a motivational poster somewhere that told me I was born perfect in every way. I am not sure that is true, but it feels good to think it. The great news for you is, if that poster was talking to me as a stranger, then it was obviously talking to you as well. So, just like me, you are a perfect being. Good for us. What this poster failed to consider, however, was our working memory. That part of us is pretty limited.

What is your working memory? Technically speaking, your working memory refers to a "limited capacity system allowing the temporary storage and manipulation of information necessary for such complex tasks as comprehension, learning and reasoning" (Baddeley, 2000, p. 418). Less technically speaking, your working memory includes your short-term memory systems (e.g., your auditory and visual short-term memory systems) and the processing systems that help you make use of your short-term memory (Cowan, 2008). Your working memory is essentially that part of your brain that allows you to remember phone numbers for the short period of time needed to transfer that information from a webpage, for example, to your telephone.

Getting back to the point, your working memory is limited. In fact, some researchers would even go so far as to claim that your working memory is inferior to that of a chimpanzee's (Inoue & Matsuzawa, 2007). To be fair, several scholars claim that this statement is not entirely true (for example, see Cook & Wilson, 2010). Still, whether or not your memory is better than an ape's, the point is that the two are similar enough for there to be a scientific debate about the differences between your ability and a chimp's ability to recall information after being exposed to it for a brief period of time. To me, that says something about the limitations of your working memory.

So just how limited is your working memory? Well, it depends on the form (i.e., auditory, visual, or tactile; Bigelow & Poremba, 2014), but generally scientists think that your short-term memory can hold somewhere between three and four units of information, and maybe up to seven (Cowan, 2001, 2008); however, some scholars limit this number to just one (see Rose, Buchsbaum, & Craik, 2014, for a brief review). How did anybody come to this conclusion? Science, baby, science. For example, scientists devise experiments that require people to do things like look at a list of scrolling numbers and, when the scientist says stop, recall as many of the numbers at the end of the list as possible. As researcher Nelson Cowan (2008) explains, when asked to complete activities like this, people generally remember between two to six numbers with the average person recalling about three or four. This reflects limits in the *quantity* of your short-term memory. Unfortunately, your short-term memory has limits on its *duration* too. According to researchers, the length of time you can keep information in your short-term memory is measured in seconds (Cowan, Saults, & Nugent, 1997; Sweller et al., 2011). And the buck doesn't stop there. In addition to its limited quantity and duration, scholars note that your working memory is limited in its *processing* capacity as well (Baddeley, 2000; Sweller et al., 2011). Your working memory's processing system essentially enables your ability to think about things in the moment and, according to researchers, is limited regarding its capacity for "organising, combining, comparing or manipulating items of information" (Sweller et al., 2011, p. 43).

So why do we care about the ideas presented here? We care about these ideas because, although long-term memory is immeasurably large (Sweller et al., 2011), information can only enter students' long-term memories if it is first processed through their working memories (Sweller, van Merrienboer, & Paas, 1998). And, speaking colloquially, if students' working memory systems are strained by instructional designs that ask them to process too much information at once, these systems run the risk of breaking down (Sweller et al., 2011). Of course, if your students' working memory systems can't handle the incoming data, their long-term memory systems have no way to gather and store the information you have taught. You can think of long-term memory as a giant parking garage and short-term memory as a one-lane road leading there. Although you might be able to park thousands of cars in the garage, those cars can only get there if you are careful about how they arrive on the road—too much traffic is likely to cause a jam.

So what does this all mean? It means that if you overwhelm your students' working memory capacities, they are not likely to learn what it is you are trying to teach. Perhaps this is why Sweller et al. (1998) argued that "the implications of working memory limitations on instructional design can hardly be overestimated" (p. 252). In fact, according to these scholars, "anything beyond the simplest cognitive activities appear to overwhelm working memory" and "any instructional design that flouts or merely ignores working memory limitations inevitably is deficient" (Sweller et al., 1998, pp. 252–253).

Okay, so we now know that students' working memory systems have major limitations that influence their ability to gather and store information in their long-term memories. At this point, the question I would be asking if I was reading this chapter is: Can we do anything about it? The answer to that question is "yes." Yes, we can. To do that, however, we have to first learn about the potential sources of "load" that might impinge on students' working memories. If we can better understand these potential sources of load, we might be able to figure out what we can do to reduce the strain we place on our students' working memory systems.

Three loads

According to cognitive load theorists, students' processing capabilities are a function of three different loads. As you will learn in what follows, one of these loads is good, one is bad, and the other is ugly—just joking, the other is pretty much neutral. Because each of these loads requires mental processing space, each should be managed, or at least considered, when creating and delivering instructional materials. Why should we think about cognitive load when we develop our teaching plans? We should do this because, according to researchers Paas, Tuovinen, Tabbers, and Van Gerven (2003), students' experiences of cognitive load represent the "major factor that determines the success of an instructional intervention" (p. 64). Let's discuss each of the loads.

Germane load

To put it simply, germane load refers to the processing space students need to think about course information in the hopes of learning it—this is the good load. Essentially, germane load refers to cognitive efforts designed to move information into students' long-term memories. What are these efforts? You already know the answer: These include any attempt to make information more meaningful by linking new information to students' current base of knowledge (Levin, 1988). In Chapter 5 we went over a few ways students can do this including trying to memorize their lessons, demonstrating their understanding through the provision of examples, applying the information they learn by engaging in activities and exercises, and evaluating various scenarios and outcomes as they relate to the lessons they have been taught.

A good way to think about germane load is to think of your students as creepy little spiders sitting in their learning webs. Spider webs are very sticky and can do a great job of catching prey like flies. As you can imagine, the more a fly gets caught in a spider's web, the more likely it is to stay caught. For example, if a single strand of spider's web caught a fly as it buzzed about, we might expect that the fly would have a decent chance of escaping. On the other hand, if the fly was caught by multiple strands of the spider's web, its chances of getting out of the trap would likely diminish. Well, the lessons your students learn are essentially like flies in a spider's web. It is just that, the web we are talking about here refers to students' stored memories. Thus, the more students can tie information from your class to the things they already know, the more likely students are to retain the information they are learning. Flies are less likely to escape when they are entangled in a spider's web. Similarly, information is less likely to escape when it is entangled in a student's base of knowledge.

Right now, you might be asking why germane load is considered a load at all. If germane load refers to the tasks of remembering and learning, why is it considered a load and not just learning? The reason germane load is considered to be a load is because it takes mental effort and processing space to engage in the activities described in the foregoing paragraphs. Sure, it would be nice if students could simply listen to class lectures and learn the material without effort. But, like most things in life, nothing is free. Thus, the first load you should consider as it applies to your students' success is their germane load.

Intrinsic load

The second type of load to keep in mind when students attempt to learn your course lessons is intrinsic load—this is the neutral load. Intrinsic load reflects the nature of the material itself and is typically thought to be a function of the number of elements in an idea and the interactivity of those elements (Sweller et al., 1998). Interactivity refers to the necessity to learn ideas simultaneously instead of through serial processing (one idea at a time). Sweller et al. (2011) discuss learning the periodic table and chemical reactions as an example. Learning the individual elements in the periodic table is thought to reflect a low level of intrinsic load because the elements can be learned independently of each other. You can literally make flashcards for each element and study these one at a time. Learning chemical reactions, on the other hand, represents a high level of intrinsic load because the equations used in the process involve several working parts that must be considered simultaneously.

If intrinsic load refers to the nature of the information to be learned, you might be asking whether or not it is possible, as a teacher, to change the intrinsic load students are faced with in your classes. According to Sweller et al. (2011), not really . . . intrinsic load is largely fixed. Well, that's not entirely true. Sweller and his colleagues note that material can become easier to learn if it is taught in a manner that allows learners to study the information one step at a time. Thus, if instructors can find a way to break their lessons into manageable chunks, the difficulty of learning course material may diminish in accordance with the reduced level of interactivity. For example, instead of teaching an entire dance at once, a teacher can try to break student learning into blocks of movements that can be learned one stage at a time. However, Sweller would caution that there are no shortcuts in learning. People who learn in steps do not learn the relations between steps which means that, in reality, they do not learn the concepts in their entirety. When students do eventually learn the relations, they must ultimately face the intrinsic interactivity of the concepts anyway.

I can attest to the truth of this logic. When I was in college, I once took a hip hop dance class with the hope of impressing others in my future nightclub endeavors. In this class, I remember we first watched the dance we would be performing in its entirety to get a feel of what we would be asked to do. Because learning the dance required too many moving parts to focus on at once, the way we learned the choreography was to memorize the various moves in a series of progressions that took us through several four- and eight-step counts. I remember that when learning the individual progressions, I was able to get each count right. However, after learning the progressions, I also remember that putting them together proved as difficult for me as it would have been to learn the dance from the start. When the music played and we were asked to perform the entire thing, I was lost. Although in the beginning the teacher was able to simplify the instruction by teaching me the individual moves one at a time, putting it all together still necessitated that I manage the interactivity of the assignment. It was too hard, I simply could not do it, and my hopes for impressing people through my cool dance moves never ended up materializing.

As you might imagine, there are some ideas that relate to a reduced intrinsic load, including the fact that intrinsic load can differ from person to person based on various levels of their personal qualities (such as a person's prior knowledge and abilities; Plass, Kalyuga, & Leutner, 2010). For instance, as it pertains to the class I mentioned earlier, learning the dance was much easier for people who were already seasoned performers and this was probably the case because they experienced a lower intrinsic load. Nevertheless, I want you to remember that, although it may differ among students, intrinsic load usually tends to remain unchangeable for teachers. As Sweller et al. (2011) explained, "for a particular task presented to learners with a particular level of knowledge, intrinsic cognitive load is fixed" (p. 65).

Extraneous load

Extraneous cognitive load refers to the load imposed on students' working memories through instructional design and is reflected in the way teachers present course material (Sweller et al., 1998)—this is the bad load. Extraneous cognitive load essentially refers to "the effort required to process poorly designed instruction" (Sweller et al., 1998, p. 259) and occurs because of the things you do as a teacher to distract, confuse, overwhelm, or otherwise teach students in a manner that leads to inefficient learning. Ultimately, course designs that impose a high extraneous load shift students' attention from engaging in elaborate processing (germane load) to other processes that do not result in learning.

Can this be possible, you ask? Could it be the case that teachers actually behave in ways that impair students' abilities to learn their course lessons? Um, yeah. As you learned in Chapter 4, there are a variety of teacher misbehaviors that ultimately disrupt student learning (e.g., Kearney, Plax, Hays, & Ivey, 1991). If you recall, when asked to report what their teachers do to irritate, demotivate, or distract them in their classrooms, instead of answering "nothing" as teachers might assume, students reported that their teachers engaged in a variety of undesirable behaviors including straying from the subject matter, rushing through material to get it done, writing illegibly on the board, and providing confusing lectures. As you might realize, these types of behaviors are detrimental to student learning (Goodboy & Bolkan, 2009). What you might not realize, however, is that these types of behaviors occur more often than you think (Bolkan & Goodboy, 2013, 2016).

Similar to what we learned in Chapter 4, the point here is that as a teacher you have a lot of power in the classroom and function as a tool for student learning. But, just like any tool, you can be used in a way that is helpful or in a way that is terribly damaging. Just as a hammer can build a house, a hammer in the wrong hands can cause a lot of physical harm. Similarly, you have to understand that as a teacher, you have a vast potential to benefit students. However, you must also be open to the idea that some of the things you do in class might be detrimental to students' educational well-being. Importantly, if you are open to this concept, then you can start behaving in ways that lead to being a better teacher.

Additivity Hypothesis

By now you might have already figured out your goal as it pertains to cognitive load. If not, let me give you a hint: Your goal as a teacher is to decrease students' extraneous load and increase their germane load, all the while keeping in mind the presence of students' intrinsic load. Okay, that wasn't a hint, it was the answer. Still, now we are on the same page. To help explain what I mean here, we need to visit the additivity hypothesis, and I'll show you an example of how it works by using the analogy of pouring liquids into a cup.

Essentially, the additivity hypothesis explains that for instruction to be effective, "intrinsic and extraneous loads together should not exceed limited working memory capacity" (Kalyuga, 2010, p. 55). In other words, in order for students to have enough processing space to learn, they cannot be overwhelmed by the combination of the difficulty of the lesson and the way it is presented. If students' intrinsic and extraneous loads take up too much space, there will be no room left over for students to think about their course lessons. To illustrate this concept, let's get to that cup example I promised.

Think of this cup as representing a student's brain . . .

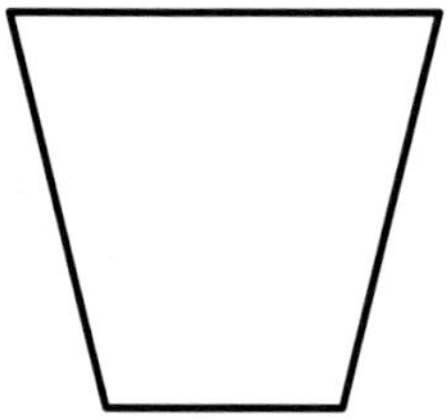

Basically, the cup represents the capacity students have in their working memories to process information. As we now know, our goal as teachers is to help students learn our course material by facilitating their germane load. Based on this, if we were playing a game of "Beer Pong," our goal would be to sink a ping pong ball into our student's cup (see below).

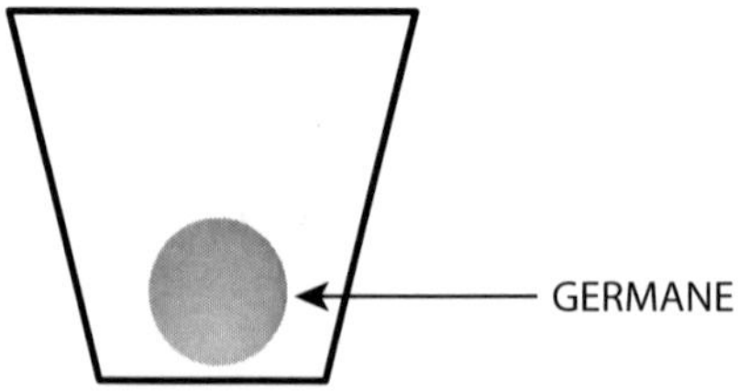

*All images Courtesy of San Bolkan

If all we had to do was sink a ball into an empty cup, it might be an easy game for us. However, there are other factors to consider. And, one of those factors includes students' intrinsic load. Therefore, in order for students to be able to think deeply about course concepts, the ball must stay in the cup in the presence of intrinsic load. In our example, intrinsic load will be shown as a dark liquid.

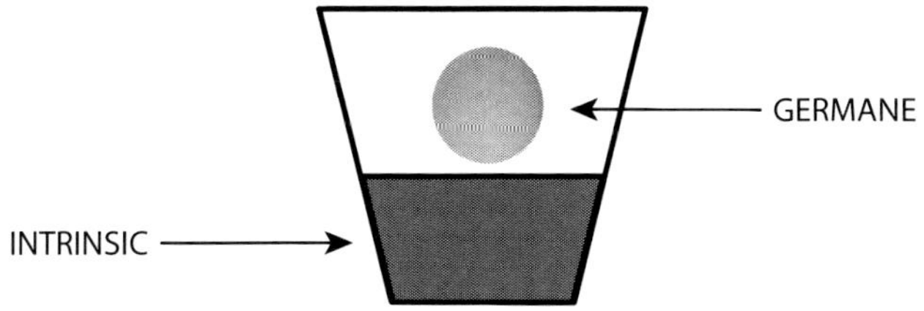

As you can see in the image presented above, as long as the ball still fits in the cup, students should be able to learn their course lessons: There is still room in their working memories for germane processing to occur.

Unfortunately, to quote late night infomercials, "that's not all!" In addition to intrinsic load, we need to take into account students' extraneous load. That comes from you as a teacher. And, although you may try your hardest to teach in a manner that reduces the extraneous cognitive load students might experience, nobody is perfect. As such, we might expect there to be some minimum amount of extraneous load in your instruction. Still, as long as there is room in the cup, your students should be able to think about their course lessons in a manner that facilitates learning. If you take a look at the next image, this is what it would look like:

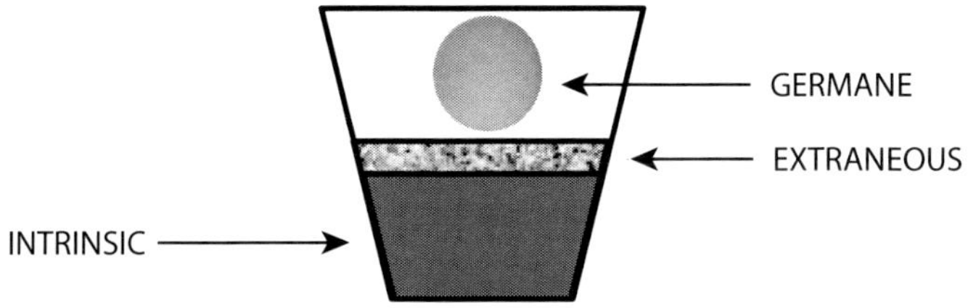

Can your students still learn at the stage represented in the previous image? Well, the ball is in the cup, right? This tells me they can. This is the additivity hypothesis in pictorial form. As long as the combination of intrinsic and extraneous loads does not overwhelm students' working memories, they should have space in their brains to process germane load.

The problem, however, occurs when your instruction is delivered in such a way as to take up so much room that your students can no longer think about your course lessons. If the load you put on your students through poor instructional design becomes too much, you will make it impossible for them to learn. An image of what this would look like is presented below:

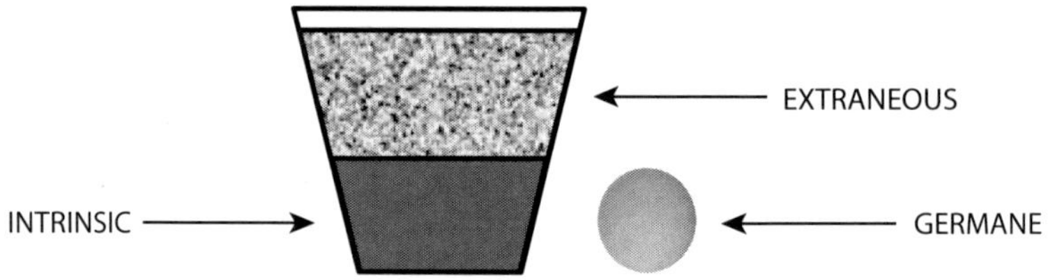

In the picture above, the ball is obviously out of the cup. What this means is that, based on your methods of instruction, you have introduced extraneous load to such an extent that there is no more room for students to process germane load. And, that's pretty much the central point of cognitive load theory: If you overwhelm students' processing capacities by inappropriately increasing students' extraneous load, they are less likely to learn their course lessons.

What Can You Do?

Now that you know a bit more about cognitive load theory, you know that by working within the limits of students' working memories, you can influence their learning outcomes in a positive manner. To achieve this goal, you might try to enhance one of two aspects related to students' academic experiences. As we already mentioned, there may not be much you can do to influence the intrinsic load students experience in your classes. Because this is the case, your efforts might be best spent focusing on increasing students' germane load and decreasing their extraneous load. So, how do you do that? Let's address each type of cognitive load in turn.

Increase students' germane load

The first thing we should do as teachers is focus on enhancing students' germane load. The idea here is that for students to think deeply about their course lessons, someone has to get that ball into the cup in the first place. I'll cover two ways to do that, these include becoming a translator and using multimedia.

Becoming a translator

As you know, germane load refers to the effort students spend linking new information to their current base of knowledge. Of course, you have also learned that some scientists refer to this as elaboration (e.g., Craik & Lockhart, 1972). The fundamental process of elaboration is making the information more meaningful, which makes it easier to remember (King, 1992). Another way of framing elaboration is to say that students tend to remember more when they make sense of the information they are being taught. Having said all of that, one of your jobs as a teacher is to make information meaningful to your students to help them make sense of what they are learning.

To explain this concept, I'm going to have you try to remember a series of letters that Cowan (2001) presented to readers in his article on short-term memory. I want you to look at the letters once, and after you have a few seconds to look at them, I want you to close your eyes and try to recall all 12 letters. Are you ready to give it a try? Remember, just look at the letters once and do so briefly. Okay, ready? Here are the letters: *fbicbsibmirs*. Okay, now look away and see how many letters you can remember . . .

Did you get them all? If not, don't worry—as you probably already know from what we learned so far, the task is difficult for most people (and chimpanzees). The task of remembering the letters you were exposed to is difficult because there are more pieces of information than your working memory can handle. That said, there is a trick to enhancing your recollection. Cowan explains that if you simply "chunk" the letters into four acronyms: FBI, CBS, IBM, and IRS, it becomes easier for you to recall all of them—remembering the letters seems easy now, right?

Why is it easier to remember the letters when you chunk them? For one, you only have to remember four things instead of 12. However, and perhaps more importantly, in addition to having fewer things to recall, it is also easier to remember the letters when they are chunked because they now have significance—they are grouped together meaningfully and linked to ideas/things you are already familiar with (Baddeley, 2000). Ultimately, it becomes easier to remember the 12 letters when you chunk them the way Cowan did because they are now associated with information in your long-term memory that aids in your recall. And, that's the point: Information becomes meaningful when it is linked to previous knowledge and, when information becomes meaningful, it is easier to remember.

Based on what we covered in this section, we might conclude that your job as a teacher is to be somewhat of a translator. In other words, your job as a teacher is to digest the information students are supposed to learn and turn it into information that is meaningful for them. Instead of simply repeating what is in some textbook, your job is to think of ways to interpret students' lessons in such a manner as to be able to turn something that might seem like gibberish (i.e., fbicbsibmirs), into something that actually makes sense to them. That's one way to get the ball into the cup.

Multimedia

A second way to get the ball into the cup and to enhance students' germane processing is by using what is referred to as the "multimedia principle" (Moreno & Mayer, 2010). Put simply, studies of the multimedia principle demonstrate that students who are exposed to information in both a visual and a verbal format enjoy more meaningful learning compared to students who receive just one or the other. There are two explanations for why the multimedia principle works. As researchers Mayer and Moreno (2003) argue, one way to explain the effect of the multimedia principle is through enhanced processing. Essentially, the idea is that humans have two information coding systems corresponding to visual and verbal channels. Based on this, if you help students learn by promoting information processing in both systems, you essentially double students' opportunities to manage their course material and create associations with previously learned information (see the modality effect in the next section). The second explanation for the benefits of the multimedia principle is that information presented both visually and verbally may be more interesting to students, which is likely to get them more engaged in, and motivated toward, their studies. Importantly, researchers have shown that students who are more motivated to think deeply about their course lessons tend to outperform their less motivated classmates on tests of retention and comprehension (e.g., Bolkan, Goodboy, & Kelsey, 2016).

In addition to the multimedia principle, other ways to enhance germane processing exist as well. In fact, we will cover a variety of methods to help motivate students in the section of the book dedicated to the "W" category of our COWs framework. For instance, in the section of our book dedicated to willingness, we will discuss how to make students self-determined, how to deliver lectures in a charismatic fashion, and what you can do to intellectually stimulate your students in the classroom. For now, however, I think it is sufficient for us to make the point that your job is to enhance germane learning to the greatest extent possible. Moreover, after reading this section, you know that two ways to do this include using your mental resources to translate class information into meaningful lessons and using multimedia presentations to engage students' visual and verbal processing systems.

Decrease students' extraneous load

As we mentioned earlier, in addition to increasing students' germane load, your goal as a teacher is to decrease students' extraneous load. There are several ways to do this, but it is impossible for me to cover them all in this short section. If you want a more comprehensive account of how to reduce students' extraneous cognitive load, you should read John Sweller, Paul Ayres, and Slava Kalyuga's (2011) excellent book titled, most appropriately, *Cognitive Load Theory*. However, let's at least cover a few ideas related to extraneous cognitive load to give you an understanding of the types of things you can do as an instructor to give your students the best opportunity to learn to their potential. In this section, we will cover ideas including: modality, split attention, worked examples, segmenting, signaling, coherence, redundancy, and teacher clarity. Let's get to it!

Modality

The first idea we'll discuss is the "modality principle" (Mayer & Moreno, 2010) or the "modality effect" (Sweller et al., 2011). To use an analogy, the modality effect basically tells teachers that if you want your students to successfully carry a bag of groceries home along with a six-pack of beer, it is better to ask them to do it with two hands instead of just one. Essentially, cognitive load researchers argue that because people have both auditory and visual processing systems, teachers can take advantage of each by spreading the cognitive load between these two formats (Mayer & Moreno, 2010; Sweller et al., 2011).

The modality effect explains why we might want to use PowerPoint or some other type of visual system in our classes. If we do this, we can off-load important information (such as the organization of the lecture) into a visual format that leaves students with enough auditory processing space to listen to our lectures. The same is true for written material. Think about how much information you would have to wade through if the example I used to explain cognitive load filling up a cup had been presented in verbal form only. By off-loading some of the explanation into a visual format, I was able to reduce your cognitive load and (hopefully) help you understand the topic I was attempting to explain. If a picture really is worth a 1,000 words, teachers who explain their course material with words *and* images are able to move that much information to a visual format which saves their students the hassle of processing it all through the auditory channel.

Split attention

The next idea I want to talk about is the "split attention effect." The split attention effect refers to extraneous cognitive load placed on students "when learners are required to split their attention between at least two sources of information that have been separated either spatially or temporally" (Sweller et al., 2011, p. 111). As an example of the split attention effect, let me tell you about something I experience in academic journals on a regular basis. When reading an article, I am often referred to a figure (or table, chart, picture, etc.) to help make sense of the text. People usually use these figures along with the text as a way of presenting information to help explain a concept. As a reader, this often works because I have two sources of information that complement each other and combine to inform me about a specific subject. It must be said, however, that when examining visual aids, I am forced to integrate these within the text to make sense of the author's objective. Still, as long as it is easy to integrate the figures and the text, the use of these visual aids in academic articles is usually helpful.

However, despite the potential usefulness of presenting text and figures together to explain a subject, if you have read an academic article lately then you know that publishers do not always present information in the most appropriate manner. Specifically, publishers sometimes place figures and tables in places that are spatially distant from the text they are meant to explain. This is a problem because, when it occurs, readers are forced to hold the information presented in the text in their working memories while they look for and examine the visual aids in another location. In the case of the journal articles to which I am referring, I sometimes have to read the text, skip a page to look at the figure, and then flip back to the text to make sense of the information being communicated. When I am asked to do this, my working memory system becomes strained and it becomes harder to make sense of the information than it would be if it was presented together.

According to Sweller et al. (2011), the way to correct for split attention is to integrate or synchronize the interacting elements of a lesson. Stated differently, when asking students to study elements *that need to be examined together for them to make sense*, these elements should be presented in such a manner that students do not have to search to find one or the other. The less searching students have to do, the better. In the case of the journal articles, the best way to present information would be to have the text and the figures next to each other. Better yet, readers would be likely to process the information more efficiently if the text and the figures were integrated with one another so there is no searching at all. Think about how this relates to the multimedia effect and the modality effect described earlier. In these cases, I told you that teachers can enhance learning when they use both words and pictures. However, according to the split attention effect, both sources of information (verbal and visual) should be presented simultaneously (to promote temporal congruity) in order to minimize the strain on students' working memories and to maximize their learning.

Before we move on, it must be stated that the split attention effect is really only applicable to information that requires two sources of information to be integrated for them both to make sense. This is why I italicized the words I did in the previous paragraph. As Sweller et al. (2011) note, if one source of information doesn't help explain the other, then you don't need to have both. Related to our example of academic articles, if all of the information can be placed in either the text *or* the figure, then having both is unnecessary; readers should be presented with either one or the other. The same is true for the information you learned that relates to the multimedia or modality effects. If you can explain information without overwhelming students by talking *or* by using visual aids alone, then you should present students with only one source of information (this idea is related to the redundancy principle discussed below).

Worked examples

The third idea I'll cover with regard to reducing students' extraneous load is the "worked example effect." To explain this idea, let me ask you to think back to the example we went over in Chapter 1 about teaching someone how to swim. In that example, I told you that without giving somebody instructions about how to swim, he or she would not be very likely to do so successfully. The reason this is true is because people who are thrown into a body of water with no instruction have to essentially use the guess-and-check method to learn how to solve their problem. If you have ever used this method of learning, you know that guessing and checking is tedious, time consuming, and hard on your working memory system. The solution then, according to Sweller et al. (2011), is to give your novice swimmer a fully worked-out example of how to swim in order to help this person build a framework upon which to base their attempts at swimming. For instance, if you provide this person with an example of someone using a freestyle stroke, he or she might figure out that in order to successfully move through the water, it is best to lay prone (instead of bobbing up and down like a pencil) while kicking one's legs and moving one's arms in a crawl-like motion. By giving an example of someone using the freestyle stroke, the person we are teaching can concentrate on learning the right way to swim instead of wasting time trying to figure out what to do in the first place. In their review of the literature, Sweller et al. (2011) give several examples of how instructors can use worked examples in their classrooms including the provision of model answers for mathematical equations and essay questions. Essentially, the idea here is that by helping students understand the right way to do something, they are more likely to do that thing right.

As Sweller et al. (2011) note, some teachers who read this section might object to the notion of providing worked examples for fear that it may lead students to copy instead of think. The truth is, however, that much of human learning, in fact, stems from copying (Sweller, 2010). And, instead of asking students to reinvent the wheel when it comes to learning a skill or solving a problem, it might be wise for us, at least at first, to help students simply observe the correct method for doing so. Of course, we want to make sure that our students don't just memorize the answers we provide—we also want them to be able to come up with answers on their own. To this end, Renkl, Hilbert, and Schworm (2009) contend that to help students learn to come up with answers on their own they should be asked to explain why the solution worked instead of just studying the fact that it did. Essentially, by asking students to explain the logic behind the solutions for themselves, you can help them use the cognitive space they saved from the reduction in extraneous load in a manner that facilitates their germane load.

Another method for helping students actively learn from worked examples includes "fading" (Sweller et al., 2011). Specifically, to help students become more active in the problem-solving process, Sweller and his colleagues suggest giving students a worked example, and once they understand how the problem is structured, allowing them to complete new problems on their own while slowly fading the help provided. For instance, if there are four steps in a problem, you can start by showing how to do all four steps and asking students to explain each. Once students understand the solution in your example, you can ask them to solve a subsequent problem with three steps completed; as you probably guessed, they have to complete the fourth step. Next, you can provide a problem with two steps completed and ask students to solve the other two. You can continue this procedure until students are able to solve an entire question on their own. Ultimately, what is being proposed here is the idea of helping students learn how to solve problems by teaching them one step at a time as opposed to asking them to do too much at once. By teaching students in this manner, you are likely to reduce the extraneous cognitive load they experience.

Segmenting, signaling, coherence, redundancy and redundancy

In addition to the three methods for reducing students' extraneous cognitive load provided earlier, there are other ways to achieve this goal as well. For example, according to researchers Mayer and Moreno (2003, 2010), one of these methods includes segmenting. Essentially, segmenting refers to the idea that you can reduce extraneous cognitive load if you give students enough time to process specific parts of an instructional message before you move on to others. In addition to segmenting, instructors can engage in what the authors call signaling. Signaling includes stressing key words and adding organization to a presentation through headings and an outline. Because students can experience extraneous cognitive load when course material is poorly laid out, signaling helps to reduce this load by making the organization of instructors' lectures more apparent.

In addition to segmenting and signaling, Mayer and Moreno also discuss the ideas of coherence and redundancy. Both ideas refer to the provision of superfluous information. As they pertain to cognitive load theory, the ideas of coherence and redundancy suggest that because students' processing capacities are limited, you are likely to enhance learning if you only expose students to information that is essential for understanding course concepts. Coherence refers to the provision of unnecessary information in course lessons. For instance, a lack of coherence might occur if teachers include superfluous facts, sounds, and visuals in their lessons. As Mayer and Moreno note, students tend to learn more when teachers remove extraneous material from their instruction because doing so gives students more cognitive space to process essential course information.

Redundancy also reflects the presence of superfluous information but refers to the unnecessary replication of information. To explain redundancy, Mayer and Moreno (2010) give the example of on-screen captions. According to the authors, when listening to a video with intelligible audio, the provision of on-screen captions is detrimental to student learning. Because the information is repetitive, students get no benefit from processing both the video and the captions and, if anything, are forced to spend more cognitive resources than necessary to make sense of their instruction.

Teacher clarity

If you are a scholar of instructional communication, you will likely recognize that many of the behaviors associated with reducing students' extraneous cognitive load closely align with the concept of instructor clarity. In fact, as I argued recently, "clear instruction has been operationalized through similar, if not identical, behaviors" (Bolkan, 2015, p. 4). Don't believe me, check it out: Scholars note that clear teachers enact a variety of behaviors to help students learn their course material including pacing instruction appropriately, teaching in steps, using examples, and using advanced organizers, transitions, previews, and reviews (for a review, see Titsworth & Mazer, 2010). That said, because there is a lot to learn about clarity, instead of trying to discuss the subject here, we will use the next chapter to explain clarity in more detail. For now however, all you need to do is relax and pat yourself on the back . . . you are almost finished with the chapter on cognitive load!

Before we finish this chapter let me just say that although there are a variety of things to think about when trying to reduce students' extraneous load, the fundamental idea to consider is this: Are you overwhelming your students' abilities to learn? Importantly, the foregoing examples suggest that some of the things you do might be subtly undermining your instruction; things like the split attention effect and redundancy aren't necessarily obvious at first glance. That said, after having learned about the variety of ways you can undermine student learning, I hope you now have the ability to take appropriate action and change the way you teach to help facilitate your students' success.

Summary

Now that you have reached the end of the chapter, it is time to reflect on what you have learned. In this chapter we have gone over the fact that you, and your students, have terrible working memories. As a result of this fact, we have to keep in mind students' processing capabilities when we attempt to transfer information into their long-term memories. Cognitive load theory helped frame this issue by dividing the processing power of the brain into three components: germane, intrinsic, and extraneous loads. In this chapter, we learned that intrinsic load is largely fixed. But as teachers, we can help students learn if we promote their germane load and reduce their extraneous load. To help you do this, I gave you a few ideas to consider when attempting to increase students' germane processing and decrease students' extraneous cognitive processing. Finally, we concluded with the idea that many of the ideas related to reducing students' extraneous load align closely with instructor clarity.

In the end, all of this was a long way of showing you that, as the teacher, you create educational opportunities for your students to thrive in their classrooms. Although you cannot communicate your course lessons with perfect fidelity by touching your students on their bodies like an alien might with its hands and its skin, by understanding how their learning systems work you *can* teach your students in a manner that functions within the limitations of their working memories.

END-OF-CHAPTER QUESTIONS

1. Which of the three loads do you think matters most for student learning? When it comes to your teaching style, which load do you think you could use the most help with to improve your teaching?
2. Based on what you learned in this chapter, what's one thing you can start doing to increase students' germane loads?
3. What is one thing you can start doing to reduce students' extraneous loads?

KEY TERMS

Working memory: A limited capacity system allowing the temporary storage and manipulation of information necessary for complex tasks such as comprehension, learning, and reasoning

Germane load: The processing space students need to use to think about course information in the hopes of learning it—the good load

Intrinsic load: The nature of the material itself, which is typically thought to be a function of the number of elements in an idea and the interactivity of those elements—the neutral load

Extraneous load: The load imposed on students' working memories through instructional design, which is reflected in the way teachers present course material—the bad load

Additivity hypothesis: As long as the combination of intrinsic and extraneous loads does not overwhelm students' working memories, they should have space in their brains to process germane load

Multimedia principle: Students who are exposed to information in both a visual and a verbal format enjoy more meaningful learning compared to students who receive just one or the other

Modality effect: Splitting cognitive processing efforts between the visual and auditory systems reduces the burden placed on any one of these systems

Segmenting: Instructors' appropriate pacing of information

Signaling: Stressing key words and adding organization to a presentation through headings and an outline

Coherence: Interesting but unnecessary information in a course lesson

Redundancy: The unnecessary replication of information

REFERENCES

Baddeley, A. (2000). The episodic buffer: A new component of working memory? *Trends in Cognitive Science, 4,* 417–423. doi:10.1016/S1364-6613(00)01538-2

Bigelow, J., & Poremba, A. (2014). Achilles' ear? Inferior human short-term and recognition memory in the auditory modality. *PLoS ONE, 9,* e89914. doi:10.1371/journal.pone.0089914

Bolkan, S. (2015). The importance of instructor clarity and its effect on student learning: Facilitating elaboration by reducing cognitive load. *Communication Reports.* Advance online publication. doi:10.1080/08934215.2015.1067708

Bolkan, S., & Goodboy, A. K. (2013). No complain, no gain: Students organizational, relational, and personal reasons for withholding rhetorical dissent from their college instructors. *Communication Education, 62,* 278–300. doi:10.1080/03634523.2013.788198

Bolkan, S., & Goodboy, A. K. (2016). Rhetorical dissent as an adaptive response to classroom problems: A test of protection motivation theory. *Communication Education, 65,* 24–43. doi:10.1080/03634523.2015.1039557

Bolkan, S., Goodboy, A. K., & Kelsey, D. (2016). Instructor clarity and student motivation: Academic performance as a product of students' ability and motivation to process instructional material. *Communication Education, 65,* 129–148. doi:10.1080/03634523.2015.1079329

Cook, P., & Wilson, M. (2010). Do young chimpanzees have extraordinary working memory? *Psychonomic Bulletin & Review, 17,* 599–600. doi:10.3758/PBR.17.4.599

Cowan, N. (2001). The magical number 4 in short-term memory: A reconsideration of mental storage capacity. *Behavioral and Brain Sciences, 24,* 87–185. doi:10.1017/S0140525X01373922

Cowan, N. (2008). What are the differences between long-term, short-term, and working memory? *Progress in Brain Research, 169,* 323–338. doi:10.1016/S0079-6123(07)00020-9

Cowan, N., Saults, J. S., & Nugent, L. D. (1997). The role of absolute and relative amounts of time in forgetting within immediate memory: The case of tone-pitch comparisons. *Psychonomic Bulletin & Review, 4,* 393–397. doi:10.3758/BF03210799

Craik, F. I. M., & Lockhart, R. S. (1972). Levels of processing: A framework for memory research. *Journal of Verbal Learning and Verbal Behavior, 11,* 671–684. doi:10.1016/S0022-5371(72)80001-X

Goodboy, A. K., & Bolkan, S. (2009). College teacher misbehaviors: Direct and indirect effects on student communication behavior and traditional learning outcomes. *Western Journal of Communication, 73,* 204–219. doi:10.1080/10570310902856089

Inoue, S., & Matsuzawa, T. (2007). Working memory of numerals in chimpanzees. *Current Biology, 17,* R1004–R1005. doi:10.1016/j.cub.2007.10.027

Kalyuga, S. (2010). Schema acquisition and sources of cognitive load. In J. L. Plass, R. Moreno, & R. Brunken (Eds.), *Cognitive load theory* (pp. 48–64). New York, NY: Cambridge University Press.

Kearney, P., Plax, T. G., Hays, L. R., & Ivey, M. J. (1991). College teacher misbehaviors: What students don't like about what teachers say or do. *Communication Quarterly, 39,* 309–324. doi:10.1080/01463379109369808

King, A. (1992). Facilitating elaborative learning through guided student-generated questioning. *Educational Psychologist, 27,* 111–126. doi:10.1207/s15326985ep2701_8

Levin, J. R. (1988). Elaboration-based learning strategies: Powerful theory = powerful application. *Contemporary Educational Psychology, 13,* 191–205. doi:10.1016/0361-476X(88)90020-3

Mayer, R. E., & Moreno, R. (2003). Nine ways to reduce cognitive load in multimedia learning. *Educational Psychologist, 38,* 43–52. doi:10.1207/S15326985EP3801_6

Mayer, R. E., & Moreno, R. (2010). Techniques that reduce extraneous cognitive load and manage intrinsic cognitive load during multimedia learning. In J. L. Plass, R. Moreno, & R. Brunken (Eds.), *Cognitive load theory* (pp. 131–152). New York, NY: Cambridge University Press.

Moreno, R., & Mayer, R. E. (2010). Techniques that increase generative processing in multimedia learning: Open questions for cognitive load research. In J. L. Plass, R. Moreno, & R. Brunken (Eds.), *Cognitive load theory* (pp. 153–177). New York, NY: Cambridge University Press.

Paas, F., Tuovinen, J. E., Tabbers, H., & Van Gerven, T. W. M. (2003). Cognitive load measurement as a means to advance cognitive load theory. *Educational Psychologist, 38,* 63–71. doi:10.1207/S15326985EP3801_8

Plass, J. L, Kalyuga, S., & Leutner, D. (2010). Individual differences and cognitive load theory. In J. L. Plass, R. Moreno, & R. Brunken (Eds.), *Cognitive load theory* (pp. 65–87). New York, NY: Cambridge University Press.

Renkl, A., Hilbert, T., & Schworm, S. (2009). Example-based learning in heuristic domains: A cognitive load theory account. *Educational Psychology Review, 21,* 67–78. doi:10.1007/s10648-008-9093-4

Rose, N. S., Buchsbaum, B. R., & Craik, F. I. M. (2014). Short-term retention of a single word relies on retrieval from long-term memory when both rehearsal and refreshing are disrupted. *Memory & Cognition, 42,* 689–700. doi:10.3758/s13421-014-0398-x

Sweller, J. (2010). Cognitive load theory: Recent theoretical advances. In J. L. Plass, R. Moreno, & R. Brunken (Eds.), *Cognitive load theory* (pp. 29–47). New York, NY: Cambridge University Press.

Sweller, J., Ayres, P., & Kalyuga, S. (2011). *Cognitive load theory.* New York, NY: Springer Publishing.

Sweller, J., van Merrienboer, J. J. G., & Paas, F. G. W. C. (1998). Cognitive architecture and instructional design. *Educational Psychology Review, 10,* 251–296. doi:10.1023/A:1022193728205

Titsworth, S., & Mazer, J. P. (2010). Clarity in teaching and learning: Conundrums, consequences, and opportunities. In D. L. Fassett & J. T. Warren (Eds.), *The SAGE handbook of communication and instruction* (pp. 241–261). Los Angeles, CA: SAGE.

SEVEN

Clarity

OBJECTIVES

By the end of this chapter, you should be a changed person in the following ways:

1. You should be able to explain the reasons scholars have had trouble defining clarity in the past
2. You should be able to articulate the five categories of clarity
3. You should be able to explain how the categories of clarity differ from one another
4. You should be able to articulate how you can increase clarity in your course lessons
5. You should be able to hold your breath for at least a minute (Never stop aiming for self-improvement!)

Clarity

As we learned in Chapter 6, it is important that instructors reduce students' extraneous cognitive load and provide them with the opportunity to learn their course lessons. Although we went over several ways to reduce students' extraneous load, I believe that instructor clarity provides the biggest opportunity for teachers to enhance student learning from this perspective. For this reason, I believe that instructor clarity is at the top of the list when it comes to instructor behaviors that have the ability to improve students' academic outcomes. In my opinion, if we were playing the childhood game of "King of the Hill," instructor clarity would stand at the top, reigning supreme. In educational contexts, clarity is the milk to your cereal, it's the gasoline to your motor vehicle, it's the champagne to your mimosa.

So what is instructor clarity, and how does it work? I thought you would never ask. Generally speaking, instructor clarity refers to the "process by which an instructor is able to effectively stimulate the desired meaning of course content . . . through the use of appropriately structured" class material (Chesebro & McCroskey, 1998, p. 262). Does this definition make sense to you? Because it shouldn't.

Do you want to know a dirty little secret about the scholars who study clarity? Here it is: Although there is a variety of research published on the topic, most researchers don't really know what it means to be a clear teacher! Ha! Essentially, what I'm telling you is that researchers typically study clarity without having a clear definition of what it means to be clear. How's that for irony? Okay, don't get me wrong; it is not as if people literally have no clue what it means to be clear. It is just that researchers tend to face two problems when it comes to studying clarity in the classroom.

The first problem is that of too much information. In particular, most definitions of instructor clarity are so broad that they might reasonably include any teaching behavior (e.g., Civikly, 1992; Sidelinger & McCroskey, 1997; Titsworth, Mazer, Goodboy, Bolkan, & Myers, 2015). Thus, it is difficult for researchers to fully capture the extent of teacher clarity without measuring long lists of specific and seemingly unrelated behaviors. The second problem is that of too little information and it manifests itself when researchers use vague definitions of clarity. For example, items in vague measures of clarity tend to ask students how much they "understand" their teachers and the extent to which their teachers are "straightforward." Unfortunately, by being vague, researchers lose important details regarding what teachers actually do to be perceived as clear. As you might reasonably conclude, these vague definitions are circular in nature and do little to inform teachers about what behaviors actually help make their instruction clear. What are we do to?

If you'll indulge me, let's ignore the problems related to the definition of clarity for the moment, we'll get back to them in a minute. For now, let's talk about the benefits of clarity in the classroom. Cool? Cool. Okay, so first, why is clarity beneficial for students? Researchers claim that clarity is beneficial because clear instruction is a necessary condition for students to "cognitively engage in learning tasks" in the classroom (Seidel, Rimmele, & Prenzel, 2005, p. 542). Specifically, as it relates to cognitive load theory (which we just learned!), unclear lectures may reduce individuals' processing capacity by taking away mental resources that could otherwise be devoted to learning (Sweller, 1988). Thus, clear teachers help keep information tidy and allow students to focus on the meaning of their lessons instead of using mental resources trying to decipher and organize the course material themselves (Mayer & Moreno, 2010). Research that I have conducted (Bolkan, 2015) has born this relationship out. Essentially, clear instructors decrease students' extraneous cognitive load and, in turn, increase their opportunities for deeply processing course information. As a result, students of clear teachers tend to be more likely to report engaging in behaviors that are typically indicative of their cognitive learning.

You probably understand that being clear is important to student learning. But you might be wondering how instructor clarity compares to other important predictors of student achievement. Well, in the experimental investigations I have conducted, teacher clarity has been shown to be the strongest predictor of students' exam scores when compared with a plethora of other important classroom variables including: teachers' enthusiasm when delivering a course lecture, students' motivation to learn the material, students' attention, students' self-discipline, and the perceived difficulty of the material. This is what I meant when I said that clarity is the king of the hill. Importantly, I am not the only one who feels this way. Other researchers argue that clear teaching is one of the most important factors related to student learning as well (e.g., Murray, 1983; Rosenshine & Furst, 1971).

Hopefully, by now we can agree that clarity is important. But, the million-dollar question is: How important? If you want a specific figure, results from studies of instructor clarity show that, taken alone, clarity tends to predict between one and two letter grades worth of students' test scores (Titsworth et al., 2015); this is roughly the equivalent of going from something like a C to a B+! That is a huge deal! Most teachers tend to figure that students' test scores are a function of students' intelligence, hard work, or some combination thereof. But, what I am trying to tell you here is that the way you communicate your course lessons is a big part of the equation too.

So, back to the problems regarding the definition of clarity… what can we do about these? Well, luckily for us a recent study has been conducted (okay, I conducted it) in an attempt to fix this situation (see Bolkan, 2016). Specifically, I was fed up with the lack of understanding related to the definition of clarity so I set out to determine what patterns of behaviors, exactly, contribute to students' perceptions of clear teaching. I wanted to do this to help researchers better understand the multidimensional nature of instructor clarity and to provide teachers like you (and me) with a simple framework for understanding the behaviors students perceive as being clear. So, what do you need to do to be a clear teacher? Keep reading!

Dude, Will I Cuddle Strangers?

If you recall, the two problems associated with the definition of clarity noted earlier included, on the one hand, the wide range of specific behaviors that might count toward being clear and, on the other hand, the extreme generality used by some researchers to define instructor clarity. To address these issues, I sought to develop a measure of instructor clarity that described specific teaching behaviors while simultaneously linking these behaviors together into bigger patterns of clear teaching practices. My goal was, essentially, to combine the two methods of defining clarity and to create a manageable list of specific behaviors linked to the different, general ways teachers can be clear in class.

To achieve this goal, I completed an exhaustive review of the literature to come up with a list of 87 items representing various definitions of instructor clarity. Next, using a statistical process called factor analysis, I looked for patterns in the data that ultimately reduced the original 87 items to a more manageable set of 20 indicators reflecting five dimensions of clarity.

So, what did I find exactly? Based on the results of my study, I found that students' perceptions of clarity stem from behaviors linked to five sets of teaching practices including avoiding *disfluency,* not overloading students' *working memories,* allowing for *interaction,* removing superfluous information to provide *coherence,* and providing *structure.* To help you remember these ideas, I came up with a memory device. The device is a mnemonic, and it is the title of the heading for this section: Dude, Will I Cuddle Strangers? So will you? You might be surprised to know that if you like cuddling strangers, you may be able to make some big money. Well, I don't know about "big money," but in Japan and the United States there are "cuddle cafes" where people pay to cuddle strangers. That could be you! Yucky.

Now that we know there are five dimensions of instructor clarity and what they are, let's go ahead and discuss each one in turn. One of my goals in the following sections is to help you better understand what it means to be clear by defining each of the dimensions. Another one of my goals is to help you learn how you can facilitate clear communication in class by giving you advice regarding specific behaviors that are linked to these various clarity dimensions.

Disfluency

Disfluency refers to instructors who have a difficult time explaining class concepts in a simple manner, who cannot create examples to explain course concepts, and who deliver course lessons in a convoluted fashion. Let me see if I can give you an example of why teachers like this make learning difficult for their students. I once had a professor in college who could not stop saying "um" during his lectures. It was not that he said it once or twice—most people forgive the occasional utterance. No, this guy had so many "ums" in his speech that I literally stopped paying attention to his lectures and started counting the number of "ums" he said per minute. At highest, the count got to 22 . . . that's per minute! As it pertains to instructor clarity, when teachers communicate in a disfluent manner, their students have a hard time focusing on the content of their course lessons. Admittedly, this is an extreme example of disfluency. However, the point is that people who include utterances such as "um" or "uh," or who otherwise have a hard time articulating themselves, make it difficult for people to follow along with their train of thought.

Based on the definition of disfluency I presented, you know that teachers who communicate in this manner tend to have other problems as well. For example, teachers who are disfluent also end up speaking in what can only be described as verbal mazes. These refer to "false starts or halts in speech" that essentially result in "tangles of words" (Smith, 1977, p. 199). For example, in one experiment, my coauthors and I manipulated verbal mazes by having a speaker introduce the topic of self-efficacy by saying the following: "Self-efficacy is ummm, self-efficacy is considered to be, or self-efficacy is defined as . . ." Compare that to the clear manipulation where the speaker simply said: "Self-efficacy is defined as . . ." Scholars refer to this type of communication as a verbal maze because, just like a person who runs through a maze and has to start over several times, communicating with false starts and unnecessary stops makes it difficult to follow a speaker's intended trajectory.

Of course, disfluency is more than just saying "um" or speaking in tangles of words. In addition to those problems, disfluency also refers to instructors who have a difficult time explaining class concepts in a simple manner and who cannot come up with appropriate examples to explain course concepts. If you want to measure students' perceptions of your disfluency, you can do so by asking your pupils the extent to which they agree or disagree with the following statements; the more students agree, the more disfluent they perceive your instruction to be:

1. My teacher has a hard time articulating his/her thoughts
2. My teacher has a hard time coming up with appropriate examples to explain course concepts
3. My teacher does not seem confident in his/her explanation of course concepts
4. My teacher has a hard time explaining things in a simple manner

Ultimately, disfluency may be detrimental to student learning and indicate a lack of clarity because it reflects the behaviors of "a performer who does not sufficiently command the facts or the understanding required for maximally effective communication" (Hiller, Fisher, & Kaess, 1969, p. 670). That said, how can we fix problems related to disfluency? Well, think about what it means to be disfluent. According to Hiller et al., disfluency provides "a clue to the speaker's command of his lesson" (p. 673) and refers to a person delivering information he or she "can't remember or never really knew" (p. 670). Taken together, these descriptions of disfluency depict somebody who is, essentially, ill-prepared. Thus, my practical advice to teachers who want to be fluent is to make sure you know what you are talking about.

Am I telling you to rehearse your lectures before you give them? Maybe, I am sure it would help. But, I think a person might enjoy more success by spending time trying to understand, and I mean really understand, the topics they are supposed to be teaching others. I know this might sound like a no-brainer, but for a variety of reasons instructors sometimes end up teaching topics that they are not altogether familiar with. When this happens, these teachers will often tell you that they can manage by staying just one chapter ahead of their students. Maybe so. However, I would caution that instead of simply reading the material one step ahead of students, teachers should also take some time to think about how they can explain course concepts in a way that will help students understand their class lessons. Knowing the material before students do is one thing. However, knowing how you are going to explain the material to someone else in a way that is easy to comprehend is another thing altogether.

Being able to explain course material in a simple fashion might take some serious thought. However, putting in the effort to think like a student will help you explain course concepts in a way that allows you to communicate both confidently and fluently. That said, before each new lesson, teachers need to spend significant time mentally planning how to explain their content to students in a simple manner that overlaps with students' experiences. How can teachers do this? Perhaps one of the best ways is by using examples.

I recently read a book by Chip and Dan Heath titled *Made to Stick* (2008) where the authors outline six steps for helping people remember information presented to them. What struck me most about their topics was that, as far as I was concerned, at least half of these essentially involved being clear. One particular step that relates to our current conversation refers to the need for communicators to make information concrete. According to the authors, making information concrete is done by making information tangible. And, according to the Heaths, using examples is one of the best ways to make information tangible. Why is this the case? Fundamentally, examples make information tangible because they turn abstract concepts into concrete ideas. As most teachers will tell you, students seem to "get it" when they are given appropriate exemplars and, as such, providing these is an important part of your job as a teacher.

So where do examples come from? From life! For instance, you can give students examples from your personal experiences (as long as they are relevant and classroom appropriate) to explain course material, or you can ask students about how the information might relate to their own experiences. Moreover, you can talk about current events, or you can show people various media clips to help give examples of course concepts. In addition to these ideas, you can use metaphors, analogies, and similes to help students understand something new in terms of something old. Whatever way you choose to use examples, the main point to remember is that the more you focus on making topics understandable by explaining them simply and in terms that overlap with students' experiences, the more your students will perceive your lectures to be clear. As I mentioned earlier, it takes time to develop good examples so don't skimp on the preparation. And, as an added benefit, the more you prepare, the less likely you are to say "um."

Working memory overload

I have a secret to tell you. I don't know if you know this about me, but I have married eight people in my life. What's more, I did it all without having to buy a single wedding ring. To make things more interesting, let me mention that I have married four men and four women in my life and one of the people I married was my sister! Weird, right? Maybe not. Do you want to know how I did this? Admittedly, it's not that crazy of a story. The thing is, I am an ordained minister. And, being ordained means that some people see you as being qualified to perform wedding ceremonies. In my case, I became ordained through the Universal Life Church which provides a free service to help people like me earn the right to marry others. Before you get too impressed, however, I have to admit that the whole process happened online and took a total of three minutes (including printing the certificate). Anyway, like I mentioned earlier, I have married eight married people in my life so far because I have had the honor of performing four wedding ceremonies to date—including the one between my sister and her husband.

Considering my background in marrying people, I want to see how good you are at memorizing wedding vows. Think you can do it? Let's try. I want you to read the statement below just once and when you are done, I want you to close your eyes and attempt to repeat it. Remember, only read it once.

> I, Paul, take you Monique, to be my wedded wife, to have and to hold from this day forward, for better for worse, for richer or poorer, in sickness and in health, to love and to cherish, 'til death do us part.

Did you read it? Great, now try to recite it. I'll give you a moment ... don't look, no cheating! Okay, so how did you do? Did you remember the whole thing? If you did, good for you. If not, don't worry, when I ask my students to try to memorize this passage in my classes, most of them can't do it either. Not being able to memorize a short passage like the foregoing one is perfectly normal; as you already learned in the section on cognitive load, your working memory is terrible.

So why did we walk through your inability to memorize wedding vows in a chapter on clarity? We did this because I wanted to prove to you that (1) it is easy to overload people's working memories, (2) if you overload people's working memories they will not have the opportunity to process the information you present, and (3) if you overload people's working memories they are not likely to remember or learn much from your lessons. It is not just me who feels this way; numerous scholars note the importance of avoiding information overload if you want to facilitate students' comprehension and their perceptions of clear teaching (e.g., Bush, Kennedy, & Cruickshank, 1977; Chesebro, 2003;

Chesebro & McCroskey, 1998; Cruickshank, 1985; Hines, Cruickshank, & Kennedy, 1985; Kennedy, Cruickshank, Bush, & Myers, 1978).

Simply put, clear teachers do not overwhelm students and are more likely to give their pupils enough time to think about the lessons they are being asked to learn. If you want to know how you are performing with regards to this aspect of clarity, you can ask your students the extent to which they agree or disagree with the following statements:

1. The amount of information presented in our lessons can be overwhelming
2. There is so much to learn during our lectures that I have a hard time keeping up in this class
3. I feel flustered trying to keep up with the amount of information presented in our lectures
4. Class lectures make me feel anxious because of the amount of information we are asked to learn all at one time

The more students agree with the statements above, the less they perceive your instruction to be clear. Essentially, the notion of working memory overload describes situations where the amount of information and the pace of class lectures outstretch students' abilities to absorb course information. Ultimately, if students cannot keep up with course material, they cannot comprehend their lessons.

So, what can you do to ensure that you do not overload your students? The first thing I would tell you to do is to engage in an out-of-body experience. No, I don't mean that you should go into the desert and smoke a pipe filled with peyote. What I mean here is that you have to try to think about your instruction from the perspective of your students. I am telling you to do this because when you know more about a subject, it is easier to absorb more information. Specifically, compared with people who know a little, people who know a lot about a subject have the ability to more easily link new information to old information to make sense of it, and group complex information into more simplified and manageable elements (Sweller, Ayres, & Kalyuga, 2011). That said, the ability to do these things makes experts more likely to be able to handle incoming information compared to novices. Thus, as an expert on a topic, it is easier to learn about new ideas, even if they come at you quickly. For example, I have married four couples in my life. As a result, I can recite the aforementioned vows in my sleep. However, just because it is easy for me to remember this information does not mean that I should move through the passage quickly when sharing it with others. I have to remember that when others see it for the first time, it is harder for them to process the information than it is for me. This idea is related to what is sometimes called the "curse of knowledge" which occurs when people forget that what is in their heads is not in the heads of other people.

Are your students experts when it comes to the academic topics you cover in your classes? Probably not. Unlike you, they have not studied the topic as closely or for as long as you have and, as such, their ability to handle incoming information is diminished compared to yours. So, when I say that you need to have an out-of-body experience, I mean that you have to think about what it would be like to learn the information in your classes for the first time, and you have to remember that when you go through it you have to go slowly.

How will you know if you are moving too quickly? Ask your students to tell you. Instruct your students to raise their hands or to otherwise speak up if they think you are moving too fast. Having your students help you direct the pace of your course lectures will enhance their ability to comprehend the information you present. In fact, several studies of student learning have demonstrated this to be the case (see Moreno & Mayer, 2007 for a review).

Another point you might consider is one that took me a long time to learn when I first started teaching. That is, sometimes *less is more*. What I mean here is that by asking students to process less information, you might help them learn more of the content you present. For instance, when I first started teaching, I wanted my students to know everything about everything. I was gung-ho about their educations and thought they would be able to keep up with my pace in the classroom. I soon found out that this was not the case. When I taught communication theory for the first time, for example, I wanted my students to understand all they could regarding theories of persuasion; I remember we had four days of instruction on the topic and I tried to introduce eight theories to my students in this time. When it came to the test, however, I noticed that my students did terribly—thanks to me. I had overwhelmed my students by asking them to do too much. Now when I teach this class, I use the same four days to teach just four theories of persuasion; one theory a day seems to be about right. And I have found that by teaching my students less, I help them understand the ideas I teach more. Researcher Marlies Baeten and her colleagues (2010) might explain my experience in the classroom by arguing that students who are given too much to learn often manage their excessive workloads by taking cognitive shortcuts. According to these authors, when there is too much information for students to manage, instead of studying course content by seeking meaning and understanding, they tend to use a surface level approach to learn only what they need to get by.

In addition to the points made above, you might consider reducing the load you place on students' working memories by off-loading information into different communication channels. This pertains to the modality effect we went over in the chapter on cognitive load. By providing a lecture along with PowerPoint, for instance, instructors may be able to off-load verbal information (for example, lecture previews and signposts) into a visual format and this should give students more cognitive space to process core content (e.g., Mayer & Moreno, 2003, 2010). That said, as I mentioned earlier, having two sources of information seems to only benefit students when the information presented is not redundant (Sweller et al., 2011). Thus, you might consider putting only key words on your slides as a way of helping organize students' thoughts. Students are not likely to benefit from having your lecture printed out verbatim on the slides while you read directly off the PowerPoint (see the redundancy principle in Chapter 6). In fact, if you teach like this, please stop . . . your students are slowly dying inside when listening to you.

Similarly, to reduce the load on students' working memories, instructors should also consider providing lecture notes or outlines to students before class. In fact, doing so has been shown to increase student success related to test scores (e.g., Raver & Maydosz, 2010). As it pertains to the current subject under consideration, this might be the case because students who are given course notes are not overloaded by the pace of instruction. Instead of concentrating on getting all of the information recorded, students can focus on thinking deeply about course concepts by making connections between new information and that which they already know. If instructors do not want to give away notes for fear of students skipping class, an alternative may be to provide students with guided as opposed to completed notes (Neef, McCord, & Ferreri, 2006).

Interaction

When you drive on the freeway, what's the first thing you do when you see a police officer point his or her radar gun at you? If you are anything like me, the first thing you do is scream. But, once I catch my breath, the second thing I do is look at my speedometer to see if I am going to get a ticket. I want to see how fast I was going to make sure I was not breaking the law. The speedometer is an important indicator of velocity and, as such, it is a critical component of any motor vehicle. This is true for avoiding tickets. However, this is true for your safety as well. You need to get feedback regarding your speed so that you can drive within the appropriate bounds of safety and order. Of course, the speedometer is not the only piece of equipment that provides feedback in your car. Some modern cars will also tell you the air pressure in your tires, alert you when your gas tank is almost empty, and some will even tell you if you are at risk for getting too sleepy! Why do cars do these things for their owners? They do all of this so that drivers have enough information to operate their vehicles to the best of their abilities. How much harder would it be to drive safely if your motor vehicle did not have any of these features?

Feedback is an important part of any experience and is helpful in just about every aspect of your life. Think about it: If you have ever tried to lose weight, I bet you jumped on a scale at some point in the process or at least noticed how your pants fit week after week. This information lets you know whether you are on track or not. Other people use feedback to help them as well. If you have gotten a back massage recently, you know that the masseuse often stops a few minutes into the experience to ask how you like the pressure. Similarly, when you go out to eat, most restaurants will send the server or the manager over to ask how the food tastes shortly after your meal is delivered. What's the point of doing any of this? The point is that feedback is essential to anybody who wants to do a good job without guessing about their performance. Feedback allows people to adjust their behaviors if their current course of action is not leading them toward the outcomes they desire.

And so it is in the classroom. At least, it should be. As teachers, we need to make a concerted effort to understand how our teaching behaviors affect our students. This may be the reason scholars assert that clear teachers do not simply lecture to their students. Instead, clear teachers take the time to assess student learning. This idea is at the heart of interaction and includes answering students' questions and asking students whether or not they comprehend course material. In the instructional communication literature, Civikly (1992) and Simonds (1997) have championed this idea. Both authors claim that clarity is a relational variable and, as Titsworth and Mazer (2010) argue, "is achieved through ongoing sequences of communication between instructors and students" (p. 256). According to Civikly (1992), interaction allows instructors to determine the level of student comprehension and permits students to signal to teachers when they are not able to follow along with course lessons.

The items used to assess interaction include the statements below. Students consider you to be clear to the extent that they agree with the following:

1. In this class, my teacher first explains things and then stops so we can ask questions
2. This teacher makes sure to ask questions to find out if we understand what we are learning
3. This teacher takes the time to answer class questions if things don't make sense
4. My teacher repeats things when we don't understand them

As you can see, at the heart of each of these statements is the idea that instructors assess student comprehension before moving on to new topics. Thus, if you want to know if you are being clear or not, the best people to tell you are the ones you are teaching. Unfortunately, unlike cars that will tell you when you are running out of fuel, students tend not to voice their needs without help from their professors (Bolkan & Goodboy, 2016). Having said that, let's cover a few ways for you to help facilitate feedback during your lessons.

First, as a teacher, you must be open to questions—you must invite them. At the beginning of every semester, for example, I tell my students that I need them to help me help them learn. I explain that, when I lecture, I usually think I am doing it well: As long as no one raises their hand to ask questions or to ask me to repeat myself, I can only assume that everything makes sense. I go on to tell my students that if they need help understanding a concept, they have to signal me so I can provide assistance. In essence, I tell my students to think of me as a lifeguard: I am willing to help, but I only do so when I think there is a problem. I try to get my students to see that my goal is to teach so that they learn the material, and if I am not being successful in my charge, they need to let me know so I can try something different. By explaining their role in the process, my goal is to empower students and to let them know that they are an integral part of the learning environment.

The above being said, you should consider doing your best to make sure your students feel comfortable when they ask questions in class or if they ask you to repeat yourself. For example, in my classrooms, whenever students ask questions, I always thank them by saying something like "thanks for your question" or "thank you for bringing that up." Similarly, when students ask me to repeat myself, I always say "sure" or "no problem." In effect, students who ask questions and who want me to repeat concepts are telling me how to make my lessons clearer for them; if anything, they are doing me a favor. Of course, the most appropriate response to someone who is trying to help you is to simply say "thank you." That's why I always thank my students for helping me do my job the best I can.

Not all teachers feel this way. I know some teachers don't want any feedback at all. For example, some teachers ignore student feedback in their courses or tell their students to "try to keep up" when asked to repeat something from their lectures. I think these teachers are missing the point: Student learning is a two-way street; students *and* teachers play a role in this process. Thus, if you want to be the best teacher for your students, you have to keep their perspectives in mind—their perception is your reality. Whether or not you think you are being clear, the truth is you are only as straightforward as your students perceive you to be.

Another way to facilitate feedback is to promote it yourself by asking students for examples. This is what we went over in the section on understanding in Chapter 5 and, in my experience, this aspect of teaching is absolutely crucial. Try it for yourself. Ask your students if they understand the topics being discussed and they will often tell you they do. However, if you ask your students to explain the concepts back to you in their own words, or to give you examples of the concepts from their own experiences, you might find that they do not know the material as well as they thought they did. As we mentioned in Chapter 5, this is what Brown, Roediger, and McDaniel (2014) refer to as the illusion of knowing. Thus, by asking students to come up with examples on their own, you can have them show you that they know their course concepts instead of simply telling you that they do. Doing this is important because if it turns out that students do not know the concepts the way you want them to, you now have the opportunity to make corrections. Of course, some teachers might complain that this takes effort and that they have too much material to get through to spend important class time going over what they just covered. If you believe this is the case, I invite you to revisit the section on working memory overload. When you do, I want you to ask yourself this question: Is your goal as a teacher to provide information or to facilitate learning? These objectives are not the same.

The point of this section is that getting students to help you make your lessons clear is an important part of the learning process. And, clear instructors are those who work with students to determine their levels of comprehension and who adjust class lectures to adapt to student understanding. In my opinion, simply relying on your personal perceptions of being clear is equivalent to removing your speedometer and driving at a speed you guess is safe. Although you may get away with it for a while, at some point you are going to get into trouble.

Coherence

Some people might tell you that a situation most loathed by teachers is when students ask us whether or not what they are learning is going to be on the test. I think teachers get upset at this question because we are interested in student development as a whole and not necessarily with their performance on an exam (although, we do, of course, like it when our students do well on their tests). We want our students to focus on mastering course concepts to develop their competencies, and we don't want them focusing solely on passing exams. Although I am sure some students certainly ask the question as a way of easing their burden for studying, I think other students ask this question genuinely. What I mean is, I think that some students who ask if the material they are being exposed to is going to be on the test are genuinely interested in trying to organize class information into meaningful categories for learning. They probably want to know what is essential to their development and are asking their teachers to give them a hand in sorting through the mountain of information they are presented with on a daily basis. In my classes, students are welcome to ask this question because I believe it's impossible for them to learn everything presented over the course of an entire semester. Because students are not going to remember everything I cover in my classes, I believe they can better spend their energy learning the key concepts if I can help them differentiate between what's crucial and what's not.

Alternatively, you can simply answer the question of whether or not a topic will be on the test by answering "yes." The way to do this and to simultaneously be genuine in your response is to teach in such a way as to make this answer true. And to make it true, you need to limit what you present to students to only the information that really matters. When you develop your course lessons, you might consider breaking the information you are thinking about presenting into the categories of "nice to know" and "need to know." Then, if you want to be able to answer "yes" to the question above, you need to discard everything in the "nice to know" pile. This idea is sometimes referred to by scholars as the "coherence principle."

Coherence refers to the necessity of instructor-provided information and describes the notion that teachers sometimes provide content that is not essential for learning course lessons (Mayer & Moreno, 2010). This idea is linked to clarity because when teachers provide superfluous information, they force students to survey the material and spend cognitive resources determining what to focus on. According to Mayer and Moreno, you can facilitate student learning by removing extraneous information from your instructional methods. Scholars have long known this to be the case. For example, in 1977, researcher Lyle Smith was able to demonstrate that student learning was reduced as a function of the irrelevant examples provided by an instructor. According to Michael Land (1979), this is because the provision of unnecessary information may confuse students, distract them from important content, and direct students' focus to unimportant aspects of their course lessons.

If you want to measure coherence as it relates to your teaching, you can ask students to report the degree to which they agree with the following statements:

1. Our teacher goes off topic when lecturing
2. This teacher goes on unrelated tangents when we are discussing ideas in class
3. In our lectures, we often receive information that is not essential to learning course concepts
4. There is a lot of unnecessary information in our lectures

I think you get it . . . it is important to cut superfluous information from your lectures. But, does that mean that you have to delete everything, and I mean *everything* that is nice to know from your lectures? Based on what I have learned about student success, I think you should try to remove most of it. Of course, that doesn't mean you should get rid of all stories, examples, and exercises. In fact, we already mentioned that these are crucial to student learning. In reality, I think the keys to following the coherence principle are necessity and relevance. Based on this, I think you should limit stories, examples, and exercises that are not necessary for student learning and get rid of those that are irrelevant or unrelated to the information you want students to learn. Let's tackle these ideas in reverse order.

What is irrelevant? Material is considered irrelevant when it is not linked specifically to students' learning objectives and when it is unrelated to your course lessons. As you can see from the items listed above, this includes going on tangents in lectures and in class discussions. Several studies have shown that the relevance of the information presented in course lessons is linked to important educational outcomes. These include studies of instructor self-disclosure (Cayanus & Martin, 2008), the provision of examples (Smith, 1977), and the use of humor in the classroom (Wanzer, Frymier, & Irwin, 2010). Thus, when delivering material to students, you can help them learn to their potential if you keep the information you present to them related to your course objectives.

Okay, so information presented to students needs to be relevant. But, something can be relevant without being necessary. Thus, in addition to eliminating irrelevant information, you should also consider limiting unnecessary information as well. What's unnecessary? If the information you provide to students does not help explain a topic, then you might consider it to be unnecessary. Do your students need to hear what trains sound like when they learn about the process of Western expansion? Probably not. When learning about lightening formation, is it necessary to include interesting facts related to the dangers of lightening? Nope. Is showing students a picture of a squirrel in a tree when talking about the foliage on your campus necessary? If you are talking about how squirrels live in the trees, then maybe. If not, then no.

Right now you might be thinking, "What's the big deal, why should I limit information in my classes. What if it's interesting? Even if it is unnecessary, as long as the information is intriguing it might help get students motivated to pay attention to my lessons." Maybe. Research does point to the notion that students tend to be "more motivated to engage in appropriate cognitive processing during learning" when their lessons are "redesigned to be more appealing" (Mayer & Estrella, 2014, p. 17). But then again, maybe not. When superfluous information is presented in class, students can spend precious processing space on unimportant information which leaves fewer resources to use for learning essential course concepts. Thus, although interesting but unnecessary details can be helpful under circumstances where students' cognitive load is relatively low, the provision of this information can be detrimental in courses that demand high levels of concentration (see Park, Moreno, Seufert, & Brunken, 2011; Park, Flowerday, & Brunken, 2015).

If you want to use interesting examples and illustrations, feel free to do so; I would just make sure that (1) they are related to the concepts you are trying to teach, and (2) the material you are presenting is not already high in cognitive load. While developing your course lessons you should think to yourself: "If a student asked me if this was going to be on the test what would I say?" If the answer is "no," you might take a step back and seriously consider the necessity of providing that information in the first place.

Structure

I have completed several cross-country driving trips in my life so far. I have driven from California to Texas, from Texas to Pennsylvania, and from Colorado to California. Think about how amazing this is: Whenever I start my journeys, my goal is to drive hundreds of miles across a series of states through a variety of different highway systems to reach a specific spot on the map—sometimes this is a place I have never been before. When I drive, I can go for hours without making a wrong turn, and I can usually pinpoint my exact location even if I feel like I am in the middle of nowhere. I usually know where I have been, where I am, and where I need to go. Because I know these things, the complex process of getting from a place like Davis, California, to another place like Austin, Texas, is a breeze. How great is that?!

Of course, all of this is possible because, despite the complexities involved in driving my body from one specific location in the world to another, the process is made easy by the navigation equipment in my car (and phone) and the signs that exist on the road. Thus, we might conclude that the complex matter of driving across the country is made simple by the provision of directions and signposts. Wouldn't you agree? Well, it turns out the same is true in teaching; clarity in your lessons can also stem from these same sources. Thus, just like clear driving directions, clear teachers are people who let their students know where they have been, where they are now, and where they are headed. In other words, clear teachers provide structure.

In addition to providing students with signposts, teachers who provide structure also present logically organized and easily manageable information in their course lessons. Easily manageable information refers to the notion that information is presented one step at a time. Logically organized information means that the sequence of steps is provided in a manner that makes sense. As an example, consider how I learned to ride a motorcycle when I signed up for a class with the Motorcycle Safety Foundation. After learning about aspects of motorcycling in the classroom, students were given the chance to hone their riding skills on real motorcycles. However, instead of letting us ride off into the sunset upon our arrival, the skills we learned were taught to us step by step. For example, the first thing we did was sit on the motorcycles to get a sense of their balance. Next, we literally walked with the motorcycles between our legs so we could get a feel of what it was like to be on them while moving. Then, once the instructors knew we would not fall off the vehicles and hurt ourselves, they allowed us to start them up and drive a short distance. Eventually, we got to ride the motorcycles in a circle, and the next day we learned how to make tight turns and avoid obstacles in an emergency. Teaching us how to ride motorcycles one step at a time made the process of learning a breeze. Moreover, helping us learn the basics before we went on to more complex lessons helped us build the core skills necessary to eventually perform more advanced maneuvers. If the instructors had not structured the class as they had and instead simply set us free, I am sure the class would have had a much harder time learning to ride.

Based on what you just read, you should have an idea of what it means to be a clear teacher who provides structure. If you want to know the extent to which your students think you do this in your classes, you can ask them to report how much they agree with the four statements presented below:

1. My teacher's lectures are well-organized
2. Our class lectures are organized into specific, manageable content blocks
3. My teacher makes class material easier to learn by teaching us one step at a time
4. It is easy to follow along with the structure of my teacher's lessons

Now, let's get to some practical advice. How can you ensure that students perceive your lessons to be well-structured? Perhaps the simplest thing to do is to add signposts to your lessons. As I have already mentioned, signposts are exactly what they sound like—aspects of your speech that help students determine where they are in a lesson. These include previews, reviews, and transitions. Most teachers know about these. But, how many of you use them? More importantly, how many of your students perceive that you use them? In order to be functional, previews, reviews, and transitions need to be made explicit. If they are not and your students do not hear them, you might as well not have included them in your lesson.

So, what do good signposts look like? In one experiment where my colleagues and I manipulated clarity, this is what we said to ensure that we had a clear preview: "Hello class, today we are going to talk about a specific theory related to health communication. This theory explains behavior change in health communication campaigns and was created by a man named Albert Bandura. The theory is called social cognitive theory. Bandura's social cognitive theory predicts behavior change through *three* key components. These components include *one,* self-efficacy; *two,* people's perceived outcomes; and *three,* perceived facilitators and impediments."

Can you find the signposts? I hope so, they were italicized. If you wanted to make the structure even more apparent, you could add emphasis to the signposts by using nonverbal communication to highlight each one. For example, you could put up an index finger when saying "one," you could hold up two fingers at "two," and so on. Having signposts is important. They allow listeners to create an outline in their minds and organize course content into an easily manageable framework of information.

When reviewing your lessons, you can do the same thing. Here is what I would say when reviewing: "Today we spoke about a specific theory related to health communication called social cognitive theory. In particular, we spoke about *three* key components of this theory. These components included *one,* self-efficacy; *two,* people's perceived outcomes; and *three,* perceived facilitators and impediments."

Are the signposts clear in the review I provided? They should be, and that's the point. If your students don't perceive that you used them, your signposts might as well have never existed. The same thing goes for transitions; you should make those explicit too. For example, by saying something like: "Now that you know about self-efficacy, let's move on to discuss perceived outcomes," you can make it clear to your students that you are introducing a new subject.

Are there any other ways to increase perceptions of your lessons' structure? Certainly. Even if you do not need to show any visual aids, you should seriously consider using PowerPoint or some other visual mechanism to help outline your lessons as you move through them. We went over this idea when we discussed the modality effect in the chapter on cognitive load, and in the current chapter when we spoke about working memory overload. Other ways to increase the clarity of your teaching include highlighting portions of your lessons to help students focus their attention on what's important and sequencing information in a logical manner to provide a framework upon which students can scaffold their knowledge. As I mentioned in the introduction to this chapter, doing these things ultimately helps your students focus on the content of their course lessons instead of using mental resources trying to organize the information themselves.

Does providing structure matter for your students? You tell me. In 2004, researchers Scott Titsworth and Kenneth Kiewra conducted an experiment to study student learning as a function of teachers' spoken organizational cues. What did they find? Turns out that compared to lectures without organizational cues, lectures with these cues boosted student note-taking (after all, students got an idea of what they were supposed to focus on) and, subsequently, students' test scores. Specifically, compared with students who did not, students who listened to a lesson with verbal cues such as the ones promoted in this chapter took down four times as many organizational points and recorded twice the number of details in their notes. Moreover, and perhaps more importantly, Titsworth and Kiewra found that providing organizational cues led to an increase in students' test scores ranging anywhere from 15% to 45%.

So, let me ask the question again: Does providing organizational cues matter to student learning? You bet it does. It is the difference between trying to guess where you are in the middle of a 1,000-mile cross-country trip and sitting back and enjoying the ride while Morgan Freeman narrates your safe passage through the directions on your map application. Whether or not I'm headed to Zihuatanejo, I'd always choose the latter.

Summary

In the beginning of this chapter, I mentioned that one of the most important things a teacher can do to develop students' opportunities to learn their course lessons is to be clear in their instruction. As I noted in the introduction, the general definition of instructor clarity is the "process by which an instructor is able to effectively stimulate the desired meaning of course content . . . through the use of appropriately structured" class material (Chesebro & McCroskey, 1998, p. 262). Although I mentioned that this definition is abhorrently broad, you now know a better way of being clear in the classroom. If you ever forget, you can simply ask yourself: "Dude, will I cuddle strangers?" You know the answer to that question.

Specifically, after reading this chapter, you now know that being clear includes avoiding disfluency, not overloading students' working memories, allowing for student interaction, providing coherence by removing superfluous information, and providing structure in your lessons by using organizational cues. It is pretty simple! If you follow the prescriptions in this chapter, I am sure that your students will learn more and will do better in your courses. Who doesn't want that?!

END-OF-CHAPTER QUESTIONS

1. In your experience, which of the five dimensions of clarity do you think makes the biggest impact on student learning? Do you think one is more important than the others?

2. Based on the teachers you have been exposed to in the past, which of the five dimensions of clarity do instructors have the most trouble with? How do you feel when exposed to unclear teachers, how does this type of instruction influence your opportunity to learn?

3. Can you explain the relationship between clarity and cognitive load?

KEY TERMS

Disfluency: Refers to instructors who have a difficult time explaining class concepts in a simple manner, who cannot create examples to explain course concepts, and who deliver course lessons in a convoluted fashion

Verbal maze: False starts or halts in speech that result in tangles of words

Working memory overload: Refers to instructors' ability to overwhelm students with instructional material

Interaction: Refers to instructors who answer students' questions and are willing to ask students whether or not they comprehend course material

Coherence: Refers to the necessity of instructor-provided information and describes the notion that teachers sometimes provide content that is not essential for learning course lessons

Structure: Refers to teachers who provide signposts and information that is organized into manageable and logical content blocks

REFERENCES

Baeten, M., Kyndt, E., Struyven, K., & Dochy, F. (2010). Using student-centered learning environments to stimulate deep approaches to learning: Factors encouraging or discouraging their effectiveness. *Educational Research Review, 5,* 243–260. doi:10.1016/j.edurev.2010.06.001

Bolkan, S. (2015). The importance of instructor clarity and its effect on student learning: Facilitating elaboration by reducing cognitive load. *Communication Reports.* Advance online publication. doi:10.1080/08934215.2015.1067708

Bolkan, S. (2016). Development and validation of the clarity indicators scale. *Communication Education.* Advance online publication. doi:10.1080/03634523.2016.1202994

Bolkan, S., & Goodboy, A. K. (2016). Rhetorical dissent as an adaptive response to classroom problems: A test of protection motivation theory. *Communication Education, 65,* 24–43. doi:10.1080/03634523.2015.1039557

Brown, P. C., Roediger, H. L., III, & McDaniel, M. A. (2014). *Make it stick: The science of successful learning.* Cambridge, MA: Harvard University Press.

Bush, A. J., Kennedy, J. J., & Cruickshank, D. R. (1977). An empirical investigation of teacher clarity. *Journal of Teacher Education, 28,* 53–58. doi:10.1177/002248717702800216

Cayanus, J. L., & Martin, M. M. (2008). Teacher self-disclosure: Amount, relevance, and negativity. *Communication Quarterly, 56,* 325–341. doi:10.1080/01463370802241492

Chesebro, J. L. (2003). Effects of teacher clarity and nonverbal immediacy on student learning, receiver apprehension, and affect. *Communication Education, 52,* 135–147. doi:10.1080/03634520302000085108

Chesebro, J. L., & McCroskey, J. C. (1998). The development of the teacher clarity short form inventory (TCSI) to measure clear teaching in the classroom. *Communication Research Reports, 15,* 262–266. doi:10.1080/08824099809362122

Civikly, J. M. (1992). Clarity: Teachers and students making sense of instruction. *Communication Education, 41,* 138–152. doi:10.1080/03634529209378876

Cruickshank, D. R. (1985). Applying research on teacher clarity. *Journal of Teacher Education, 36,* 44–48. doi:10.1177/002248718503600210

Heath, C., & Heath, D. (2008). *Made to stick: Why some ideas survive and others die.* New York, NY: Random House.

Hiller, J. H., Fisher, G. A., & Kaess, W. (1969). A computer investigation of verbal characteristics of effective classroom lecturing. *American Educational Research Journal, 6,* 661–675. doi:10.2307/1162258

Hines, C. V., Cruickshank, D. R., & Kennedy, J. J. (1985). Teacher clarity and its relationship to student achievement and satisfaction. *American Educational Research Journal, 22,* 87–99. doi:10.3102/00028312022001087

Kennedy, J. J., Cruickshank, D. R., Bush, A. J., & Myers, B. (1978). Additional investigations into the nature of teacher clarity. *The Journal of Educational Research, 72,* 3–10. doi:10.1080/00220671.1978.10885109

Land, M. L. (1979). Low-inference variables of teacher clarity: Effects on student concept learning. *Journal of Educational Psychology, 71,* 795–799. doi:10.1037/0022-0663.71.6.795

Mayer, R. E., & Estrella, G. (2014). Benefits of emotional design in multimedia instruction. *Learning and Instruction, 33,* 12–18. doi:10.1016/j.learninstruc.2014.02.004

Mayer, R. E., & Moreno, R. (2003). Nine ways to reduce cognitive load in multimedia learning. *Educational Psychologist, 38,* 43–52. doi:10.1207/S15326985EP3801_6

Mayer, R. E., & Moreno, R. (2010). Techniques that reduce extraneous cognitive load and manage intrinsic cognitive load during multimedia learning. In J. L. Plass, R. Moreno, & R. Brunken (Eds.), *Cognitive load theory* (pp. 131–152). New York, NY: Cambridge University Press.

Moreno, R., & Mayer, R. (2007). Interactive multimodal learning environments. *Educational Psychology Review, 19,* 309–326. doi:10.1007/s10648-007-9047-2

Murray, H. G. (1983). Low-inference classroom teaching behaviors and student ratings of college teaching effectiveness. *Journal of Educational Psychology, 75,* 138–149. doi:10.1037/0022-0663.75.1.138

Neef, N. A., McCord, B. E., Ferreri, S. J. (2006). Effects of guided notes versus completed notes during lectures on college students' quiz performance. *Journal of Applied Behavior Analysis, 39,* 123–130. doi:10.1901/jaba.2006.94-04

Park, B., Flowerday, T., & Brunken, R. (2015). Cognitive and affective effects of seductive details in multimedia. *Computers in Human Behavior, 44,* 267–278. doi:10.1016/j.chb.2014.10.061

Park, B., Moreno, R., Seufert, T., & Brunken, R. (2011). Does cognitive load moderate the seductive details effect? A multimedia study. *Computers in Human Behavior, 27,* 5–10. doi:10.1016/j.chb.2010.05.006

Raver, S. A., & Maydosz, A. D. (2010). Impact of the provision and timing of instructor-provided notes on university students' learning. *Active Learning in Higher Education, 11,* 189–200. doi:10.1177/1469787410379682

Rosenshine, B. V., & Furst, N. F. (1971). Research on teacher performance criteria. In B. O. Smith (Ed.), *Research in teacher education* (pp. 27–72). Englewood Cliffs, NJ: Prentice-Hall.

Seidel, T., Rimmele, R., & Prenzel, M. (2005). Clarity and coherence of lesson goals as a scaffold for student learning. *Learning and Instruction, 15,* 539–556. doi:10.1016/j.learninstruc.2005.08.004

Sidelinger, R. J., & McCroskey, J. C. (1997). Communication correlates of teacher clarity in the classroom. *Communication Research Reports, 14,* 1–10. doi:10.1080/08824099709388640

Smith, L. R. (1977). Aspects of teacher discourse and student achievement in mathematics. *Journal for Research in Mathematics Education, 8,* 195–204. doi:10.2307/748520

Simonds, C. J. (1997). Classroom understanding: An expanded notion of teacher clarity. *Communication Research Reports, 14,* 279–290. doi:10.1080/08824099709388671

Sweller, J. (1988). Cognitive load during problem solving: Effects on learning. *Cognitive Science, 12,* 257–285. doi:10.1207/s15516709cog1202_4

Sweller, J., Ayres, P., & Kalyuga, S. (2011). *Cognitive load theory.* New York, NY: Springer Publishing.

Titsworth, B. S., & Kiewra, K. A. (2004). Spoken organizational lecture cues and student notetaking as facilitators of student learning. *Contemporary Educational Psychology, 29,* 447–461. doi:10.1016/j.cedpsych.2003.12.001

Titsworth, S., & Mazer, J. P. (2010). Clarity in teaching and learning: Conundrums, consequences, and opportunities. In D. L. Fassett & J. T. Warren (Eds.), *The SAGE handbook of communication and instruction* (pp. 241–261). Los Angeles, CA: SAGE.

Titsworth, S., Mazer, J. P., Goodboy, A. K., Bolkan, S., & Myers, S. A. (2015). Two meta-analyses exploring the relationship between teacher clarity and student learning. *Communication Education, 64,* 385–418. doi:10.1080/03634523.2015.1041998

Wanzer, M. B., Frymier, A. B., & Irwin, J. (2010). An explanation of the relationship between instructor humor and student learning: Instructional humor processing theory. *Communication Education, 59,* 1–18. doi:10.1080/03634520903367238

Additional References

Portions of this chapter have appeared in some of my journal articles including:

Bolkan, S. (2016). Development and validation of the clarity indicators scale. *Communication Education*. Advance online publication. doi:10.1080/03634523.2016.1202994

Bolkan, S. Goodboy, A. G., & Kelsey, D. (2016). Instructor clarity and student motivation: Academic performance as a product of students' ability and motivation to process instructional material. *Communication Education, 65*, 129–148. doi:10.1080/03634523.2015.1079329

SECTION III

Willingness

Two sections down and one to go! The last section in our COWs framework covers students' willingness to study their course lessons. In the next three chapters, we'll go over how to get your students autonomously motivated, what you can do to be charismatic in the classroom, and what tactics you can employ to get students excited about school and learning. So, are you ready to do it? Well, let's do it then… these chapters aren't going to read themselves!

EIGHT

Self-Determination

OBJECTIVES

By the end of this chapter, you should be a changed person in the following ways:

1. You should know the three fundamental human needs
2. You should be able to articulate various ways you can help students fulfill their fundamental needs
3. You should be able to explain the difference between autonomous and controlled motivation
4. You should be able to articulate the benefits of autonomous motivation
5. You should be able to stretch to the point where you can touch your toes (I still cannot do this)

Self-Determination

To start this chapter, I want you to imagine that I gave you $1,000 to place on a bet. If you win the bet, you get to keep the money. If you lose, you get nothing. The bet you have to place is on one of two runners: Bob or Darrin. These individuals are going to run a half marathon, and I want you to guess who is going to win. For the most part, both runners are identical: Bob and Darrin are the same height and weight, they have the exact same VO_2 max (ability to use oxygen to fuel their athletic efforts), and they have trained for exactly the same amount of time. I want you to imagine that everything about these two men is identical except that Bob is hungry, hasn't slept in two days, and is also dehydrated. Darrin, on the other hand, is not hungry, has had a full eight hours of sleep every night for the past week, and is perfectly hydrated. Got it? Okay, given the foregoing information, who would you bet on to win the race?

If you are like most people, you would probably put your money on Darrin. All else being equal, having his physical needs met will allow Darrin to outperform Bob who is likely to experience something short of his personal best. Having their physical needs met is crucial if runners are going to perform a physical act to their potential, and the same goes for you, of course. If you were going to go for a jog, head out for a hike, lift weights, or go for a swim, and had the choice to do so while hungry, tired, and thirsty—or not—most of us would choose "not." If you have ever felt like you were not at your physical best because you were hungover, dehydrated, or otherwise depleted, you know that having your physical needs met facilitates your ability to perform to your potential.

Using physical performance as an analogy, we might argue that if we want students to learn at their best and reach their potential in school, we must ensure that they too have their needs met. Just as runners require that their *physical* needs are fulfilled before they can perform to their physical potential, scholars argue students require that their *psychological* needs are met before they can learn to their cognitive potential. Whereas meeting runners' bodily needs helps to energize their physical pursuits, meeting students' psychological needs helps to energize their mental pursuits. Why should this be the case? Essentially, scholars argue that by fulfilling students' psychological needs, teachers can help students become self-motivated, and this type of motivation is central to helping students' achieve their full potential in their academic endeavors.

Though you may agree with the foregoing, at this point we are still faced with somewhat of a dilemma: Despite the fact that it might be relatively easy to come up with a list of physical needs that should be met to ensure a person runs their best, when it comes to fulfilling students' fundamental psychological needs, it might be more difficult to articulate what they require. Fortunately, we don't have to reinvent the wheel; scientists (i.e., Edward Deci, Richard Ryan, and others) have spent their careers researching what students need if they are to learn to their potential. And, although the list of possible psychological requirements may seem like it should be a long one, these scholars have articulated just three fundamental psychological needs: competence, relatedness, and autonomy.

So, just as running coaches might work hard to ensure their runners' physical needs are met so they can be ready to race at their best, as teachers, we should work hard to ensure that our students' psychological needs are met so they can be ready to learn at their best. This chapter was designed to help you do just that. In this chapter we'll cover the ideas of intrinsic and autonomous motivation, and we'll go over the definitions of the three fundamental psychological needs. In addition, we'll discuss why the needs are important in school, and we'll go over what you can do to fulfill your students' needs in your classes.

The Three Needs

The idea that there are three basic psychological needs stems from self-determination theory which argues that in order for people to enjoy a sense of well-being and optimal functioning they must first experience a sense of competence, relatedness, and autonomy (Deci & Ryan, 2000). According to scholars, this is true across a variety of life's domains including: personal relationships, school, work, and leisure activities (Milyavskaya & Koestner, 2011). Stated differently, the basic idea at the heart of self-determination theory is that in order for people to thrive in their various endeavors, it is important that they experience a sense of proficiency, belongingness, and personal choice/control.

As it pertains to the classroom, self-determination theorists argue that, by nature, people are intrinsically motivated and inspired to learn. Intrinsic motivation refers to doing something out of curiosity, interest, enjoyment, novelty, challenge, or satisfaction (Ryan & Deci, 2000a). Essentially, self-determination researchers argue that people are naturally motivated toward personal growth and development and that the social contexts they are faced with either thwart or support these inclinations (Ryan & Deci, 2000b). In the classroom, this boils down to the idea that learning is something students seek out naturally and that instructors need only to facilitate the process by supporting students' three fundamental needs (Rigby, Deci, Patrick, & Ryan, 1992; Ryan & Deci, 2002). If you have ever experienced learning as an enjoyable activity and something to look forward to, then you know that education and personal growth can be experiences that are both energizing and fulfilling. That said, self-determination scholars might argue that, as a teacher, one of your most important tasks is simply to stoke the fire of your students' enthusiasm by creating environments where students can learn while feeling capable, connected, and in control. Easy, right? Maybe not.

Unfortunately, educators often fail to facilitate students' natural drive toward learning and instead try to regulate student development by implementing various external controls (Ryan & Deci, 2009). Instead of facilitating positive relationships and student initiative, for example, some educators use pressure and forced compliance to get students to behave in certain ways. Ultimately, the use of pressure and force decimate student motivation (Guay, Ratelle, & Chanal, 2008). And, as a result, teachers' attempts to control and corral students' educational experiences typically lead to perceptions of learning as a task to be completed ruefully instead of as an activity to be experienced joyfully.

Luckily for us, this doesn't have to be the case. Researchers have spent their careers figuring out what it takes to get students to become self-motivated, and we can borrow from their expertise to inform our teaching practices. As I mentioned earlier, the way to help facilitate students' natural intrinsic motivation in your classrooms is to simply ensure that you meet their three fundamental psychological needs. What are these needs again? The three needs are: competence, relatedness, and autonomy.

Competence reflects "individuals' inherent desire to feel effective" (Van den Broeck, Vansteenkiste, De Witte, Soenens, & Lens, 2010, p. 982) and has been operationalized as being good at certain tasks, feeling confident regarding one's performance, and believing that one can accomplish something. In essence, competence may be defined as self-efficacy (Deci, Vallerand, Pelletier, & Ryan, 1991), which relates to a person's belief in their ability to accomplish some goal (Bandura, 1997). So, what does it mean to feel competent? It simply means that you believe you can do something well.

Relatedness is defined as experiencing "a sense of belongingness and connectedness to the persons, group, or culture disseminating a goal" (Ryan & Deci, 2000a, p. 64). In the classroom, this is often reflected in students' relationships with their teachers (Ryan, Stiller, & Lynch, 1994). Relatedness is the idea that people experience secure and meaningful relationships with important others (Deci et al., 1991) and, in the context of scholastic achievement, researchers argue that these relationships form the motivational foundation for getting students to engage in various educational activities (Ryan & Deci, 2000a).

Autonomy represents "individuals' inherent desire to feel volitional and to experience a sense of choice" (Van den Broeck et al., 2010, p. 982). Stated differently, autonomy refers to a sense of control when engaging in activities. In various contexts, autonomy has been operationalized as feeling free from having to follow other people's commands and engaging in activities that one really wants to do (e.g., Van den Broeck et al.).

Organismic Integration

Admittedly, the idea that students enter our classrooms inherently motivated to master the course content represents a best-case scenario. It would be nice if our students were dying to learn what we had to teach, and all we had to do to facilitate this process was to provide for their three fundamental psychological needs. As many teachers might attest, however, this is not usually the case; in our classrooms, it can often seem as if students are not naturally very excited to learn their course material.

If you agree with the sentiments expressed in the previous paragraph, you will be glad to know that self-determination researchers do too. For example, Reeve (2002) acknowledges that students might not always be intrinsically motivated to study their course material. Similarly, Ryan and Deci (2000b) note that many of our adult experiences are not marked by intrinsic motivation and argue that most people do not have the luxury of only engaging in activities that they find personally interesting and satisfying. As a result, these researchers argue that much of our behavior might be considered controlled to some extent. It is important to mention this because it may be unrealistic to assume that teachers can always intrinsically motivate their students (Ryan & Deci, 2000a). This is especially the case because "many of the tasks that educators want their students to perform are not inherently interesting or enjoyable" (Ryan & Deci, 2000a, p. 55).

Uh oh, if someone is not intrinsically motivated or naturally inclined to engage in an activity, then what can we do to get him or her engaged? The answer is that we can use extrinsic motivation. Extrinsic motivation is defined as motivation that arises as a result of some outside pressure or force; prototypical examples include doing something to earn a reward or avoiding doing something to stay out of trouble (Ryan & Deci, 2000b). Thus, if we cannot facilitate students' intrinsic motivation because it does not exist in the first place, we might consider helping students along by providing some type of extrinsic motivation.

Although most people might think of extrinsic motivation as being a singular concept, self-determination scholars note that extrinsic motivation can, in fact, vary in degrees of control. More specifically, researchers consider extrinsic motivation to occur in four forms including external regulation, introjection, identification, and integration. Each of these motives is thought to lie on a continuum ranging from most controlled (i.e., external regulation) to least controlled (i.e., integration).

First, *external regulation* is the idea that people might behave in a certain fashion in order to earn a reward or to stay out of trouble. An example of external regulation might include driving the speed limit when a police officer is around. In this instance, driving the speed limit is something that you do because you will be punished if you do not, and you are forced to do it because it is a rule (Ryan & Connell, 1989). External regulation is considered the most controlled type of motivation on the extrinsic continuum because, when motivated in this fashion, a person performs an act owing to sources that are completely external to their person (i.e., the police officer in our example).

The second type of extrinsic motivation is *introjection.* As Ryan and Deci (2000b) note, introjection refers to external pressure that has been internalized by an individual. Examples of introjection include going to your grandma's birthday party because you would feel guilty if you did not, and watching the television show "Jeopardy" because you want others to think you are smart (Ryan & Connell, 1989). In the case of introjection, there is still an outside pressure or force controlling your behavior (in our examples, this might be the perceived judgment of other people); it is just that this pressure or force has been internalized by you (i.e., it's all in your head). According to Ryan and Deci (2000b), these first two types of extrinsic motivation (i.e., external regulation and introjection) are considered *controlled* because they reference some external source that directs an individual's behavior.

The second two types of motivation, although technically still extrinsic in nature, are considered more *autonomous* than the two just described. This is because these types of motivation stem from sources that reflect self-direction or personal choice. The first type of autonomous motivation is *identification.* Identification stems from linking a behavior to an outcome of personal significance (Ryan & Deci, 2000b). Going to college because it will help you get a job is an example of identified regulation. The second type of autonomous motivation is *integration.* Integration occurs when you behave in a certain manner because it is a part of who you are or because the behavior is linked to your personal values (Deci & Ryan, 2000). An example might be your willingness to help somebody move their belongings from one residence to another. You might do this, not because you like boxing up belongings and driving moving vans, but because you consider helping friends to be an important part of your personal philosophy.

To summarize then, there are four types of extrinsic motivation that, along with intrinsic motivation, might promote desired behaviors in our students. Again, the four types of extrinsic motivation, in order from the most controlled to the most autonomous include: external regulation, introjection, identification, and integration. As I mentioned, it is possible to group the first two types of motivation into the category of controlled motivation and the second two types (plus intrinsic motivation) into the category of autonomous motivation (Deci & Ryan, 2008).

There are two reasons I went through the trouble of explaining the potential sources of students' motivation. First, it is important to know that instead of talking about motives in terms of the specific extrinsic or intrinsic drivers of human behaviors, self-determination scholars tend to speak in broader terms of controlled versus autonomous motivation. Second, as we discussed already, most students are not naturally intrinsically motivated to engage in your class lessons. As a result, you might have to use extrinsic motivation to get your students to work hard in their courses. Because this is the case, self-determination scholars argue that your focus as a teacher should be on how to move your pupils from being controlled (i.e., promoting external regulation and introjection) to behaving in a more autonomous fashion (i.e., promoting identification and integration; Deci, Eghral, Patrick, & Leone, 1994).

Okay, so how do we get students to move from controlled to more autonomous forms of motivation? You already know the answer . . . through the fulfillment of their fundamental needs (Deci & Ryan, 2000, 2008; Ryan & Deci, 2009). Just as competence, relatedness, and autonomy help facilitate students' natural intrinsic drive toward learning, fulfilling these three needs is also crucial as it pertains to getting students to experience other forms of autonomous motivation as well.

Benefits of autonomous motivation

The difference between controlled regulation and autonomous motivation is the difference between compliance and choice (Deci et al., 1991). And having choice matters in academic endeavors because, compared with people who are controlled by external forces, students who are autonomously motivated tend to experience better outcomes including: greater enjoyment in school, greater conceptual learning, more academic persistence, and enhanced academic achievement (Deci & Ryan, 2000; Guay et al., 2008). In addition to these benefits, autonomously motivated students also enjoy higher self-worth, greater cognitive flexibility, and exhibit more creativity (Reeve, 2002).

As if that were not enough, Kusurkar, Ten Cate, Vos, Westers, and Croiset (2013) found that being autonomously motivated promoted students' deep learning strategies (i.e., integrating information into one's knowledge base). Perhaps due to their use of superior study strategies, students who are autonomously motivated have also been found be less likely to forget what they learned at a later date (Grolnick & Ryan, 1987). Specifically, Grolnick and Ryan note that when students are externally incentivized, they are more likely to engage in what the researchers call the "core-dump" phenomenon in which students study for a test and then subsequently forget what they learned. Although teachers may loathe for this to happen, it is sensible from a students' perspective. If students prepare for an exam based on some external incentive, it seems reasonable that their goal would be to meet a specific set of standards and then move on with their lives. If, on the other hand, students learn their course material because they think it is interesting, important, or valuable, it makes sense that they would be more likely to study in ways that allow them to master the information. Results from a study conducted by Koestner, Ryan, Bernieri, and Holt (1984) seem to support this conclusion: compared to internally motivated students, students who felt controlled by their teachers produced lower-quality work and were less motivated to engage in recommended tasks.

Ultimately, the reason students who are self-motivated do better in academic environments is because they end up learning for themselves as opposed to for somebody (or something) else. Consequently, students who are motivated from within have their efforts sustained by their interests, values, and goals. Essentially, students benefit from self-determined motivation because people who are self-motivated experience school differently compared with, and are more likely to direct their behaviors toward learning activities in ways that are qualitatively different than, externally controlled individuals. In support of this assertion, Ryan and Deci (2000b) report that, compared with teachers who were controlling, teachers who promoted autonomous motivation also encouraged "greater curiosity and desire for challenge" (p. 70). In addition, various scholars have found that, compared with learning environments that do not support students' autonomous motivation, environments that do lead to greater interest, satisfaction, and enjoyment (Black & Deci, 2000;

Hardre & Reeve, 2003; Grolnick & Ryan, 1987; Jang, Reeve, Ryan, & Kim, 2009; Reeve & Hyungshim, 2006).

What Can You Do?

Now that we know what the fundamental needs are and why they are important for our students, the next step we need to take is to figure out what we can do to fulfill students' needs when they are in our classrooms. We'll cover some of the major ideas related to fulfilling students' needs in the next few chapters when we talk about instructor charisma (which fulfills students' needs for relatedness and autonomy; Chapter 9) and intellectual stimulation (which fulfills students' needs for competence and autonomy; Chapter 10). However, for now, let's focus on some other ways we can help students feel competent, related, and autonomous.

Competence

According to Lim and Bowers (1991), competence can be facilitated to the extent that one's abilities are respected, and is maintained by communicating positive evaluations, providing recognition, and avoiding criticism. This style of communication is called "approbation," and includes minimizing personal blame for problems or unsuccessful operations, and maximizing praise and positive feedback. Although there are several ways to support students' need for competence, in this section we will focus on doing so by communicating student progress when providing feedback, communicating informational aspects of a performance when critiquing it, and being careful when providing incentives or rewards in our classrooms.

First, as it pertains to providing feedback to students, it is important that we do not forget that, in addition to pointing out what students need to work on, we should also encourage them to continue demonstrating the aspects of their educations they have already mastered. Stated differently, as teachers, our jobs are not just about telling students where they need improvement; in addition to helping students correct their mistakes, it is also important that we tell our students what they are doing well. This is because, if all we do is tell students what they have to work on, we run the risk of making students feel like they might never be successful. If you have ever given up on something because you felt like you would never be able do it, then you know what I am talking about. The same is true for your pupils—if students never feel like they are making progress, they might ultimately give up for a lack of perceived self-efficacy. Just like you, if they do not believe they can do something, they might eventually stop trying.

So think about it: The last time you graded your students' assignments, what was the ratio of criticisms to compliments? If there were more of the former compared to the latter, then you might consider re-visiting their papers. I have to do this all the time. My natural inclination when grading students' papers is to tell them everything they need to fix. However, I constantly have to remind myself to go back through students' assignments to comment on the portions of their work that were done correctly. In addition to telling students what needs work, I have to remind myself to make sure I also praise them for the things they have done well. That said, when it comes to positive feedback, there are various ways to communicate praise that are known to have differing effects. Specifically, when it comes to choosing your messages, you should know that praise is better spent helping students see how they used classroom information and/or learning strategies correctly as opposed to generic compliments such as "you did a good job" (Hattie & Timperley, 2007).

Of course, students do, in fact, need to know what steps are needed to continue making progress toward their goals (Hattie & Timperley, 2007). Thus, one of your jobs as a teacher *is* to help students correct their mistakes. Still, teachers can provide corrective feedback in at least two ways. According to researchers, feedback can occur in a controlling/evaluative manner or in an informative manner (Deci, Koestner, & Ryan, 1999; Koestner et al., 1984). Controlling and evaluative messages are those that communicate a lack of competence and use directives (Koestner et al., 1984). An example of controlling/evaluative feedback might include a teacher writing something like this to students: "This is *not* what we learned in class, you need to work on this response."

On the other hand, informational messages are those that convey respect, acceptance, and a focus on development (Kerssen-Griep, 2001; Koestner et al., 1984). For example, a teacher might write to a student something like: "Good effort, if you develop your answer a bit more thoroughly you will be better able to showcase what you have learned in this class so far." Although the specifics of what you write may obviously differ, you should consider communicating instructional messages to students that are rich in information and low on control and evaluation. As you probably already guessed, the way you provide feedback is important because the more controlling and evaluative your messages are perceived to be, the less your students are likely to experience autonomous motivation (Deci et al., 1999; Koestner et al., 1984).

Some readers might resent the comments presented here because they make it seem like teachers have to walk on eggshells when interacting with students. This is not the case. All I'm advocating here is that teachers consider being sensitive to the human side of their pupils. This is important because scholars argue that being sensitive to students' interpersonal needs is the key to creating optimal learning environments (Kerssen-Griep, Trees, & Hess, 2008). In fact, according to Kerssen-Griep et al. (2008), students and teachers "continually negotiate social identities . . . so competent instruction must include the ability to mitigate face threats and negotiate mutually acceptable identities" (p. 314). As Kerssen-Griep, Hess, and Trees (2003) argue, teachers engage in a number of acts that threaten students' fundamental needs and thus the way instructors communicate with their students plays a major role in teachers' ability to facilitate these. Essentially, the point here is that, as a teacher, you have the ability to communicate the same information to students in a variety of different ways. That being said, when speaking to your students you can support their need for competence by communicating praise and feedback in a supportive and informational manner and avoiding evaluative and coercive statements (Reeve, 2006; Reeve, Jang, Carrell, Jeon, & Barch, 2004).

Finally, when it comes to competence, teachers should also consider being cautious when designating incentives and/or rewards for performance because the information these provide to students can either benefit or detract from their autonomous motivation. As it pertains to competence, incentives and rewards can benefit students when they provide information related to students' progress and development. If, on the other hand, incentives and rewards communicate a lack of competence, teachers might find their provision to be detrimental to students' autonomous motivation. For example, in their meta-analysis examining the impact of tangible rewards on intrinsic motivation, Deci et al. (1999) found that when a tiered reward system was used to incentivize people, getting less than the maximum led to diminished intrinsic motivation. Why would this be the case? Because people who received less than the maximum reward were essentially told that they did not do as well as they could have.

The same type of result can be observed if teachers are not careful when they use competition to incentivize student behavior. Specifically, competition can facilitate intrinsic motivation to the extent that it helps individuals focus on performing well under challenging conditions (Deci et al., 1999), and can help those who win feel more competent (Reeve & Deci, 1996). On the other hand, if competition emphasizes winning at the expense of thoughtful performance, people might perceive these situations as controlling and, as a result, experience less autonomous motivation (Reeve & Deci, 1996). Not to mention, as may seem obvious to readers, people who lose competitions tend to feel less competent relative to winners (Reeve & Deci, 1996).

Relatedness

Relatedness refers to the idea that students feel respected and cared for in their classrooms (Ryan & Deci, 2000a). In the instructional communication literature, this idea may be reflected in the notion of instructor–student rapport operationalized through students' enjoyable interactions and personal connections with their teachers (Frisby & Martin, 2010). According to researchers Brandi Frisby and Matthew Martin, rapport can be built to the extent that instructors take a personal interest in students and make their interactions with students comfortable. Why is this important? Well, in their study, Frisby and Martin found that a positive interpersonal climate between students and teachers was related to students' participation, positive feelings toward the class and the instructor, and perceptions of learning throughout the course of an academic semester. Other researchers support the importance of instructor–student rapport and have found that positive relationships between students and teachers are linked to students' motivation for class and also to their final course grades (Wilson & Ryan, 2013).

Why should the relationship between students and teachers enhance student learning? As my colleague Alan Goodboy and I argued (2015), the reason this might be the case is because students who like their professors enjoy coming to class and engage in behaviors that ultimately lead to student learning. Specifically, we argued that when instructors build a positive climate for students by promoting positive affective experiences, they foster genuine enthusiasm for learning which leads to behaviors that increase students' chances for being successful in their classes. Results from the study conducted by Wilson and Ryan (2013) mentioned in the previous paragraph corroborate this conclusion insofar as students who experienced rapport with their professors reported being more engaged in their classes and skipping fewer classes over the course of a semester.

Conversely, when instructors fail to build rapport with their students, they create a negative classroom climate that subsequently leads to reduced student motivation and positive affect (Goodboy & Bolkan, 2009). Based on the information presented above then, we might conclude that teachers who create positive interpersonal climates help their pupils feel more autonomous because classes stop being a chore to attend and instead reflect enjoyable experiences that students want to be a part of. This type of classroom atmosphere is crucial in academia because students' experiences of positive affect are associated positively with a host of important educational outcomes including students' intrinsic motivation, effort, cognitive elaboration, self-regulation, and grade point averages (Pekrun, Goetz, Frenzel, Barchfeld, & Perry, 2011).

So now we know that developing positive relationships with students can help facilitate their educational achievement. At this point, however, you might be wondering what you can do to build these relationships with students. Thankfully, building rapport does not mean that you have to take your students out to the movies and buy them birthday presents. On the contrary, the things teachers do to develop positive relationships with students don't really take much work at all. In the next chapter, we will discuss the ideas of nonverbal immediacy, humor, confirming students, and caring. But for now, let's focus on some other behaviors you might employ to develop positive personal relationships with students.

According to research conducted by Virginia Richmond (1990), some of these behaviors might include facilitating enjoyment (e.g., attempting to make class interesting for students), assuming equality (i.e., avoiding the perception of being superior to students), and communicating optimism (e.g., staying cheerful and positive in class). Admittedly, that last idea regarding staying cheerful in class can be difficult to employ because teachers experience life just like everybody else. In other words, just like other people, we experience days where we might feel more melancholy than others. Still, as professional public speakers, our jobs require us to look past our personal feelings (at least for the time being) and deliver information to our students in a manner that reflects a certain level of professionalism and optimism: In fact, coming to class moody is considered by some researchers to be a teacher misbehavior (Kearney, Plax, Hays, & Ivey, 1991). As teachers, we are in the service industry and the service we provide is instruction. That said, just as you expect a certain level of professionalism from the service providers you encounter, your students expect the same from you. If the pizza guy, the man at the supermarket, or the lady working as a bank teller were having a bad day, I bet you would expect them to smile and serve you with enthusiasm regardless, right? Well, guess what? The same thing is true for you.

Another behavior you might consider employing to create a sense of interpersonal closeness includes facilitating students' self-disclosure (Frymier, 1994). According to Richmond (1990), this involves talking to students in a genuine effort to get to know them. Just like any relationship, engaging in conversations with others is key to developing interpersonal rapport (Bell & Daly, 1984). Thus, teachers who are good at creating a sense of interpersonal relatedness are instructors who are willing to talk to students about their interests, opinions, and feelings. Again, you do not have to go to great lengths to make this happen. Nobody expects you to take your students to the beach to have heartfelt conversations at sunset. Instead, to facilitate these conversations, you can simply come to class early or stay late to talk to students and get to know them as people—you might even be surprised at just how interesting your students are.

For me, this is one of the most rewarding parts about being a teacher; by getting to know my students, I get to build meaningful relationships with them, and I often have the opportunity to learn from them as well. For example, by talking to my students before class over the years, I have learned that one of my students won the Stanley Cup with the Anaheim Ducks. One woman told me about her experiences flying small airplanes. And another student told me about his experience getting thrown into a Mexican prison when his fishing boat drifted out of California waters! The point here is that if you spend time getting to know your students, you will begin to build rapport with them and, as a side benefit, you might even find yourself enjoying the experience!

Autonomy

Autonomy relates to the idea of being free from the imposition of others. According to Reeve Bolt and Cai (1999), teachers can promote autonomy in a variety of ways that might ultimately be consolidated into two major categories. The first category refers to what I consider *promoting student agency* and includes behaviors such as: supporting student initiative, avoiding the use of directives, and providing choice. The second category refers to *facilitating internalization* and includes: providing a rationale for engaging in academic tasks, promoting the value of academic tasks, and promoting interest in academic tasks. As it pertains to facilitating the internalization of students' course lessons, we already learned how to provide a rationale for, and promote the value of, engaging in academic tasks when we discussed the notions of students' long-term goals and content relevance in the chapter on self-control (Chapter 2). Moreover, we will discuss various behaviors related to promoting interest in academic tasks in the chapters that follow. For now, however, I want us to focus on some of the things we can do as teachers to promote student agency.

As it pertains to the classroom, it may not surprise you to learn that autonomy can be maintained to the extent that teachers give students options and refrain from blunt commands (Lim & Bowers, 1991). According to Lim and Bowers, this can be achieved by using conventional politeness techniques such as saying "please," requesting an action (e.g., "do you think you can you fix this?") instead of ordering someone to do something (e.g., "fix this!"), and sharing responsibility when asking for some outcome (e.g., "let's fix this"). Although some people might argue that teachers have the right to command their students and demand their compliance, it may be worthwhile for teachers to minimize the pressure they put on students and to instead acknowledge their perspectives and provide choice. This is true insofar as these latter behaviors have been associated with students' increased interest, enjoyment, and performance in their courses (Black & Deci, 2000).

Evidence from studies of classroom communication support the conclusion articulated above: Teachers who are autonomy-supportive have been found to be less likely to give directives by saying things like "should" and "must" to their students (Reeve et al., 1999; Reeve & Hyungshim, 2006). For example, Vansteenkiste and his colleagues (e.g., Vansteenkiste, Simons, Lens, Sheldon, & Deci, 2004) found that learning climates in which words such as "you can," "you might," "if you choose," "we ask you to," "we invite you to," "you might want to," and "you can decide for yourself" were perceived by students to be more autonomy-supportive compared with climates where students were told things such as "you should," "you have to," "you'd better," "you are expected to," and "you must" (see also Vansteenkiste, Simons, Lens, Soenens, & Matos, 2005; Vansteenkiste, Simons, Soenens, & Lens, 2004).

The differences in the word choices noted above are admittedly small, but research demonstrates that this simple reframing of instructional messages can make a big impact on the way they are perceived and, subsequently, the way students react. For example, compared with controlling messages, autonomy-supportive messages that are manipulated through the different forms of communication noted above have been associated with increases in students' task involvement, perceptions of personal autonomy, and conceptual learning at both short- and long-term intervals (Vansteenkiste et al., 2005). The central idea here is a simple one and refers to the way you structure your messages to avoid the perception of force. In reality, you cannot make your students do anything; and as far as self-determination scholars are concerned, you shouldn't try to do so in the first place.

Of course, although avoiding unnecessary pressure is desirable, teachers also need to make sure they don't introduce ambiguity in the pursuit of politeness. Thus, you might consider balancing the clarity of your instructional messages with an appropriate sense of imposition (Blum-Kulka, 1987). Essentially, the reason I bring this up is to help you understand that when communicating with students, you may want to avoid the use of unnecessary coercion. However, you should also ensure that when you communicate this way, your objective is still clear. In academic settings, this might translate to you asking students to "please consider completing the homework thoughtfully" instead of hinting to them that "it might be wise if you were to think about attending to the homework" or aggressively telling them that they "need to be thoughtful when completing the homework!"

The concepts noted in the foregoing paragraphs are important to students' perceptions of autonomy because they communicate the provision of choice. Of course, students can be given choices in other ways as well. For example, in my classes I often provide students with at least one optional assignment they can choose to complete or not. Usually, this assignment is a written project, and if students choose to complete it, they have the chance to change the nature of their semester-long evaluation. For example, imagine I have three tests each worth 50 points in one class. If students in my class choose not to complete the optional assignment, their semester scores will simply be the percentage of correct test questions they were able to answer, which will be X/150. However, if students choose to complete the optional written assignment that is worth 50 points, their semester score will be the percentage of points earned on the tests plus the optional assignment: X/200. Self-determination scholars would argue that by giving them a choice regarding the best method of evaluation, I am able to facilitate my students' autonomous motivation. Other ways to provide choice for students exist as well and might include a variety of teaching practices such as requesting student feedback on mid-semester evaluations and allowing students to choose their own research topics (perhaps, with your final approval).

Finally, similar to competence, teachers who wish to support student autonomy need to be strategic with their use of incentives and rewards. This is because incentives and rewards that are perceived to be controlling or pressuring limit the utility of these provisions by undermining individuals' sense of autonomy (Deci et al., 1999). In reality, the idea that extrinsic rewards can undermine intrinsic motivation only applies if there is intrinsic motivation to undermine in the first place (Deci et al., 1999). That said, as long as there is, researchers have shown that providing rewards and incentives for various behaviors can, in fact, diminish this type of motivation. For example, providing people with an expected tangible reward as an incentive to engage in or to complete a task has been shown to undermine individuals' interest in that activity and their subsequent free-choice behavior in relation to that activity (Deci et al., 1999). This is true not just in the short term, but in the long term as well.

The reason incentives can undermine autonomous motivation is because people who come to expect rewards for a behavior may begin to think of themselves as acting a certain way simply to gain the promised outcome. In a sense, once a freely chosen behavior becomes monetized, the utility of this behavior changes from being an end in itself to a means to an end. And importantly, once the incentive to engage in the behavior is no longer present, you might find that people's motivation to engage in that behavior disappears as well. Of course, similar to positive incentives, negative incentives such as deadlines, grades, and other evaluations can be detrimental to individuals' autonomous motivation for these same reasons.

Having said the above, it might be hard to teach your students without incentives such as grades, deadlines, and tests. However, as it pertains to grades and other incentives that are usually expected in academic environments, emphasizing autonomy can still be accomplished in the same way I advocated when promoting competence earlier. Specifically, teachers might consider de-emphasizing the controlling nature of their evaluations by framing grades (and other incentives) as important pieces of informational feedback regarding student growth and development instead of as rewards or punishments that drive behavior (Grolnick & Ryan, 1987). For example, scholars have found that teachers can support students' perceptions of autonomy to the extent that they provide a rationale for undesirable activities like tests, quizzes, or class assignments (i.e., helping people understand the personal utility of a recommended activity), and acknowledge the conflict between what is being asked and what people want to do (i.e., acknowledging students' experiences of negative affect instead of challenging it; Deci et al., 1994; Reeve et al., 1999, 2004). Thus, by empathizing with students and articulating how various assignments and incentives help them learn, teachers may be able to help students identify the value or importance of activities that might otherwise be experienced as unpleasant or controlling.

Summary

In this chapter, we spoke about the benefits of self-determined motivation and its relationship to students' three fundamental psychological needs. Specifically, I argued that by fulfilling students' needs for competence, relatedness, and autonomy, teachers can help them develop autonomous motivation, which is beneficial in the classroom for a variety of reasons. As you continue in your teaching endeavors, you might try to remember that even small changes in your approach to interacting with students can make big differences in the way they pursue their educations.

As Ryan and Deci (2009) note, fulfilling students' needs occurs when classrooms feel "accepting, supportive, and encouraging" (p. 183), instead of controlling and pressuring. Crucially, you play a major role here: The most important predictor of the classroom climate is the way teachers interact with their students (Ryan & Deci, 2009). In other words, a lot of what it means to facilitate students' needs stems from teachers' interpersonal styles (Reeve et al., 1999). That said, now that you have finished this chapter, you know that if you want to provide a classroom climate that supports students' autonomous motivation, you can do so by engaging in behaviors that demonstrate your desire to build connections with students, and that support their self-efficacy and self-direction.

Think back to the beginning of this chapter where I introduced two runners named Darrin and Bob. Both of these runners were equally fit and had identical physical attributes. Still, as we discussed, Darrin was more likely to perform at his best because he had his needs fulfilled. The same is true for your pupils. After reading this chapter, you now know that you can help maximize students' academic potential by doing your best to help them fulfill their psychological needs for competence, relatedness, and autonomy. Congrats on that.

END-OF-CHAPTER QUESTIONS

1. In your experience, do teachers do a good job facilitating their students' fundamental needs? Which of the three fundamental needs do teachers have the hardest time promoting?

2. What are your thoughts on students' need for relatedness? Are teachers within their rights to thumb their noses at developing student–teacher rapport?

3. Can you name something for which you are motivated by introjection? What about identification? Do you notice a difference in the way you approach activities because of differences in your motivation?

KEY TERMS

Fundamental psychological needs: Competence, relatedness, and autonomy

Need for competence: An individual's inherent desire to feel effective

Need for relatedness: An individual's need to feel a sense of belongingness and connectedness to the persons, group, or culture disseminating a goal

Need for autonomy: An individual's inherent desire to feel free from imposition and to experience a sense of choice

External regulation: Motivation that stems from the desire to earn a reward or avoid punishment

Introjection: Motivation that stems from external pressure that has been internalized by an individual (e.g., guilt)

Controlled motivation: Motivation that stems from some external source (i.e., external regulation and introjection)

Identification: Motivation that stems from linking behaviors to an outcome of personal significance

Integration: Motivation that stems from linking behaviors to personal values

Intrinsic motivation: Motivation that stems from curiosity, interest, enjoyment, novelty, challenge, or satisfaction

Autonomous motivation: Motivation that stems from identification, integration, and/or intrinsic interest/value

REFERENCES

Bandura, A. (1997). *Self-efficacy: The exercise of control.* New York, NY: W. H. Freeman and Company.

Bell, R. A., & Daly, J. A. (1984). The affinity-seeking function of communication. *Communication Monographs, 51,* 91–115. doi:10.1080/03637758409390188

Black, A. E., & Deci, E. L. (2000). The effects of instructors' autonomy support and students' autonomous motivation on learning organic chemistry: A self-determination perspective. *Science Education, 84,* 740–756. doi:10.1002/1098-237X(200011)84:6<740::AID-SCE4>3.0.CO;2-3

Blum-Kulka, S. (1987). Indirectness and politeness in requests: Same or different? *Journal of Pragmatics, 11,* 131–146. doi:10.1016/0378-2166(87)90192-5

Bolkan, S., & Goodboy, A. K. (2015). Exploratory theoretical tests of the instructor humor-student learning link. *Communication Education, 64,* 45–64. doi:10.1080/03634523.2014.978793

Deci, E. L., Eghral, H., Patrick, B. C., & Leone, D. R. (1994). Facilitating internalization: The self-determination theory perspective. *Journal of Personality, 62,* 119–142. doi:10.1111/j.1467-6494.1994.tb00797.x

Deci, E. L., Koestner, R., & Ryan, R. M. (1999). A meta-analytic review of experiments examining the effects of extrinsic rewards on intrinsic motivation. *Psychological Bulletin, 125,* 627–668. doi:10.1037/0033-2909.125.6.627

Deci, E. L., & Ryan, R. M. (2000). The "what" and "why" of goal pursuits: Human needs and the self-determination of behavior. *Psychological Inquiry: An International Journal for the Advancement of Psychological Theory, 11,* 227–268. doi:10.1207/S15327965PLI1104_01

Deci, E. L., & Ryan, R. M. (2008). Facilitating optimal motivation and psychological well-being across life's domains. *Canadian Psychology, 49,* 14–23. doi:10.1037/0708-5591.49.1.14

Deci, E. L., Vallerand, R. J., Pelletier, L. G., & Ryan, R. M. (1991). Motivation and education: The self-determination perspective. *Educational Psychologist, 26,* 325–346. doi:10.1080/00461520.1991.9653137

Frisby, B. N., & Martin, M. M. (2010). Instructor-student and student-student rapport in the classroom. *Communication Education, 59,* 146–164. doi:10.1080/03634520903564362

Frymier, A. B. (1994). The use of affinity-seeking in producing liking and learning in the classroom. *Journal of Applied Communication Research, 22,* 87–105. doi:10.1080/00909889409365391

Goodboy, A. K., & Bolkan, S. (2009). College teacher misbehaviors: Direct and indirect effects on student communication behavior and traditional learning outcomes. *Western Journal of Communication, 73,* 204–219. doi:10.1080/10570310902856089

Grolnick, W. S., & Ryan, R. M. (1987). Autonomy in children's learning: An experimental and individual difference investigation. *Journal of Personality and Social Psychology, 52,* 890–898. doi:10.1037/0022-3514.52.5.890

Guay, F., Ratelle, C. F., & Chanal, J. (2008). Optimal learning in optimal contexts: The role of self-determination in education. *Canadian Psychology, 49,* 233–240. doi:10.1037/a0012758

Hardre, P. L., & Reeve, J. (2003). A motivational model of rural students' intentions to persist in, versus drop out of, high school. *Journal of Educational Psychology, 95,* 347–356. doi:10.1037/0022-0663.95.2.347

Hattie, J., & Timperley, H. (2007). The power of feedback. *Review of Education Research, 77,* 81–112. doi:10.3102/003465430298487

Jang, H., Reeve, J., Ryan, R. M., & Kim, A. (2009). Can self-determination theory explain what underlies the productive, satisfying learning experiences of collectivistically oriented Korean students? *Journal of Educational Psychology, 101,* 644–661. doi:10.1037/a0014241

Kearney, P., Plax, T. G., Hays, E. R., & Ivey, M. J. (1991). College teacher misbehaviors: What students don't like about what teachers say and do. *Communication Quarterly, 39,* 309–324. doi:10.1080/01463379109369808

Kerssen-Griep, J. (2001). Teacher communication activities relevant to student motivation: Classroom facework and instructional communication competence. *Communication Education, 50,* 256–273. doi:10.1080/03634520109379252

Kerssen-Griep, J., Hess, J. A., & Trees, A. R. (2003). Sustaining the desire to learn: Dimensions of perceived instructional facework related to student involvement and motivation to learn. *Western Journal of Communication, 67,* 357–381. doi:10.1080/10570310309374779

Kerssen-Griep, J., Trees, A. R., & Hess, J. A. (2008). Attentive facework during instructional feedback: Key to perceiving mentorship and an optimal learning environment. *Communication Education, 57,* 312–332. doi:10.1080/03634520802027347

Koestner, R., Ryan, R. M., Bernieri, F., & Holt, K. (1984). Setting limits on children's behavior: The differential effects of controlling vs. informational styles on intrinsic motivation. *Journal of Personality, 52,* 233–248. doi:10.1111/j.1467-6494.1984.tb00879.x

Kusurkar, R. A., Ten Cate, Th. J., Vos, C. M. P., Westers, P., & Croiset, G. (2013). How motivation affects academic performance: A structural equation modelling analysis. *Advances in Health Science Education, 18,* 57–69. doi:10.1007/s10459-012-9354-3

Lim, T., & Bowers, J. W. (1991). Facework: Solidarity, approbation, and tact. *Human Communication Research, 17,* 415–450. doi:10.1111/j.1468-2958.1991.tb00239.x

Milyavskaya, M., & Koestner, R. (2011). Psychological needs, motivation, and well-being: A test of self-determination theory across multiple domains. *Personality and Individual Differences, 50,* 387–391. doi:10.1016/j.paid.2010.10.029

Pekrun, R., Goetz, T., Frenzel, A. C., Barchfeld, P., & Perry, R. P. (2011). Measuring emotions in students' learning and performance: The achievement emotions questionnaire (AEQ). *Contemporary Educational Psychology, 36,* 36–48. doi:10.1016/j.cedpsych.2010.10.002

Reeve, J. (2002). Self-determination theory applied to educational settings. In E. L. Deci & R. M. Ryan (Eds.), *Handbook of self-determination research* (pp. 183–203). Rochester, NY: University of Rochester Press.

Reeve, J. (2006). Teachers as facilitators: What autonomy-supportive teachers do and why their students benefit. *The Elementary School Journal, 106,* 225–236. doi:10.1086/501484

Reeve, J., Bolt, E., & Cai, Y. (1999). Autonomy-supportive teachers: How they teach and motivate students. *Journal of Educational Psychology, 91,* 537–548. doi:10.1037/0022-0663.91.3.537

Reeve, J., & Deci, E. L. (1996). Elements of the competitive situation that affect intrinsic motivation. *Personality and Social Psychology Bulletin, 22,* 24–33. doi:10.1177/0146167296221003

Reeve, J., & Hyungshim, J. (2006). What teachers say and do to support students' autonomy during a learning activity. *Journal of Educational Psychology, 98,* 209–218. doi:10.1037/0022-0663.98.1.209

Reeve, J., Jang, H., Carrell, D., Jeon, S., & Barch, J. (2004). Enhancing students' engagement by increasing teachers' autonomy support. *Motivation and Emotion, 28,* 147–169. doi:10.1023/B:MOEM.0000032312.95499.6f

Richmond, V. P. (1990). Communication in the classroom: Power and motivation. *Communication Education, 39,* 181–195. doi:10.1080/03634529009378801

Rigby, C. S., Deci, E. L., Patrick, B. C., & Ryan, R. M. (1992). Beyond the intrinsic-extrinsic dichotomy: Self-determination in motivation and learning. *Motivation and Emotion, 16,* 165–185. doi:10.1007/BF00991650

Ryan, R. M., & Connell, J. P. (1989). Perceived locus of causality and internalization: Examining reasons for acting in two domains. *Journal of Personality and Social Psychology, 57,* 749–761. doi:10.1037/0022-3514.57.5.749

Ryan, R. M., & Deci, E. L. (2000a). Intrinsic and extrinsic motivations: Classic definitions and new directions. *Contemporary Educational Psychology, 25,* 54–67. doi:10.1006/ceps.1999.1020

Ryan, R. M., & Deci, E. L. (2000b). Self-determination theory and the facilitation of intrinsic motivation, social development, and well-being. *American Psychologist, 5,* 68–78. doi:10.1037110003-066X.55.1.68

Ryan, R. M., & Deci, E. L. (2002). Overview of self-determination theory: An organismic perspective. In E. L. Deci & R. M. Ryan (Eds.), *Handbook of self-determination research* (pp. 3–33). Rochester, NY: University of Rochester Press.

Ryan, R. M., & Deci, E. L. (2009). Promoting self-determined school engagement: Motivation, learning, and well-being. In K. R. Wentzel & A. Wigfield (Eds.), *Handbook of motivation at school* (pp. 171–196). New York, NY: Routledge.

Ryan, R. M., Stiller, J. D., & Lynch, J. H. (1994). Representations of relationships to teachers, parents, and friends as predictors of academic motivation and self-esteem. *The Journal of Early Adolescence, 14,* 226–249. doi:10.1177/027243169401400207

Van den Broeck, A., Vansteenkiste, M., De Witte, H., Soenens, B., & Lens, W. (2010). Capturing autonomy, competence, and relatedness at work: Construction and initial validation of the work-related basic need satisfaction scale. *Journal of Occupational Psychology, 83,* 981–1002. doi:10.1348/096317909X481382

Vansteenkiste, M., Simons, J., Lens, W., Sheldon, K. M., & Deci, E. L. (2004). Motivating learning, performance, and persistence: The synergistic effects of intrinsic goal contents and autonomy-supportive contexts. *Journal of Personality and Social Psychology, 87,* 246–260. doi:10.1037/0022-3514.87.2.246

Vansteenkiste, M., Simons, J., Lens, W., Soenens, B., & Matos, L. (2005). Examining the motivational impact of intrinsic versus extrinsic goal framing and autonomy-supportive versus internally controlling communication style on early adolescents' academic achievement. *Child Development, 76,* 483–501. doi:10.1111/j.1467-8624.2005.00858.x

Vansteenkiste, M., Simons, J., Soenens, B., & Lens, W. (2004). How to become a persevering exerciser? Providing a clear, future intrinsic goal in an autonomy-supportive way. *Journal of Sport & Exercise Psychology, 26,* 232–249.

Wilson, J. H., & Ryan, R. G. (2013). Professor-student rapport scale: Six items predict student outcomes. *Teaching of Psychology, 40,* 130–133. doi:10.1177/0098628312475033

NINE

Charisma

OBJECTIVES

By the end of this chapter, you should be a changed person in the following ways:

1. You should know the four aspects of charismatic teaching
2. You should be able to articulate how the four aspects of charisma combine into the patterns of delivering information well and building relationships with students
3. You should be able to articulate the connection between self-determination and charisma
4. You should be able to explain how to increase students' perceptions of your charisma
5. You should be able to articulate what you want for your birthday this year

Charisma

I elected to spend the first semester of my senior year of college in Madrid, Spain, so I could finally achieve one of my academic goals of studying abroad. The trip was, for the most part, a good one, and I enjoyed meeting new people and learning new things. For example, I learned about the history of Andalucia, the benefits of having a siesta in the afternoon, and about the delicious taste of "Calimocho" (sometimes known as "Kalimotxo" or "Rioja Libre"). Don't know what Calimocho is? It's a drink made up of (basically) half red wine and half cola. I know it sounds crazy at first, but try it before you knock it—you might like it!

Another thing I learned when I was in Spain was the language. Well, I tried to learn it at least. To help me do this, the program I was with set me up to live with a Spanish family who did not speak any English. I guess that was the point: Their lack of English forced me to try to use what little Spanish I knew to communicate. Although I liked living with my Spanish family and was glad for the opportunity to practice the language, I found it difficult and often made mistakes along the way. So, in an effort to help myself improve faster, I tried doing everything I could to get accustomed to the language. For instance, I remember trying to talk to strangers in the street (who would usually walk away as quickly as possible), and I also did my best to listen to Spanish rap songs (which did not help produce any usable vocabulary). Perhaps the best thing I did to help myself learn the language, however, was watch TV with my Spanish family. Doing so allowed me to listen to a variety of new words in a relatively safe and comfortable environment.

Without a doubt, whenever we watched TV, my favorite show was *Gente con Chispa.* "Gente con Chispa" roughly translates to "people who have a spark" and references the celebrity nature of the guests invited to play a game show. As far as I could tell, the show essentially consisted of Spanish celebrities playing games to win prize money for the charities of their choice. The show was hilarious because the celebrities were asked to play some pretty funny games. The one I remember the most was one I called "feel what it is with your hand and your arm." In this game, celebrities were blindfolded and asked to touch something inside a glass box.

Basically, the goal of this game was for the celebrities to reach into a box, feel an object, and guess what it was. What made this game so funny was that the box would be covered with a cloth at first, and when it was time to begin, the cloth would be removed to the horrifying screams of the audience. Regardless of the objects inside the box, the audience would always yell bloody murder, which, obviously, made the blindfolded celebrities hesitant to reach their hands inside. Sometimes the objects were mundane like stuffed animals, caterpillars, or a bunch of frogs. But at other times, the objects were intense and included things like electric wires, tarantulas, or baby crocodiles. Of course, after hearing the audience scream, the celebrities would make a big deal out of reaching into the box, and the way they behaved during the game made it endlessly entertaining. Essentially, because of the "sparky" nature of the celebrities' behavior, the game show was always lively, interesting, and fun to watch. In fact, I recall that whenever the show was over, I would wish that one day I too could be a person with chispa.

The problem with trying to get chispa, however, was that I didn't really know what chispa was. Now, when I say that I didn't know what chispa was, I don't mean that I didn't know the translation. I knew that people who had chispa had a spark, and that in the United States we would say they have charisma. So, the problem wasn't that I couldn't understand what the term meant. Instead, the problem was that I didn't know what a person does, exactly, to be perceived as charismatic. Think about it, do you? If you had to help someone develop the skills necessary to become a charismatic person, what, exactly, would you tell him/her to do? Obviously, most of us know when someone has a special spark, and when we see it we can't miss it. But, at least for me, it was difficult to articulate what it was, exactly, that actually made people perceive others to possess this quality.

Ultimately, this matters because if you don't know what it takes to behave in a charismatic manner, you cannot teach yourself (or others) to increase their charisma. I knew this was a problem; so after returning to America, I set about trying to learn what people do to be charismatic. Of course, because I study instructional communication, my eventual focus was on what teachers do to promote perceptions of charisma in the classroom, and how these perceptions relate to students' educational experiences. I figured that if people who have a spark could be so interesting on TV, then maybe teachers who have a spark can similarly command students' attention in their classrooms.

In this chapter, we will go over what I have learned regarding charisma and how it applies in academic settings. Specifically, in the next few pages I will cover charisma to define what it is, explain how teachers behave to express it, and articulate how it helps in the classroom. Although you might not ever have the chance to participate in a Spanish game show, perhaps by reading this chapter your students will at least one day refer to you as a teacher con chispa. This is my hope.

What Is Charisma?

What is charisma? Let's ask the people who study it. According to Conger (1999), there are three streams of research that have informed the investigation of the topic. Generally speaking, these research traditions tend to examine charisma in the context of organizational leadership and include the Bass tradition, the Conger and Kanungo tradition, and the Shamir and House tradition. To learn what it takes to be charismatic, let's go over each.

To understand what charisma is and how it's defined, we'll first turn to one of the original charismatic theorists, Bernard Bass. In 1985, Bass wrote a book titled *Leadership and Performance Beyond Expectations*. In this book, Bass defined charisma as a component of transformational leadership. According to Bass, transformational leadership is defined by behaviors that help subordinates become motivated to work beyond, well as the book title suggests, their expectations. More specifically, based on Burns' (1978) conceptualization of the idea, Bass (1985) suggested that transformational leadership occurs when leaders get employees to accept the mission of the group and when they inspire and intellectually stimulate employees to be their best. Transformational leaders are people who motivate individuals to do more than they originally expected to do by challenging and encouraging subordinates to reach their full potential (Bass & Riggio, 2006). Although there might be a variety of ways for a person to be transformational, Bass asserted that this type of leadership is a constellation of three components including *charisma, individualized consideration,* and *intellectual stimulation.*

So, what do transformational leaders do to be perceived as charismatic? According to Bass (1985), charismatic individuals have insights into the needs and values of their followers and build on these needs and values to push people to reach their potential. In particular, Bass suggests that charismatic leaders are inspirational, self-confident, and optimistic about followers' potential, and also command respect and loyalty from followers while arousing a sense of achievement and affiliation. Moreover, Bass asserts that charismatic leadership occurs to the extent that leaders instill a sense of enthusiasm in subordinates, inspire trust in their capacity to overcome challenges and obstacles, and have a sense of mission which they are able to transmit to their followers.

That's a lot to remember, but unfortunately there's more. The information presented above describes how Bass defines charisma, but other scholars define the idea somewhat differently. For example, according to Conger and Kanungo's model of charismatic leadership, followers are motivated by leaders' character as opposed to their authority. This is true to the extent that charismatic leaders are able to articulate an inspirational vision to their followers and give the impression that they are engaged in something extraordinary (Conger, Kanungo, & Menon, 2000). The specific components of Conger and Kanungo's (1994) charismatic leadership model include: *vision and articulation* (e.g., speaking well in public, communicating inspiring goals), *environmental sensitivity* (e.g., recognizing the skills of organizational members and being aware of constraints as well as the opportunities presented to the organization), *unconventional behavior* (e.g., being willing to use nontraditional means to achieve their goals), *personal risk* (e.g., being willing to make personal sacrifices for others), *sensitivity to member needs* (e.g., expressing personal concern for people in the organization), and *not maintaining the status quo* (e.g., being willing to try new things for the good of the organization).

The list of charismatic behaviors doesn't stop there. Shamir, House, and Arthur (1993) have their own conceptualization of what it means to be a charismatic leader including: *increasing the intrinsic value of activities* (e.g., associating organizational goals with important personal values), *increasing expectations of effort and accomplishment* (e.g., pushing followers to be their best and communicating confidence in their ability to perform at a high level), *increasing the value of accomplishing goals* (e.g., increasing the meaningfulness of the goals being pursued), *instilling faith in a better future* (e.g., emphasizing important long-term goals), and *creating personal commitment* (relating followers' goals to the goals of the organization).

Wow. Okay so, In addition to Bass's conceptualization of charisma and Conger and Kanungo's six categories of charismatic behaviors, we now have to add five more ideas to our definition of the construct. That's a lot to remember. But, perhaps there are some places where these scholars' ideas overlap. If so, that will make it easier for us to identify core behaviors that influence perceptions of charismatic leadership. The good news here is that, according to Conger (1999), the three streams of research reported earlier do, in fact, overlap. Hooray! The bad news is, they share no less than nine components. Oh no! These components include: (1) articulating a vision, (2) promoting inspiration, (3) leading by example, (4) helping subordinates think deeply about organizational problems, (5) linking work to core values, (6) focusing on subordinates' higher-order needs, (7) empowering followers, (8) setting high expectations, and (9) creating a sense of togetherness. Overwhelmed yet? Well, it might upset you to know that there's more—charisma has been studied in other academic fields as well.

The famous philosopher Snoop Dogg once noted: "It ain't no fun if the homies can't have none." So, let's let the communication homies have a little fun with charisma too. After all, scholars have asserted that the way information is communicated has more to do with perceptions of charisma than does the content of what is communicated (Holladay & Coombs, 1994). So, what have communication scholars found? According to researchers Kenneth Levine, Robert Muenchen, and Abby Brooks (2010), among other things, charismatic individuals are people who are: outgoing, motivating, confident, enthusiastic, energetic, determined, humorous, empathetic, interesting, comfortable, perceptive, powerful, poised, charming, interested in what others think and feel, open to the ideas of others, and strong speakers.

Holy shit. If you were not overwhelmed by the plethora of things a person can do to be charismatic before we let the communication researchers into the fray, then I bet you are now. And, do you want to hear something crazy? This is by no means a comprehensive list of the things a person can do to enhance perceptions of their charisma!

In my opinion, being charismatic seems to encompass so many things that if asked to display charisma in the classroom, it would be hard for most people to know where to start. The problem I faced when I watched the show *Gente con Chispa* was that I didn't know what it meant to be charismatic. However, the problem we face now, after being exposed to all of the different definitions of charisma, is that it is easy to be overwhelmed by what it means to be charismatic. If charisma encompasses so many ideas at once, how can anybody behave in such a way as to ensure they are being charismatic without forgetting one of the behaviors listed here?

In addition to the seemingly unending list of behaviors, as far as our needs are concerned, two other problems exist with the definitions of charisma noted earlier. First, most of the definitions cited here come from investigations of charisma in business-like situations. Because this is the case, we can't be sure if the behaviors we noted also work in educational contexts. Second, some of the ideas seem a little ambiguous. For example, communication researchers know that charismatic people are individuals who display confidence, but what do you need to do, exactly, to make others perceive you as being confident? The same thing goes for the idea of inspiring trust. What, exactly, can you do to inspire trust in others? Not knowing the specific behaviors that create perceptions of being charismatic is a major problem for people who want to improve this aspect of their teaching.

Charisma in the Classroom

Having been frustrated for too long regarding the definition of charisma, and not knowing what it means to be charismatic in the classroom, I set out to determine if I could define what, exactly, it means to be a charismatic teacher. To make sense of the ways teachers could be charismatic in educational contexts, I recruited my colleague Alan Goodboy and we started our research on the topic from the ground up. In one of our first studies of charisma in the classroom (Bolkan & Goodboy, 2011a), we provided a definition of charisma and asked students to tell us what, exactly, their teachers did to help create this perception. Specifically, we conducted a study where we presented students with the following prompt based on Bass's (1985) definition of charisma: "Some students have teachers they look up to and who have charisma. These teachers inspire loyalty through their personalities and have the ability to make students feel good to be around them while at the same time commanding respect." After students read this statement, we asked them to tell us what their instructors did or said that reflected this description.

What were the results? Turns out that, for the most part, students think their teachers communicate charisma in one of four ways including: being nonverbally immediate, being humorous, confirming students, and caring for students. First, students reported that instructors used a variety of *nonverbal immediacy* behaviors that were considered to be charismatic. For instance, students reported that they believed instructors were charismatic when they communicated with vocal variety; one student wrote that a professor "would get louder when trying to stress a point." Other examples included reports of instructors who: smiled, used gestures in class, were outgoing, demonstrated an interest in the course material, and who decreased the physical distance between themselves and their students (e.g., sitting on a desk instead of behind it).

Second, instructors were perceived to be charismatic when they used *humor* in the classroom and made learning fun. These instructors were considered "funny" and "hysterical" and were able to make students feel comfortable and relaxed through their use of comedy in the classroom. For example, a student wrote that "when professors joke around with their students they show that they have a sense of humor. This puts the student at ease and makes it easier to learn."

Third, instructors were perceived to be charismatic when they were *confirming*, which occurred when they demonstrated an interest in students and communicated their belief in students' abilities to succeed. For example, charismatic teachers were people who interacted with their students to hear their points of view, communicated that students had a high probability of success in their classes, were optimistic about student success, and used interactive teaching materials to get students excited about learning. As it pertains to the idea of confirmation, one student wrote that her instructor "never put students down and always encouraged them that they can succeed and will succeed."

Finally, instructors were also perceived as being charismatic to the extent that they communicated *caring*. Generally, instructors ommunicated caring to students by being thoughtful and by going the extra mile to help students both academically and personally. Specifically, instructors were considered caring for a variety of reasons including: helping students with their other classes or other goals that were not class-related (e.g., helping students with personal problems), being willing to help students who ask for it, getting to know students on a personal level (e.g., getting to know students' names, getting to know students' backgrounds, asking students how their weekends were), recognizing students on campus while out of class, and, in one instance, by bringing cookies to class. How does caring relate to charisma? As one student explained, "a teacher who does not care will not inspire anyone. If the instructor does not show they care about the students, the students will not care either."

Alright! So now you know that being charismatic in the classroom is a function of your nonverbal immediacy, humor, confirmation, and caring. I bet you can remember those four ideas. If not, I am going to make it even easier. If you think you see a pattern in the data reported here, then you are not alone. Alan and I also saw a pattern and noted that these behaviors combine to form two higher-order constructs of *delivering information well* and *building relationships with students* (Bolkan & Goodboy, 2014).

Importantly, the behaviors we found in our study are similar to what previous researchers found, although our results are a little less numbered. Specifically, as it pertains to being able to deliver information well, this notion is similar to communication researchers' ideas of being: a strong speaker, outgoing, motivating, confident, enthusiastic, energetic, and humorous. Being able to deliver information well is also linked to research on charismatic leadership in organizations including promoting a vision and being inspiring. The second concept, building relationships with students, is similar to communication scholars' notions of being: empathetic, perceptive, interested in what others think and feel, and open to the ideas of others. Moreover, compared to the ideas articulated by organizational scholars, building relationships with students is similar to focusing on subordinates' higher-order needs and empowering followers. Thus, although we did not find a plethora of variables in our study, the ones we did uncover are aligned with components of charisma found in other research projects and indicate that people experience charisma in the classroom in a manner similar to how they experience charisma across a variety of other domains.

Now that you know what charismatic teaching includes, you probably want to know if charismatic behaviors are beneficial in the classroom. Guess what? Based on what you learned about self-determination theory (Chapter 8), you already know they are! Because of its focus on developing relationships with students, charisma is likely related to the concept of student–teacher rapport and, therefore, linked to students' fundamental need of relatedness. Moreover, because of its emphasis on delivering information well, charismatic teachers create learning environments that students are excited to be a part of and is therefore likely related to their fundamental need of autonomy. Based on this, it should be no surprise to learn that charismatic teaching has been linked to students' positive emotional experiences in the classroom, their satisfaction with class, and their participation (Bolkan & Goodboy, 2009). In addition, charismatic teaching has been shown to reduce student resistance in the classroom as well (Bolkan & Goodboy, 2011b). As we might predict from self-determination theory, these outcomes ultimately indicate that students who experience charismatic teaching tend to be more autonomously motivated in class. In support of this conclusion, Alan and I have linked charismatic teaching to students' intrinsic motivation demonstrating that this is, indeed, the case (Bolkan & Goodboy, 2014).

Importantly, these are just the results from some of the recent studies on charisma; if you took a look at the independent effects of each of the behaviors linked to charisma, you would notice that they have been consistently associated with a host of positive academic outcomes. To prove it to you, we'll turn our attention to the four aspects of charismatic teaching next.

Delivery

Nonverbal Immediacy

For those of you who are unfamiliar with the term, nonverbal immediacy was introduced to the field of instructional communication by Janice Andersen and refers to "behaviors that reduce physical and/or psychological distance between teachers and students" (Andersen,

1979, p. 543). This concept was originally studied because of its presumed ability to influence students' positive emotional experiences in class. This outcome is important because, although some people might argue that students are in class to learn and not to "feel good" about their academic experiences, researchers have found that students' emotional experiences in class do matter and can influence student learning in important ways (see Pekrun & Linnenbrink-Garcia, 2014 for a comprehensive review). As researchers Mottet, Frymier, and Beebe (2006) argue, students enter our classrooms with both practical *and* personal needs and, as such, teachers are optimally effective when they help students satisfy both.

So what is nonverbal immediacy? Again, nonverbal immediacy refers to the behaviors teachers enact that reduce the physical and/or psychological distance between themselves and their students. As Andersen (1979) reports, this includes standing near your students as opposed to being far away from them, being relaxed (e.g., avoiding fidgeting or fiddling with an object such as a pen), smiling, and using appropriate eye contact. To this list, we might add gesturing while talking, using vocal variety, and moving around the class when speaking (McCroskey, Richmond, Sallinen, Fayer, & Barraclough, 1995). Other behaviors include standing in front of as opposed to behind a podium, standing in front of instead of sitting behind a desk, and avoiding looking at the board or at your notes when speaking to the class (Richmond, Gorham, & McCroskey, 1987). Essentially, the behaviors reported here are behaviors that are perceived to be warm, friendly, and enthusiastic. Thus, stated differently, one of the ways to be charismatic in the classroom is to behave in a manner that signals your closeness to students and promotes a sense of engagement.

What does nonverbal immediacy do for you as a teacher? Well, for starters, there is a significant relationship between teachers' nonverbal immediacy and teaching evaluations (e.g., Feeley, 2002; Richmond, 2002). Moreover, nonverbal immediacy is also associated with students' sense of empowerment including their perceptions of meaningfulness, competence, and impact in class (Frymier, Shulman, & Houser, 1996). In addition, nonverbal immediacy has been connected to students' increased out-of-class communication (Jaasma & Koper, 1999), perceptions of instructor credibility, and even students' intent to persist in college (Witt,

Schrodt, Wheeless, & Bryand, 2014). Furthermore, nonverbal immediacy has been related to increased teacher liking, reduced student resistance, increased perceptions of teacher competence, increased student attention, increased perceptions of teacher approachability, and reduced student anxiety (for a review, see Richmond, 2002).

The provision of nonverbal immediacy also seems particularly important for student motivation (e.g., Christophel, 1990; Zhang, Oetzel, Gao, Wilcox, & Takai, 2007). In fact, according to Gorham and Millette (1997), students report that one of the biggest demotivators in the classroom stems from their teachers having poor presentational abilities in general, and a lack of enthusiasm when presenting course material in specific. In other words, students report that their lack of motivation in class often stems from their teachers' absence of nonverbal immediacy behaviors (see also Christophel & Gorham, 1995).

Although the evidence suggests that nonverbal immediacy impacts students' emotional and motivational experiences in class, one question we might want to ask is whether or not immediacy behaviors also influence student learning. To make a long story short, most of the research points to the conclusion of "not really." In their meta-analysis (i.e., a study that combines the results of several studies), Witt, Wheeless, and Allen (2004) found that while nonverbal immediacy was strongly linked to students' positive emotional experiences in class, it was only weakly linked to their actual learning. Some of my own studies corroborate this conclusion. In fact, in one of my more recent studies, I found that nonverbal immediacy behaviors were not directly linked to learning at all (Bolkan, Goodboy, & Myers, in press).

Uh oh. I just made the case that charisma is important for academic achievement, and now we know that one of its core components (nonverbal immediacy) does not strongly influence student learning. What gives? I think a couple of explanations are in order. First, nonverbal immediacy may influence learning indirectly, and for a select group of students. I just mentioned that I conducted a study and found that nonverbal immediacy did not influence student learning. To be precise, I found no *direct* influence . . . there was an indirect influence. Specifically, I did find that, when paired with clear teaching, nonverbal immediacy can influence the attention students pay to a lecture and that this extra attention, in turn, can make a small impact on students' test scores.

However, removing immediacy only really hurt students who scored low on measures of self-control. In other words, nonverbal immediacy seems to benefit students when it is paired with clear teaching, but it is mostly beneficial for students who cannot otherwise make themselves pay attention to class lectures.

Second, as Witt et al. (2004) noted, most of the studies that have examined nonverbal immediacy and learning focus on short-term results. That is, most of these studies (including mine) are experimental in nature and do not allow for the long-term cumulative results of positive affect to influence their measurement. So, for example, although we may not expect more eye contact to lead to increased learning in a 50-minute lecture, students exposed to teachers who use nonverbal immediacy to create a positive educational climate may be more likely to do things over the long term that ultimately lead to learning—such as coming to class and paying attention to their lectures. Thus, although nonverbal immediacy behaviors may not have strong and direct relationships with learning in the short term, you might still consider employing these behaviors in your classes because of their indirect and long-term effects. Besides, as I reported earlier, there are still significant positive associations between nonverbal immediacy and a host of other important academic outcomes.

So, what can you do to increase your immediacy? Easy, become aware of your behaviors to ensure that you teach in a nonverbally immediate manner. Essentially, my first piece of advice to you is the same advice I give to my public speaking students: In order to control for unintended behaviors and to be in control of your presentation, you must focus on your delivery and not take it for granted. In other words, you should be deliberate in the delivery of your presentations. What I mean by this is that you should not go into "autopilot" when delivering your lectures. Instead, try to watch every word that comes out of your mouth and try to behave in ways that are intentionally designed to create a sense of warmth and enthusiasm. If you want to seem friendly in class, for example, do not simply think friendly thoughts. Instead, you need to make a conscious effort to smile at your students to make this impression. The same goes for any of the other behaviors discussed earlier. If you need reminders, you can write the words "smile" or "move closer to students" on your lecture notes to help you do these things.

Most people spend a significant amount of time preparing the content of their presentations and pay less attention to how they deliver them. That said, although taking time to prepare the content of your lessons is a great habit, I suggest that you try to be just as deliberate in the delivery of your information you are in your selection of it.

My second piece of advice is to find out what you look like when you teach. I don't mean that you should try to discover just how good your hair looks when you deliver your lectures. I'm sure your hair looks fine. Instead, I mean that you might consider watching yourself from your students' point of view to see how they perceive you when you deliver your course lessons. Why? Because there is usually a difference between what you think you are doing and what people experience you doing, and it is important to be able to align your perception of reality with that of your students. For example, whenever I teach public speaking, I ask my students to write down the level of enthusiasm and friendliness they think they portray when speaking to others. Then, I videotape my students speaking and ask them to rate themselves on these qualities. Usually, after this exercise, people recognize that what they think they are doing and what people experience them as doing are two different things. Specifically, people tend to report seeing themselves as less friendly and enthusiastic when they watch themselves on video than they thought they were being when speaking. Of course, the same is likely true for you. So, why not have someone record one of your lectures so you can see how you act for yourself? You have a smartphone, right? Give it to a student and ask them to record you; even a few minutes will be helpful. Watching yourself deliver a presentation might give you some important insights regarding your ability to create the atmosphere you intend for your classrooms.

Humor

As an effective teaching behavior, humor has been studied for some time (e.g., Kaplan & Pascoe, 1977; Ziv, 1988). And, scientists have found that, for the most part, humor is beneficial in the classroom. Humor has been shown to be beneficial in a variety of ways including its ability to entertain students, alleviate anxiety, create a positive academic climate, increase student motivation, and increase student learning. Moreover, researchers report that humor can increase perceptions of group cohesion and create an enjoyable learning environment (for a review, see Banas, Dunbar, Rodriguez, & Liu 2011). Although these benefits reflect gains students might enjoy, humor is important for instructors too. According to Banas et al. (2011), the use of humor in the classroom bolsters students' affinity for instructors, boosts instructor credibility, and increases positive instructor evaluations as well. In addition, Houser, Cowan, and West (2007) note that humor is associated positively with students' perceptions of instructors' extroversion, sociability, and character.

Okay, you know that humor can be beneficial in the classroom, but how does this work? I'm glad you asked. Humor might operate in the classroom through two mechanisms: one general and one specific. The first way humor might work is through its general ability to make class an enjoyable experience and to subsequently fulfill students' three fundamental needs (Bolkan & Goodboy, 2015). Particularly, when students like their classes more they may be more likely to: behave in ways that help them perform better in their courses (i.e., competence), feel a connection with their instructors (i.e., relatedness), and believe they are involved in an activity they actually want to be a part of (i.e., autonomy). As you already know, when classroom environments fulfill their needs, students can become more engaged in, and autonomously motivated toward, their course work (Jang, Reeve, Ryan, & Kim, 2009).

The second way humor might operate is by enhancing the memorability of specific course content. As researchers Kaplan and Pascoe (1977) found, lectures that incorporated humorous examples were better remembered six weeks later compared to lectures that did not. Admittedly, Kaplan and Pascoe argued that students' "general comprehension and retention of a classroom message is not improved by the use of humor" (pp. 64–65). Instead, Kaplan and Pascoe noted that "a positive effect of humorous examples only results when test items are based on those particular examples" (p. 65). According to the researchers then, humorous examples essentially cue students' memories for the specific information tied to the use of humor in class. Thus, the second reason humor might be beneficial in the classroom is because it helps make some information more distinctive and therefore more memorable.

Great! Now that you know humor is important and now that you have an idea about how it works, you might be wondering what you should do to be humorous in the classroom. First, let me tell you that you can relax knowing that you do not have to be a standup comedian to make a positive impression on your students. As Banas et al. (2011) discussed, most teachers use humor in their classrooms sparingly; it *is* possible for you to distract students if you try to provide too much of a good thing. That said, if forced to put a number on it, we might conclude that teachers who are considered to be funny tend to employ humor somewhere between four and seven times in an hour-long lecture (see Banas et al., 2011 for a discussion). That seems reasonable, doesn't it? I think this is doable, especially considering the ways a person can be humorous in the classroom are almost limitless. According to Banas et al. (2011), some ways to be funny include the use of humorous stories, funny comments, using funny facial expressions, and using props or illustrations.

Regardless of whether humorous teachers need to be funny three times, four times, or even seven times in a single class period, people who are naturally funny might find doing the things mentioned above to be effortless. For these individuals, promoting humor might be no big deal. If humor comes naturally to you and being funny describes your personality or your teaching style, then good for you. But what should you do if you are not naturally funny? My advice is to not worry about it; there are plenty of funny people in the world you can lean on. In particular, if you want to infuse humor into your lessons but do not consider yourself to be humorous, you can borrow it from other people. For example, you might consider borrowing humor from others in the form of comics, videos, or other multimedia sources such as gifs or memes. Importantly, having a few "fun" items that you gather from others might relieve some of the pressure to be spontaneously funny yourself.

What's more, you might create activities that allow students to laugh at themselves. For example, in my public speaking classes I have one activity where I teach my students to focus on nonverbal immediacy by making them stand and simply look at fellow classmates for 10 seconds while smiling—no talking allowed. I have students do this with several partners for a total of several minutes. I tell students that they have to overcome the feeling of awkwardness that comes with looking and smiling at their classmates and that practicing like this will help them reach their goal of being able to deliver speeches while looking and smiling at their audience. Whenever I have students engage in this activity, they always crack up laughing. Most of my students have a hard time keeping a straight face when smiling and looking deep into the eyes of their classmates—I would too! As a result, I am able to help my students laugh without having to be funny myself. In my opinion, the experience of humor in the classroom is really just a reflection of students enjoying class. Having said that, if you are not naturally funny you should feel confident knowing that there are several ways to help your students enjoy class; you simply have to get creative with your lesson plans.

Before we leave this section I have to answer the important question of whether all humor is considered beneficial for student learning. My response is "nope," various types of humor are not created equal. Humor is not a unidimensional concept. Instead, there are a variety of types that instructors might employ in their classrooms including: funny stories, impersonation, nonverbal humor, jokes, unplanned humor, self-disparaging humor, and aggressive humor (Banas et al., 2011). That said, some humor may be considered irrelevant to student success. For instance, humor that is unrelated to classroom content (e.g., telling funny stories unrelated to the course; Frymier, Wanzer, & Wojtaszczyk, 2008) or that is considered inappropriate or offensive (e.g., disparaging towards students or social groups, covering topics such as sex or drugs; Wanzer, Frymier, Wojtaszczyk, & Smith, 2006) has been shown to be unrelated to indicators of student learning (Wanzer, Frymier, & Irwin, 2010). The bottom line? Comedy can be beneficial in educational contexts. But don't force it with unrelated, offensive, or inappropriate humor.

Relationship formation

Confirmation

As teachers, we usually know that our jobs involve communicating course content to our students. But, I think we often forget that we do this as humans for other humans. Because of the nature of our humanity, we have to remember that all communication has two elements to it: an instrumental and a relational part. Thus, although our goal as teachers may be to communicate information to our students, we have to keep in mind that when we do we also communicate our feelings of accepting or rejecting students as well. This is important to remember because the way we communicate with students indicates our attitudes toward them as people (Teven & McCroskey, 1997).

Having said the above, the third idea related to teacher charisma is confirmation. Confirmation refers to the notion that "teachers communicate to students that they are valuable, significant individuals" (Ellis, 2000, p. 265). Essentially, confirming students reflects the idea that we communicate our support to students whenever possible. More specifically, we are confirming when we recognize and endorse students as individuals, and this occurs to the extent that we show interest in our students, communicate our acceptance of them, and demonstrate respect toward them (Ellis, 2000).

According to researcher Kathleen Ellis (2000, 2004), confirming students happens when teachers do four things. These include: (1) responding to students' questions (i.e., listening to students' questions and communicating that we appreciate student contributions), (2) showing an interest in student development (i.e., indicating an interest in student learning and communicating the belief that students can do well), and (3) delivering information in a manner that includes students (i.e., having an interactive classroom and asking students for feedback). Moreover, confirmation also occurs to the extent that (4) teachers avoid being demeaning and disrespectful (i.e., avoiding being arrogant, embarrassing students, or being rude to students). Ultimately, the ideas here converge on supporting students' identities and letting them know that we appreciate them as important human beings.

At this point, you might be on board with the idea that confirming students can help them feel better in class, but you might also be wondering if confirmation affects their learning experiences. It sure does. Teacher confirmation has been linked to students' positive affective experiences in class (Ellis, 2000) and also to a reduction in their negative affective experiences including apprehension (Ellis, 2004). Moreover, confirmation has been associated with an increase in students' emotional interest (Goldman & Goodboy, 2014), and students' increased communication satisfaction, out-of-class communication, and feelings of empowerment (Goodboy, Martin, & Bolkan, 2009). In addition, confirmation has been linked to students' increased willingness to participate in class, satisfaction with teachers, perceived cognitive learning (Goodboy & Myers, 2008), feelings of being understood by instructors, perceptions of teacher credibility, and perceptions of overall teaching effectiveness (Schrodt, Turman, and Soliz, 2006).

How can confirming students do all of this you ask? Confirmation does this by helping teachers develop healthy relationships with their students (Schrodt et al., 2006). And, considering student–teacher relationships matter in instruction (Frymier & Houser, 2000), the better the relationships you have with your students, the more likely they are to be at ease and to be motivated in your classrooms (Ellis, 2004). This should come as no surprise considering what you learned about instructor–student rapport in the previous chapter. Of course, the same is likely true for you, isn't it? Think about the relationships you have with your superiors. Do you work harder and operate more successfully when your bosses communicate that they like you and believe in you, or when they are rude, dismissive, and don't acknowledge you?

Hopefully, by now you agree that confirmation is important. But, what can you do to help create a confirming environment for your students? There are two things you might consider. The first idea includes responding to students in a manner that supports their identities. When students participate in class or communicate with you outside of class, for example, they put themselves in a conspicuous position where you have the power to support them as individuals or damage their self-esteem. Thus, to be confirming you need to focus on endorsing students in these situations. Instead of being curt with students or being dismissive of their viewpoints, you should practice what I call the ABCs of confirming. ABC in this instance stands for "Always Be Complimenting." For example, when students ask questions in class or share their experiences, you can say things like: "good question;" "great example, thank you for sharing;" or if they send an e-mail, you can say something as simple as "thanks for the note." Moreover, you can do your best to respond in ways that acknowledge student contributions by linking their questions or comments to class material and following up with students to make sure you have answered their questions completely. Whatever you do, the main idea is really just to be patient with students, to help them see that their contributions are valuable, and to endorse their experiences and perspectives as being significant.

The second thing you can do to help confirm students is to communicate that you are interested in their learning your course material and to communicate you believe your students can do well in your classes. The idea is to show support for your students' success and to communicate your interest in their development. In this regard, one of your roles as a teacher includes being something like a cheerleader for your students. Well, maybe not a cheerleader so much as a team captain because, in reality, you should help students see that you are in the learning process with them. Sometimes, the simple act of telling students that you believe in their abilities and that you are here to help them the best you can is all it takes to get them to believe in themselves. By creating a positive and supportive climate for your students, you can help establish an atmosphere that motivates students to succeed to the best of their abilities.

Caring

Finally, caring is the last component of teacher charisma we'll discuss. Caring is defined as showing concern for the welfare of students and their success, and is important in the classroom because, as Jason Teven and James McCroskey (1997) argue, the more teachers care about their students, the more students end up caring about their classes. Other researchers agree with this conclusion and claim that "in order to maximize learning, it is essential for teachers to develop good relationships with their students" (Teven & Gorham, 1998, p. 288).

There are several ways to promote caring in your classrooms. For example, Teven (2001) found that teachers who were helpful, sympathetic, compassionate, and friendly were perceived by students to be caring. Moreover, teachers can demonstrate caring through understanding (i.e., being sensitive to students' problems in class and outside of class as well) and responsiveness (i.e., being attentive to students and responding to their needs quickly; Teven & McCroskey, 1997). Other ideas for promoting caring include demonstrating a concern for students' positive performance in class (i.e., being available for help including helping students study for tests), and demonstrating a concern for teaching well (i.e., showing a concern for being able to help students learn; Teven & Gorham, 1998).

Is caring important to students' learning outcomes? Several scholars think it is. For example, researchers have found that teacher caring is linked to students' positive feelings toward class, positive feelings toward their instructors (Teven & McCroskey, 1997), and to students' perceptions of teachers' competence and trustworthiness (Teven, 2007). In reality, it is not that caring helps students learn their course content better because your positive feelings toward them make students any smarter. Instead, as we learned in Chapter 8, the connection between teacher caring and student performance likely stems from the ability for caring to motivate students in the classroom (e.g., Comadena, Hunt, & Simonds, 2007) through its fulfillment of students' fundamental needs.

So, what can you do to enhance caring? Similar to what we noted for confirmation, one thing we know from the literature is that teachers who show caring are those people who demonstrate a concern for their students' academic development (Teven & Gorham, 1998). That said, teachers can show caring for their students by helping them prepare for tests and by demonstrating an interest in their doing well in class. Some ways to help make this impression include making study guides for students, reviewing for exams before students take them, and helping students study for tests or revise their papers during office hours if they need the extra help. In addition, you might consider demonstrating your care for students' deep and conceptual learning as well. One way to do this is to go over students' exams and assignments in class after students hand them in. By helping students review what they did correctly and what they did not, you can show your concern for their ability to actually learn the concepts in your courses. Finally, another way to show that you care about student development is by being responsive to their needs (Teven & McCroskey, 1997). For example, you can try to e-mail students back within one business day of receiving an e-mail, you can grade students' papers, assignments and tests within a week of their being turned in (if not sooner), and you can even help students when they come to you with personal projects or questions for which they deem your expertise relevant.

In addition to the ideas presented above, learning students' names and finding out about their interests is paramount for demonstrating caring. Although remembering students' names may mean little to us as teachers, it means the world to our students. Admittedly, learning students' names can be tough, especially when you have large classes. However, there is one trick you can use to make the process easy . . . have them help you study! Here's what I do: In the beginning of each semester, I ask my students to create a flashcard for me so I can study their names and learn more about them. Specifically, on the first day of class, I give students homework and ask them to bring in a 4 × 6 or a 3 × 5 card with their names on the front and a picture of themselves on the back. In addition to the picture, I ask students to report an interesting fact about themselves, something I wouldn't know just by looking at them. This assignment fulfills two goals for me. First, it gives me a mechanism to study their names and faces, and with this method I can usually learn hundreds of students' names in a matter of weeks. Second, it helps me get to know my students as interesting individuals, and it gives me something to talk about when I see them before class or in the hallways. Sometimes, I think that we forget that students are just like us with dreams, fears, and lives outside of class. Using the notecard method to get a glimpse into their worlds allows us to recognize students as the important people they really are.

Finally, when it comes to showing students that you care, one of the best things you can do is demonstrate that you are concerned with teaching well (Teven & Gorham, 1998). One way to do this is to solicit your students' feedback once you have been teaching for a couple of weeks. We already went over a few ways to collect information about your teaching in the chapter on teacher misbehaviors. However, let me take a moment to give you another mechanism for soliciting feedback that one of my professors taught me. According to this professor, a quick way to collect feedback from students is to ask them to write the words "keep," "start," and "stop" at the top, middle, and bottom of a piece of paper. Basically, the idea here is to ask students to (anonymously) report one thing we should keep doing, one thing we should start doing, and one thing we should stop doing to help them learn to their potential. Engaging in this activity shows students that you care because it lets them know that you are interested in their feedback and in creating a learning environment that suits their needs. Of course, as we have already learned, once we receive this feedback, it is important to report back to our students so we can demonstrate our willingness to change for the better. For example, when I receive feedback I make sure that if I can change something, I do it and report the change in class. Alternatively, if I cannot change something, I at least explain my rationale and alert students to the fact that I appreciate their positions. Although this tactic for soliciting feedback is simple, you might be surprised at the constructive feedback you get from your pupils using this method. In fact, some of the best teaching advice I have ever received has come from soliciting feedback from my students in the manner just described. In addition, allowing your students to influence your teaching practices and demonstrating your willingness to change based on their needs is a powerful way to communicate to your students that you care about their academic experiences.

Summary

In this chapter, we went over what it takes to be a charismatic teacher. Specifically, we learned that, although the possibilities for being charismatic are almost limitless, there are four things you can do to promote this perception in the classroom including being: nonverbally immediate, humorous, confirming, and caring. Of course, as you know, these four ideas can be combined into two dimensions of charismatic teaching which include delivering information well and building relationships with students.

For some people, being charismatic may come naturally. However, most of us have to work at it. That said, even though the behaviors I outlined in this chapter might not be easy for you to employ, as a human being you have the ability to make choices that can help you overcome your natural behavioral tendencies. For example, even if you are not a naturally nonverbally immediate person (i.e., someone who looks at others and smiles while talking), you can still *act* nonverbally immediate in the classroom. And, at the end of the day, students only know what you show them, not what you feel inside.

Before we move on, let me make one last point. As you already learned, the reason charismatic teachers help students learn is most likely through the indirect effect of charismatic behaviors on student motivation. Thus, if people argue that charismatic teaching doesn't lead to learning directly, they may be correct. Technically, it impacts student motivation and that is what leads to student learning. Still, as you learned from the COWs model in the first chapter, students have to be motivated if they are to make full use out of their learning potential. And, having said that, charismatic teaching is a great way to get students excited about class!

At the beginning of this chapter I told you that when I was in Spain, I had no idea what it meant to be charismatic. That said, based on what you read in this chapter you now do. Although being charismatic in the classroom might seem like something only celebrities can make possible, the truth of the matter is that anybody can behave in ways that spark students' interest and motivation. To make this happen, you just have to focus on delivering information well and building relationships with your students. It is that simple.

Okay, that's it for now . . . the chapter is done! You learned a lot here so why don't you treat yourself for a job well done. Go ahead and celebrate by going onto YouTube, finding an episode of *Gente con Chispa,* and having yourself a Calimocho. You deserve it!

END-OF-CHAPTER QUESTIONS

1. Which aspect of charisma do you struggle with most in the classroom? Why?

2. As a student, which component of charismatic teaching do you think benefits you the most? In other words, which component is the most motivating for you?

3. Besides delivery and relationship formation, can you think of other behaviors that might influence students' perceptions of teacher charisma? Did we leave anything out?

KEY TERMS

Transformational leadership: Leadership behaviors that stimulate, empower, and inspire followers

Charismatic teachers: Teachers who inspire loyalty through their personalities and who have the ability to make students feel good to be around them while at the same time commanding respect

Nonverbal immediacy: Behaviors that reduce physical and/or psychological distance between teachers and students

Confirmation: Communicating to students that they are valuable, significant individuals

REFERENCES

Andersen, J. F. (1979). Teacher immediacy as a predictor of teaching effectiveness. In B. D. Ruben (Ed.), *Communication yearbook* (Vol. 3, pp. 534–559). New Brunswick, NJ: Transaction Books.

Banas, J. A., Dunbar, N., Rodriguez, D., & Liu, S-J. (2011). A review of humor in educational settings: Four decades of research. *Communication Education, 60,* 115–144. doi:10.1080/03634523.2010.496867

Bass, B. M. (1985). *Leadership and performance beyond expectations.* New York: Free Press.

Bass, B. M., & Riggio, R. E. (2006). *Transformational leadership.* New York, NY: Taylor & Francis.

Bolkan, S., & Goodboy, A. K. (2009). Transformational leadership in the classroom: Fostering student learning, student participation, and teacher credibility. *Journal of Instructional Psychology, 36,* 296–306.

Bolkan, S., & Goodboy, A. K. (2011a). Behavioral indicators of transformational leadership in the college classroom. *Qualitative Research Reports in Communication, 12,* 10–18. doi:10.1080/17459435.2011.601520

Bolkan, S., & Goodboy, A. K. (2011b). Leadership in the college classroom: The use of charismatic leadership as a deterrent to student resistance strategies. *Journal of Classroom Interaction, 46,* 4–10.

Bolkan, S., & Goodboy, A. K. (2014). Communicating charisma in instructional settings: Indicators and effects of charismatic teaching. *College Teaching, 62,* 136–142. doi:10.1080/87567555.2014.956039

Bolkan, S., & Goodboy, A. K. (2015). Exploratory theoretical tests of the instructor humor-student learning link. *Communication Education, 64,* 45–64. doi:10.1080/03634523.2014.978793

Bolkan, S., Goodboy, A. K., & Myers, S. A. (in press). Conditional processes of effective instructor communication and increases in students' cognitive learning. Manuscript in press in *Communication Education.*

Burns, J. M. (1978). *Leadership.* New York, NY: Harper Row.

Christophel, D. M. (1990). The relationships among teacher immediacy behaviors, student motivation, and learning. *Communication Education, 39,* 323–340. doi:10.1080/03634529009378813

Christophel, D. M., & Gorham, J. (1995). A test-retest analysis of student motivation, teacher immediacy, and perceived sources of motivation and demotivation in college classes. *Communication Education, 44,* 292–306. doi:10.1080/03634529509379020

Comadena, M. E., Hunt, S. K., & Simonds, C. J. (2007). The effects of teacher clarity, nonverbal immediacy, and caring on student motivation, affective, and cognitive learning. *Communication Research Reports, 24,* 241–248. doi:10.1080/08824090701446617

Conger, J. A. (1999). Charismatic and transformational leadership in organizations: An insider's perspective on these developing streams of research. *Leadership Quarterly, 10,* 145–179. doi:10.1016/S1048-9843(99)00012-0

Conger, J. A., & Kanungo, R. N. (1994). Charismatic leadership in organizations: Perceived behavioral attributes and their measurement. *Journal of Organizational Behavior, 15,* 439–452. doi:10.1002/job.4030150508

Conger, J. A., Kanungo, R. N., & Menon, S. T. (2000). Charismatic leadership and follower effects. *Journal of Organizational Behavior, 21,* 747–767. doi:10.1002/1099-1379(200011)21:7<747::AID-JOB46>3.0.CO;2-J

Ellis, K. (2000). Perceived teacher confirmation: The development and validation of an instrument and two studies of the relationship to cognitive and affective learning. *Human Communication Research, 26,* 264–291. doi:10.1111/j.1468-2958.2000.tb00758.x

Ellis, K. (2004). The impact of perceived teacher confirmation on receiver apprehension, motivation, and learning. *Communication Education, 53,* 1–20. doi:10.10/0363452032000135742

Feeley, T. H. (2002). Evidence of halo effects in student evaluations of communication instruction. *Communication Education, 51,* 225–236. doi:10.1080/03634520216519

Frymier, A. B., & Houser, M. L. (2000). The teacher-student relationship as an interpersonal relationship. *Communication Education, 49,* 207–219. doi:10.1080/03634520009379209

Frymier, A. B., Shulman, G. M., & Houser, M. (1996). The development of a learner empowerment measure. *Communication Education, 45,* 181–199. doi:10.1080/03634529609379048

Frymier, A. B., Wanzer, M. B., & Wojtaszczyk, A. M. (2008). Assessing students' perceptions of inappropriate and appropriate teacher humor. *Communication Education, 57,* 266–288. doi:10.1080/03634520701687183

Goldman, Z. W., & Goodboy, A. K. (2014). Making students feel better: Examining the relationship between teacher confirmation and college students' emotional outcomes. *Communication Education, 63,* 259–277. doi:10.1080/03634523.2014.920091

Goodboy, A. K., Martin, M. M., & Bolkan, S. (2009). The development and validation of the student communication satisfaction scale. *Communication Education, 58,* 372–396. doi:10.1080/03634520902755441

Goodboy, A. K., & Myers, S. A. (2008). The effect of teacher confirmation on student communication and learning outcomes. *Communication Education, 57,* 153–179. doi:10.1080/03634520701787777

Gorham, J., & Millette, D. M. (1997). A comparative analysis of teacher and student perceptions of sources of motivation and demotivation in college classes. *Communication Education, 46,* 245–261. doi:10.1080/03634529709379099

Holladay, S. J., & Coombs, W. T. (1994). Speaking of visions and visions being spoken: An exploration of the effects of content and delivery on perceptions of leader charisma. *Management Communication Quarterly, 8,* 165–189. doi:10.1177/0893318994008002002

Houser, M. L., Cowan, R. L., & West, D. A. (2007). Investigating a new education frontier: Instructor communication behavior in CD-ROM texts—Do traditionally positive behaviors translate into this new environment? *Communication Quarterly, 55,* 19–38. doi:10.1080/01463370600998319

Jaasma, M. A., & Koper, R. J. (1999). The relationship of student-faculty out-of-class communication to instructor immediacy and trust and to student motivation. *Communication Education, 48,* 41–47. doi:10.1080/03634529909379151

Jang, H., Reeve, J., Ryan, R. M., & Kim, A. (2009). Can self-determination theory explain what underlies the productive, satisfying learning experiences of collectivistically oriented Korean students? *Journal of Educational Psychology, 101,* 644–661. doi:10.1037/a0014241

Kaplan, R. M., & Pascoe, G. C. (1977). Humorous lectures and humorous examples: Some effects upon comprehension and retention. *Journal of Educational Psychology, 69,* 61–65. doi:10.1037/0022-0663.69.1.61

Levine, K. J., Muenchen, R. A., & Brooks, A. M. (2010). Measuring transformational and charismatic leadership: Why isn't charisma measured? *Communication Monographs, 77,* 576–591. doi:10.1080/03637751.2010.499368

McCroskey, J. C., Richmond, V. P., Sallinen, A., Fayer, J. M., & Barraclough, R. A. (1995). A cross-cultural and multi-behavioral analysis of the relationship between nonverbal immediacy and teacher evaluation. *Communication Education, 44,* 281–291. doi:10.1080/03634529509379019

Mottet, T. P., Frymier, A. B., & Beebe, S. A. (2006). Theorizing about instructional communication. In T. P. Mottet, V. P. Richmond, & J. C. McCroskey (Eds.), *Handbook of instructional communication: Rhetorical and relational perspectives* (pp. 255–282). Boston, MA: Pearson.

Pekrun, R., & Linnenbrink-Garcia, L. (Eds.). (2014). *International handbook of emotions in education.* New York, NY: Routledge.

Richmond, V. P. (2002). Teacher nonverbal immediacy: Uses and outcomes. In J. L. Chesebro & J. C. McCroskey (Eds.) *Communication for teachers* (pp. 65–82). Boston, MA: Allyn & Bacon.

Richmond, V. P., Gorham, J. S., & McCroskey, J. C. (1987). The relationship between selected immediacy behaviors and cognitive learning. In M. L. McLaughlin (Ed.), *Communication yearbook 10* (pp. 574–590). Newbury Park, CA: SAGE.

Schrodt, P., Turman, P. D., & Soliz, J. (2006). Perceived understanding as a mediator of perceived teacher confirmation and students' ratings of instruction. *Communication Education, 55,* 370–388. doi:10.1080/03634520600879196

Shamir, B., House, R. J., & Arthur, M. B. (1993). The motivational effects of charismatic leadership: A self-concept based theory. *Organizational Science, 4,* 577–594. doi:10.1287/orsc.4.4.577

Teven, J. J. (2001). The relationships among teacher characteristics and perceived caring. *Communication Education, 50,* 159–169. doi:10.1080/03634520109379241

Teven, J. J. (2007). Teacher caring and classroom behavior: Relationships with student affect and perceptions of teacher competence and trustworthiness. *Communication Quarterly, 55,* 433–450. doi:10.1080/01463370701658077

Teven, J. J., & Gorham, J. (1998). A qualitative analysis of low-inference student perceptions of teacher caring and non-caring behaviors within the college classroom. *Communication Research Reports, 15,* 288–298. doi:10.1080/08824099809362125

Teven, J. J., & McCroskey, J. C. (1997). The relationship of perceived teacher caring with student learning and teacher evaluation. *Communication Education, 46,* 1–9. doi:10.1080/03634529709379069

Wanzer, M. B., Frymier, A. B., & Irwin, J. (2010). An explanation of the relationship between instructor humor and student learning: Instructional humor processing theory. *Communication Education, 59,* 1–18. doi:10.1080/03634520903367238

Wanzer, M. B., Frymier, A. B., Wojtaszczyk, A. M., & Smith, T. (2006). Appropriate and inappropriate uses of humor by instructors. *Communication Education, 55,* 178–196. doi:10.1080/03634520600566132

Witt, P. L., Schrodt, P., Wheeless, V., & Bryand, M. (2014). Students' intent to persist in college: Moderating the negative effects of receiver apprehension with instructor credibility and nonverbal immediacy. *Communication Studies, 65,* 330–352. doi:10.1080/10510974.2013.811428

Witt, P. L., Wheeless, L. R., & Allen, M. (2004). A meta-analytical review of the relationship between teacher immediacy and student learning. *Communication Monographs, 71,* 184–207. doi:10.1080/036452042000228054

Zhang, Q., Oetzel, J. G., Gao, X., Wilcox, R. G., & Takai, J. (2007). A further test of immediacy-learning models: A cross-cultural investigation. *Journal of Intercultural Communication Research, 36,* 1–13. doi:10.1080/17475750701265209

Ziv, A. (1988). Teaching and learning with humor: Experiment and replication. *Journal of Experimental Education, 57,* 5–15.

Additional References

Portions of this chapter have appeared in some of my journal articles including:

Bolkan, S., & Goodboy, A. K. (2011). Behavioral indicators of transformational leadership in the college classroom. *Qualitative Research Reports in Communication, 12,* 10–18. doi:10.1080/17459435.2011.601520

Bolkan, S., & Goodboy, A. K. (2015). Exploratory theoretical tests of the instructor humor-student learning link. *Communication Education, 64,* 45–64. doi:10.1080/03634523.2014.978793

TEN

Intellectual Stimulation

OBJECTIVES

By the end of this chapter, you should be a changed person in the following ways:

1. You should know the three aspects of intellectual stimulation and behaviors associated with these
2. You should be able to articulate how the three aspects of intellectual stimulation influence students
3. You should be able to articulate various ways that you can personally foster intellectual stimulation
4. You should be able to explain how intellectual stimulation relates to the fulfillment of students' fundamental needs
5. You should know the average height of men and women in America (How do you stack up?)

Intellectual Stimulation

I want to begin the last chapter of this book by asking for your opinion regarding students' motivation in your classrooms. There are currently two sides to a debate, and I want you to weigh in on the discussion. Here's the scenario: Some people might claim that university instructors experience a challenge of maintaining intellectual rigor in the face of students' expectations for reduced workloads (e.g., Mottet, Parker-Raley, Beebe, & Cunningham, 2007). As Mottet and his colleagues note, these people might argue that it is difficult for instructors to demand much from their pupils because students expect their academic experiences to be akin to something like "college lite." Essentially, the first position in this debate is that, as a teacher, your job is a difficult one because most of your students don't want to put forth the effort necessary to pass classes that demand intellectual rigor.

On the other hand, the second position in this debate is that students appreciate and prefer instructors who provide challenging classroom atmospheres (e.g., Gillmore, 2001). People who support this position claim that the notion of students wanting an easy education is a myth, and might support this assertion with evidence that difficult and challenging courses tend to be evaluated more favorably by students (Marsh, 2001). According to this argument, students "value learning and achievement more highly when it involves a substantial degree of challenge and commitment," and "if success is too easily won as a result of an overly light workload," people who support the second position would claim that "students may lose interest and not value such learning" (Marsh, 2001, p. 185).

So, what do you think? Do you support the first position or the second? Do college students prefer to get things done with the least amount of effort possible, or do they enjoy being pushed to learn course material? Do you think your students would prefer to enroll in college lite, or do you think they have signed up for college to experience the challenges and demands of a rigorous academic schedule? Which one is it? Before you move on, I want you to really think about how you might answer these questions.

When I first looked into the question of whether students want to work hard or prefer to hardly work, I did not expect to find the answer I did. But now that I know what students want, the answer seems pretty obvious: Students want to be challenged, but they want to be challenged *with purpose*. Put simply, if the tasks they are asked to do are considered by students to be meaningful, they tend to prefer to work hard. If not, students prefer college lite. In other words, students' preferences for challenge are not related to their workloads as a general construct. Instead, their preferences for challenge are a function of good (or useful) workloads (i.e., time spent on course material that is considered to be important to advancing their educations) versus bad workloads (i.e., busywork or work not deemed important to advancing their educations). Although overall teacher ratings, perceived learning, and appreciation of a field of study are correlated positively with good workloads, the same outcomes are negatively related to bad workloads (Marsh, 2001). As Mottet et al. (2007) note, it seems that the *quality* of work instructors ask their students to engage in ultimately affects how students react to the *quantity* of work they are asked to do.

If you think about the notion of good and bad workloads, I bet you will find that this conclusion is true for you too. I know it's true for me, let me explain. I am sure some of you are aware that part of a professor's job is to be a good university citizen and to "donate" your time to various service organizations on campus. This includes joining committees that help plan curriculum, committees that select scholarship recipients, and committees that manage university resources, etc. I have been on several of these committees and, as you might imagine, I find some to be more purposeful than others. For example, I have literally sat through meetings where professors have argued over the placement of the word "the" in university documents for over 30 minutes. On the other hand, I have also sat in on meetings that have helped shape college- and university-level decisions regarding how to increase student graduation rates on campus. In my opinion, some of these meetings were a waste of time, and others were invigorating.

If you were to ask the dean of my college (i.e., my boss) whether he thought I prefer to work hard or enjoy "professor lite," his answer would probably depend on what meeting he saw me in. If he saw me in the meeting where people were debating the importance of the word "the," his answer would probably be that I prefer professor lite. I sat in those meetings watching the clock and checking my phone just like a "bad" student would do. If, instead, he saw me in the meetings where we discussed student success, he would probably tell you that I like to work hard. In those meetings I was alert, focused, and engaged. Just like students then, it turns out that I appreciate meaningful challenges and resent busy work that lacks real purpose. I'm sure most people feel the same way, don't you? Do you appreciate having meaningless tasks poured onto your desk and do you like engaging in mundane activities just because someone told you to get them done? I doubt it.

Having said the above, it's important that we think about the way we structure our courses so we can be sure that we create classroom climates that help students learn with purpose. One way to do this involves the provision of intellectual stimulation. Intellectual stimulation refers to the ability for teachers to get students involved in their course lessons and to get students thinking critically about what they are learning. Specifically, intellectually stimulating teachers are instructors who help their students reconsider old ways of doing things, help students challenge their own ideas to provide them with new ways of thinking, and help promote deep thought and imagination in an effort to solve meaningful problems. Ultimately, by intellectually stimulating your students, you might find that they experience their lessons as meaningful, and as a result, enjoy their classes more and become autonomously motivated to work hard in your courses.

To help you learn how to be intellectually stimulating in the classroom and to explain why you should do it, this chapter will cover a variety of topics including what it means to be an intellectually stimulating teacher, how your students benefit from being intellectually stimulated, and what you can do to be intellectually stimulating. So, first things first, what is intellectual stimulation?

Intellectual Stimulation

Like charisma, intellectual stimulation is a component of transformational leadership (see Bass, 1985) and, in the classroom, relates to teachers' abilities to get students personally engaged in the learning process. So what, exactly, do teachers do to influence students' perceptions that they behave in intellectually stimulating ways? My colleague, Alan Goodboy, and I were two of the first people to look into this question and, just like we did with charisma, we attempted to find an answer by asking students what their teachers did to facilitate this impression (e.g., Bolkan & Goodboy, 2011).

In response to our inquiry, students told us that their teachers did several things that were intellectually stimulating. And, contrary to experiences that might lead to the desire for college lite, these behaviors generally reflected getting students involved in the learning process in meaningful ways. Essentially, intellectually stimulating behaviors reflected an instructor's ability to get students excited about learning and to challenge students to assert themselves in the classroom. Although there are a variety of things students reported that their teachers did in this regard, to make things more manageable, Alan and I grouped these behaviors into three categories including: having an interactive teaching style, challenging students, and encouraging independent thought.

The first idea related to intellectual stimulation is having an *interactive teaching style.* Basically, instructors who have an interactive teaching style get their students engaged in, and excited about, their academic experiences. In our study, students reported examples of instructors using an interactive teaching style when they taught students through the provision of games, activities, skits, movies, visual aids, exercises outside of class, and when they asked students to teach their classmates. These activities were used to help students learn their course material in novel ways, and when asked to participate in these endeavors, students reported they were more interested in, and excited about, their learning tasks. In practice, having an interactive teaching style is the difference between making students sit in their chairs and take notes while you lecture, and allowing students to participate in the creation of their own knowledge.

If you want to assess intellectual stimulation in your classroom, you will be glad to know that Alan and I developed a measure to help you accomplish this goal (Bolkan & Goodboy, 2010). That said, if you want to know if your students consider your instruction to reflect an interactive teaching style, you can ask them to report the extent to which they agree or disagree with the following statements:

1. My teacher uses unique activities to get the class involved with the course material
2. My teacher uses exciting teaching techniques in class
3. My teacher helps students get excited about learning through classroom activities
4. My teacher stimulates students to help us get involved in the learning process in a variety of ways

I want you to really think about how your students would respond to these questions. If your students would disagree with the majority of them, you might be surprised to know that your students do not believe that they are being intellectually stimulated in a significant way ☹.

Now that we've covered what it means to have an interactive teaching style, let's turn to the idea of *challenging students*. Whenever I think of challenging my students, an image pops into my mind of me standing in an arena, gladiator style, while students rush toward me with their weapons drawn. Of course, in this thought experience, I destroy my students like Russell Crowe's Maximus did his opponents. And, when I am done, I return back to my barracks to rest, plot against Commodus, and prepare for my next bout.

As the foregoing story relates, the idea of challenging others tends to evoke in me the notions of murder, conflict, aggression, fighting, and hurt feelings (just joking about the first one). However, this doesn't have to be the case—especially not in the classroom. Challenging students' ideas and challenging their identities are two different things. In the case of the former, communication scholars would say that you are being assertive. In the case of the latter, we would say you are being aggressive. As you might already know, you can be assertive in your interactions with others without being aggressive (Infante & Rancer, 1982). This matters because people who behave in ways that challenge the ideas of others tend to be seen in a positive light, whereas people who behave in ways that challenge the identities of others tend to be seen negatively (for a review, see Rancer, Whitecap, Kosberg, & Avtgis, 1997). I guess all of this is just a long way of saying that, although you should try to avoid challenging your students' self-concepts, you should not be afraid to challenge your students' ideas.

So, what does it mean to challenge students in an intellectually stimulating manner? It means that you challenge your students' ideas to help them build their academic proficiency. For example, several students in our original study mentioned that they perceived their instructors to be intellectually stimulating when they challenged students to be their best through demanding (but relevant and doable) assignments, provided challenging procedures (such as grading and strict deadlines), when they challenged students to see things from new perspectives, or when they challenged students to support their beliefs with evidence. Each of these ideas refers to instructors who ask their students to think through classroom assignments, problems, and discussions in a thoughtful and thorough manner. More specifically, instead of accepting students' initial efforts, teachers who challenge their students: promote differing viewpoints, ask students to support their positions instead of taking them at face value, and push students to go beyond their first try when completing class assignments.

To ascertain the level of challenge that you offer in your courses, you can ask your students the extent to which they agree or disagree with the following statements:

1. My teacher challenges me to be the best student I can be
2. My teacher makes me work hard to ensure that I really know the material well
3. My teacher helps me realize that my hard work is worth it

If I could offer some preliminary advice regarding challenging students, it would be to reframe the way you think about the activity. Instead of thinking of challenging students as a gladiator would—standing in an arena poised to defeat those who stand in your way, you might instead think of challenging students as a personal trainer would—creating resistance to increase a person's strength. Thus, by challenging your students in small but acceptable ways, you can help them develop a stronger repertoire of cognitive skills that will ultimately help them achieve their academic potential (Johnson & Johnson, 2009).

The third idea related to intellectual stimulation is *encouraging independent thought.* Essentially, encouraging independent thought involves asking students to think through course-related problems in order to come to their own conclusions. Students in our study mentioned that their teachers did this in several ways. For example, students noted that instructors who encouraged independent thought asked their students to come to their own conclusions by posing questions to their pupils and requesting personal examples of classroom lessons. Moreover, instructors facilitated the development of independent thought by using a variety of probing questions to get students to look into the concepts and theories being learned in a thoughtful manner. In addition, instructors who encouraged independent thought provided case studies or other activities that asked students to work under various conditions and required them to come to their own conclusions while utilizing a variety of different problem-solving skills.

If you wanted to measure the extent to which your students perceive you to encourage independent thought, you could ask them to respond to the following statements:

1. My teacher helps me think deeply about the concepts taught in class
2. My teacher encourages me to come to my own conclusions about course material
3. My teacher wants me to think critically about what we are learning

In my opinion, encouraging independent thought is similar to helping a person learn how to ride a bike on his or her own: Eventually, you are going to have to take off the training wheels. Using this analogy, teachers who help students come to their own conclusions regarding course lessons ultimately allow their students to learn how to "ride on their own" with the class material. This is important if you ever want your students to grow to be independent thinkers and to use the lessons they learned from you in various settings outside of class. Admittedly, this might be frightening for some students. I know that having to perform on my own was scary for me when I learned how to ride a bicycle—the first time my dad let me ride my bike without training wheels I remember making small errors and almost falling down and being frightened that I would not be able to do it. But that experience helped teach me what I needed to do on my own. And now, as an adult, I can ride my bike down the street without needing to have my dad nearby. Of course, I still have him watch me in case I fall and scrape my knees, but the point is I do not *need* him to be there. The same thing should be true (for the most part) for your students.

What does it do and how does it work?

At this point, you might be wondering if intellectually stimulating students in your classrooms will lead to any tangible benefits. The answer to this question is that it certainly will, muchacho; there are positive associations between students' perceptions of experiencing an intellectually stimulating learning environment and a host of favorable educational outcomes (see Bolkan & Goodboy, 2009). For example, students who experience their classrooms as intellectually stimulating perceive that they learn more in these classes and report liking these classes more as well. What's more, students report that they are more motivated for class, more satisfied with class, and participate more in class when they experience intellectually stimulating environments.

In addition to these outcomes, intellectually stimulating teaching behaviors have been associated with students' experiences of empowerment (Bolkan & Goodboy, 2010), and also with students' intrinsic motivation, and their deep and strategic study strategies (Bolkan, Goodboy, & Griffin, 2011). Moreover, students who are exposed to intellectually stimulating teachers tend to pay more attention in class, work harder in class, and experience less boredom in class (Bolkan, 2015). As if that were not enough, by doing things like providing intellectual stimulation and helping students get involved in the learning process, teachers can help students increase their learning gains as well (Michael, 2006; Prince, 2004). Finally, teachers who employ an intellectually stimulating teaching style benefit too: Intellectual stimulation has been associated with students' liking for their teachers and also with students' perceptions of their teachers' credibility (Bolkan, 2015; Bolkan & Goodboy, 2009).

So how does intellectual stimulation work to create all these benefits? You are going to like this answer. Based on my understanding of the phenomenon, intellectual stimulation is likely beneficial in classroom environments because it satisfies at least two of students' three fundamental needs. First, intellectual stimulation is closely related to the need for competence. Operationally speaking, teachers who promote intellectual stimulation do three things: They use unique activities to get students involved with the course material, they challenge students to be the best they can be, and they encourage students' independent thought. That said, intellectual stimulation is likely related to students' need for competence because activities like the ones just described help individuals develop and successfully utilize their cognitive abilities in the pursuit of various course objectives.

Second, I expect intellectual stimulation influences students' perceptions of autonomy as well. This is true insofar as students who experience intellectual stimulation in the classroom are likely to believe that the tasks they are asked to do are in line with what they really want to be doing (Van den Broeck, Vansteenkiste, De Witte, Soenens, & Lens, 2010). In other words, students most likely don't feel like they are being forced to participate in events they would rather not be a part of when experiencing intellectually stimulating course activities. This conclusion has support from scholars who have shown that intellectual stimulation positively affects students' appreciation for class (Bolkan, 2015; Bolkan & Goodboy, 2009, 2010) and creates "an environment that naturally engages student interests" (Bolkan et al., 2011, p. 343).

Thus, we might conclude that the positive effects of intellectual stimulation stem from its ability to satisfy students' fundamental needs. And, based on what you already know about students' needs, you might expect that by satisfying these for students, intellectually stimulating teachers have the ability to foster autonomous motivation which is beneficial in academic environments (see Chapter 8 for a refresher). In support of this rationale, research has confirmed that intellectually stimulating teaching behaviors are, indeed, linked to students' autonomous motivation (Bolkan, 2015). Ultimately, the takeaway from this section is that intellectually stimulating teaching behaviors help students have enjoyable and enriching experiences in the classroom, and experiences like these have several benefits for student learning.

What Can You Do?

As you now know, intellectual stimulation is beneficial for students. At this point, the next thing you might want to know is how you can help students experience intellectual stimulation. To answer that question, let's take a look at some of the things you can do to provide an interactive teaching style, challenge students, and encourage independent thought.

Interactive teaching style

Developing an interactive teaching style refers to a teacher's ability to present information in novel, memorable, and engaging ways. As I mentioned in other parts of this book, your job as a teacher is not to simply disseminate information—a robot, a parrot, or a talking cat could do that. Instead, your job is to translate information into meaningful course lessons that allow your students to understand and make sense of the underlying concepts you are attempting to teach. Having said that, if you want to get your students engaged in their course lessons, it is going to take some creativity—it's up to you to dream up ways to present information in an interactive manner. Well, perhaps not entirely, you can borrow ideas from other people if you want. But, the point is that *you* have to take the time to develop and research various methods for turning course lessons into experiences that students will not forget.

So, where do these ideas come from? Importantly, most of these ideas will not come from the textbooks you use. Instead, they'll come from talking to your colleagues, researching various methods other people use to teach similar courses, and perhaps even your own imagination. Whatever the source, just remember that your goal is to get your students to be involved and active participants in their educations. Let me give you a few examples of what I do in my classrooms to accomplish this objective.

In several of my classes, I want students to learn the importance of perspective taking when they communicate with others. Essentially, the idea I want students to learn is that what is in their heads may not exist in the heads of other people. I want students to understand this idea because problems in communication can occur when we assume too much of our conversational partners. In particular, when we assume that others know what we know, this can result in either under-communication or over-communication. As it pertains to the former, we sometimes fail to give people enough information when we speak with them. For instance, telling someone to "grab you a drink" may be ambiguous when there are several to choose from. Pertaining to the latter, we sometimes do not realize that others might not know what we know, or how much we know. This might occur, for example, when we get upset with people who give us directions for something we already know how to do.

To help students understand the importance of perspective taking, I talk to them about an idea called theory of mind. Essentially, theory of mind explains that as we get older, we start to learn that what goes on inside our heads is different from what might occur in objective reality. Relatedly, theory of mind helps us understand that if we only have one version of reality in our heads, other people might have different versions of reality in their heads as well. Tests related to the theory of mind typically involve "false-belief" experiments (see de Villiers, 2007; Wellman, Cross, & Watson, 2001) that work something like this: I show you a door with a picture of a goat on it and ask you to tell me what animal you think might be behind the door. Looking at the picture you, quite reasonably, guess a goat. Once you say goat, I open the door to reveal a duck. After you see the duck, I tell you that I am going to bring in someone else who has never played the game to look at the same door. Then, I ask you to tell me what animal you think he or she will guess is behind the door. People who say "goat" are thought to have a developed theory of mind. They understand that, although there is really a duck back there, the new person doesn't know that. Conversely, people who say "duck" are not thought to have a developed theory of mind because they fail to realize that objective reality and subjective reality can differ. Essentially, these people do not recognize that what's in their heads can substantially differ from what's inside the heads of other people, and they fail to realize that the other person has no way of knowing about the duck behind the door.

Explaining the theory of mind in the manner I just did might help students learn it. But, is it likely to stick? Does teaching the theory of mind with a simple explanation represent a unique or exciting teaching technique? Hardly. So, this is what I do instead ... borrowing from Chip and Dan Heath's (2008) example drawn from Elizabeth Newton's dissertation, I have students play what I call the "tapping game." Here's how it works: First, I ask students to choose a partner and to designate one person as a listener. Once this is done, I tell students that the other person should be labeled as the tapper. After students have done this, I tell the listeners to look away while I show the tappers the name of a song. I typically try to pick something everyone knows, but I also try to pick a song that is fun and ridiculous. My go-to is usually Sisqo's *Thong Song.* Once the song has been picked, I tell the tappers that their goal is to use their pencils to tap out the beat of the song without giving any other clues—no humming, no dancing, and, in this case, no pointing to people's thongs. The objective of the game is for listeners to pay attention to the taps and then to guess the name of the song being tapped. Once students do this activity for a minute or so, we switch tappers with listeners and repeat the process with a different song.

So, what's happening, and why do I have students go through all of this trouble? Well, what's happening is that when they are tapping the *Thong Song,* tappers are, in their heads, also singing along with the taps of their pencils. Thus, because they "hear the song" as they tap it, they are usually amazed that listeners cannot guess the name of the tune—the beat is so obvious, how could anybody miss it? Of course, the people listening do not have access to the songs being sung the in tappers' heads, and all they hear are a bunch of noisy taps being drowned out by other people in the room tapping similar noises at various intervals. Tappers tend to get frustrated because they fail to realize that listeners don't share the musical information that exists in their heads, and they get upset when their partners cannot guess such a simple song. Listeners, on the other hand, get frustrated because they cannot believe that tappers think they are providing enough information to make a reasonable guess.

The point of engaging in the tapping game is for students to realize that, although most of us develop a theory of mind at about four years of age (Wellman et al., 2001), we don't always think about the differences between what is in our heads and what is in the heads of others when we communicate with them. I want students to live this through the experiment because it allows them to *experience* the frustration of trying to communicate without regard for the theory of mind. By using this exercise, my goal is to help students attach meaning to the theory of mind as it pertains to human communication, and this type of experiential learning is at the heart of what it means to teach with an interactive style.

Of course, tapping out songs about thongs is not the only option I have for creating an interactive classroom. When studying group communication, for example, I have students engage in a "lost-on-the-moon" activity where they first work individually and then in teams to rank a set of 15 items in terms of importance for surviving a 200-mile trek across the lighted side of the moon. Groups usually do better than the individuals on this task, and once the activity is done, I explain why this might be the case. Similarly, when it comes to studying ideas related to listening and feedback, I also try to use an interactive teaching style. Specifically, instead of telling students about the impact that feedback has on a speaker, I have students deliver short presentations while instructing the audience to pay various levels of attention. Usually, we find that when we don't pay attention to what speakers have to say, they have a difficult time saying it.

These are just a few examples of what I do in my classrooms, and I only share these as a way of illustrating some of the possibilities for making class interactive. Importantly, there are several other ways to promote an interactive teaching style that don't necessitate activities like the ones just discussed. For example, some of these include: class discussions, team-based assignments, student performances, problem-solving exercises, and in-class or online demonstrations, to name a few. Moreover, even taking a few breaks during class and asking students to clarify their notes with a partner can get students engaged in their learning environments in meaningful ways (for a discussion see Prince, 2004).

Before we move on, let me just say one more thing about having an interactive teaching style. Sometimes, teachers ask me to tell them how many activities they should include for a specific period of time. I don't know if I can come up with an exact answer to this question; however, breaking your classes into 10- or 15-minute "sections" is a strategy recommended by some scholars (e.g., Medina, 2008). This means that you might consider having activities or exercises, or simply changing the nature of the learning experience several times in each class session. Admittedly, getting students actively involved in the learning process to this extent will take foresight, planning, and effort. But, the rewards you will experience pertaining to your students' interest, engagement, and learning are well worth the struggle.

Challenging students

For nearly four decades, David and Roger Johnson have studied how challenging students' ideas in the classroom can enhance students' academic experiences. Based on their program of research, the authors have concluded that intellectual conflict is an "essential tool that energizes student efforts to learn" (Johnson & Johnson, 2009, p. 37). Put simply, the authors suggest that students benefit from being presented with alternative perspectives that are incompatible with the positions they currently hold. Challenging students is important because it helps students "engage in cognitive rehearsal and higher-level reasoning strategies" (Johnson & Johnson, 2009, p. 41). In addition to thinking deeply about their own positions, exposing students to the positions of others can also induce curiosity, which is likely to result in their searching for more information about a topic and their consideration of varying perspectives. What's more, the Johnson's argue that compared with students whose beliefs are not, students' whose beliefs are challenged tend to enjoy greater: retention, deep thinking, transfer, perspective taking, open-mindedness, creativity, task involvement, and motivation to continue learning about classroom issues. Moreover, students exposed to this type of educational experience also tend to like the people they participate in the controversies with more as well.

Generally speaking, the Johnsons argue that teachers can challenge students to the extent that they require their pupils to justify their opinions, use reasoning to articulate their conclusions, and provide evidence to support their assertions. The way we can help students do this is simple but delicate. First, the simple part. Johnson and Johnson (2009) state that to help students experience challenge, we simply have to ask them to articulate their positions thoughtfully and engage them in open discussions where they are forced to consider alternative perspectives. So, when students articulate their positions, instead of taking them at face value, the Johnsons argue that we should ask them to explain the logic behind their conclusions. That is, instead of taking their positions for granted, we should ask students to think through the reasoning behind their ideas to ensure they start with thoughtful arguments. Specifically, to help students think critically about their attitudes, we can ask them to articulate why they support an argument, to provide evidence or examples that support their opinions, and to detail the steps they took to reach a specific conclusion.

Once we are convinced that the reasoning behind students' ideas is both logical and thoughtful, Johnson and Johnson (2009) argue that students should be exposed to alternative perspectives. These alternative perspectives can come from you as the teacher, from other students who offer different opinions, or even from asking the original students to come up with some themselves. The idea here is to help students come to the conclusion that, as one of my students once framed it, perhaps their way isn't the only way.

After students have been exposed to alternative perspectives, the Johnsons note that we should encourage them to think through all the claims made and, instead of simply arguing to support an original position, use the available evidence to come to what they perceive to be the most appropriate conclusion. According to the Johnsons, we can help students do this by: asking students to argue from alternative perspectives instead of from their own, asking students to think about how their original ideas fare in the face of competing explanations, and asking students to synthesize the positions they hold with the positions of other individuals to help them see how new, creative solutions may be possible.

We just went over the simple part of helping students experience challenge; now on to the delicate part. The delicate part involves our ability to create an atmosphere where doing all of the above feels safe. To help us achieve this goal, the Johnsons offer several pieces of advice. First, the authors argue that we should try to create a context where we frame disagreements as helpful for coming to correct conclusions. That is, instead of framing challenges as attacks on the positions of others, we should frame them as a collective effort to use what we know to come to accurate conclusions about the world. In other words, we should help students perceive the experience of challenging others' ideas through the lens of answering questions instead of advocating for, or taking, sides. To aid in this process, we can help students understand that changing their minds is okay; they should hold positions owing to logic, reason, and evidence—not simply for the purposes of being dogmatic.

Second, Johnson and Johnson (2009) note that we should build a community of challenge that values politeness and respect. As the authors put it, students should be encouraged to challenge the ideas of others "while confirming their competence and value as individuals" (p. 42). Of course, if you are the person doing the challenging (as the teacher), this applies to you as well. Specifically, while offering alternative perspectives, you can help affirm students' sense of self-worth by expressing respect for them as people and for the positions they hold. Moreover, we should develop the same community of respect when students speak to each other as well.

Ultimately, being delicate when facilitating challenge really means that we should concentrate on creating a cooperative experience and avoiding a competitive environment. Doing so will help us promote thinking and reasoning instead of closed-mindedness and defensiveness. As Johnson and Johnson argue, we should help students see that the value in challenging positions comes not from proving that one person is right while another person is wrong, but instead from thinking critically about what we believe and coming to conclusions based on sound logic and valid evidence.

Before we conclude this section, I have to make one last comment related to your willingness to engage with the ideas promoted above. Simply put, you need to be open to having your ideas challenged and supporting your positions with reasoning and evidence as well! In particular, it is important that, as teachers, we are able listen to the ideas of others even if, and perhaps especially if, we disagree. One of my favorite professors in graduate school used to tell us that he believed he could learn as much from us (as students) as we could from him (as the instructor). Having that mentality is important as a teacher because it allows us to approach conversations in our courses with open minds instead of defaulting to a position of defensiveness when students challenge our ideas.

Encouraging independent thought

Recall that the notion of encouraging independent thought involves helping students come to their own conclusions in class. Based on this definition, promoting independent thought might include facilitating students' expression of personal opinions, positions, and original examples in class. Thus, one way teachers might be able to promote students' independent thought is by helping students participate in class.

Participation in classroom discussions is essential because it has the potential to enhance students' academic outcomes in important ways. For example, in her review of the literature, Kelly Rocca (2010) found that participation in class was linked to student motivation, grades, and enhanced critical thinking. Importantly, not all researchers agree that oral participation is the best way to get students engaged in classroom activities (e.g., Frymier & Houser, 2016). These scholars claim that students can demonstrate their engagement in a variety of ways and argue that oral participation might not lead to the outcomes most researchers purport they do. Although this argument certainly has merit, one of the reasons oral participation may not lead to student engagement is because not all oral participation is productive. As researchers Dallimore, Hertenstein, and Platt (2004) note, the manner in which teachers facilitate student participation can either make for effective or ineffective classroom discussions.

According to Dallimore et al. (2004), there are a variety of behaviors that facilitate effective classroom discussions and that reduce the probability of promoting ineffective discussions. First, teachers who facilitate effective discussions ask open-ended questions instead of looking to students to come up with the "right" answer. Thus, when students provide their perspectives, these teachers allow for and encourage multiple viewpoints instead of pushing a preset agenda. One way to facilitate this type of discussion is to ask questions of interpretation, opinion, or experience. Not only will you be able to encourage multiple viewpoints by doing so, but students are also more likely to share when responding to these types of questions as opposed to those that require the provision of facts with right or wrong answers.

Second, Dallimore et al. (2004) note that effective discussions are those in which instructors expand upon students' ideas. This is the equivalent of having a deep conversation with somebody as opposed to a superficial one. If you have ever had a conversation with someone who was distracted by something else, then you know what I am talking about. These people do not respond to your messages appropriately, do not build off the conversation in constructive ways, and they sometimes ignore your comments altogether. When I encounter conversations like this, I tend to want to escape the interaction as soon as possible, and the same is likely true for your students. So, instead of calling on students and then moving on with indifference, consider expanding on students' ideas by clarifying the thoughts they bring up, relating them to your course materials, and building off students' comments to spark a class discussion by playing the devil's advocate or by asking students who disagree to speak up.

Third, Dallimore and colleagues note that effective discussions are those that are structured. If you have ever sat through a class where the discussion has broken down into individuals promoting tangential ideas, then you understand how destabilizing this can be for a coherent dialog. Thus, teachers who promote discussions in their classrooms can help make these meaningful by guiding participants' disclosures toward the material being covered in the course instead of letting them digress into topics that are not essential for learning class concepts.

Okay, now we know that student participation is important and, if promoted thoughtfully, can lead to effective class discussions. However, as a teacher, I bet you have experienced at least one situation where students did not participate as much as you wished they would. Thus, you might be wondering what you can do to get people to speak up more. There are several things you may consider to achieve this outcome. According to Rocca (2010), one of these things includes building a comfortable atmosphere where students feel safe sharing their opinions. For example, to create a comfortable class atmosphere you can get to know students by name, interact with students before class, and deliver course lectures in a nonverbally immediate manner. Moreover, students are more likely to participate in course discussions when teachers are friendly, supportive, open-minded, and respectful. These findings are similar to those of other researchers who have found instructor–student rapport to be a positive predictor of student participation in class (Frisby & Martin, 2010).

Additionally, Rocca argues that students learn to participate based on teachers' reactions to their contributions. Specifically, students are less likely to contribute to class discussions when teachers do not pay attention to their participation or when teachers are critical of their responses. On the other hand, as we learned previously, students are more likely to participate when teachers communicate the value of their sharing by doing things such as thanking students for their opinions, building deeper discussions from students' comments, and otherwise affirming students who share.

In addition to inviting students to participate by creating a safe environment, another method for getting students to participate in class is "cold calling." In essence, cold calling entails calling on students without waiting on them to raise their hands (Dallimore et al., 2004). Admittedly, there can be some potentially negative outcomes with cold calling. For example, if you cold-call students by asking them to participate without any warning, the people you call on might not have enough time to prepare a thoughtful response. Moreover, the practice might also make your students anxious and, if this is the case, may prove to be demotivating for some individuals.

Thus, because of the issues that can exist with cold calling, you might consider doing what I call "warm calling" instead. Warm calling is just like cold calling with one exception: you allow your students to prepare for the call. One way to change a cold call into a warm call is to alert your students to the fact that you employ this method in class (perhaps on the syllabus or in the first lecture). Essentially, by letting them know you call on people without regard to the traditional raising of hands, you can help your students prepare for this experience and make their participation less unexpected. Even if this is impossible and students are asked to participate on the spot with little time for preparation, you might change a cold call into a warm call by giving them a few seconds to formulate their thoughts. For example, instead of being called on out of the blue, allowing students to think about their answers for a few seconds and perhaps even asking them to write them down or share them with classmates before you call on them will provide students with the time they need to prepare thoughtful responses to your questions.

At this point, you might be wondering if there is any best way to enact the cold/warm calling technique to ensure its fairness. There sure is: Allred and Swenson (2006) note that calling on students through a random selection process can be helpful in this regard. Not only is random selection fair, but it also encourages students to prepare their comments because your selections are uncertain. That said, when you employ this method of picking students, you might consider making the process transparent. Allowing students to see that the process is truly random (e.g., you can use a random number generator from something like random.org) will make the process appear more equitable.

Although some people might think otherwise, students report that the use of cold/warm calling is an effective means of helping them prepare for class (Allred & Swenson, 2006; Dallimore et al., 2004). This is because if students know they might get called on, it is in their best interest to be ready to respond. Moreover, Dallimore and colleagues report that calling on students helps to involve individuals who are less likely to speak up on their own. This is particularly important considering that a few students can often end up being the only ones who participate regularly (Rocca, 2010).

In essence, the bottom line in this section is that you should try to get your students to participate in their course lessons because doing so can encourage their independent thinking. Of course, as the instructor, you play a major role in your students' willingness to speak up in class. That said, after reading this section you know that there are several things you can do to facilitate students' productive participation. By being cognizant of your influence in the process, you might be more successful in creating an atmosphere where students feel safe and feel free to articulate their points of view in ways that lead to effective learning experiences.

Summary

Do you ever wonder why your classes seem to go by quickly when you teach them while students look at the clock as if time is standing still? In my opinion, one of the reasons time moves more quickly for you is because when you teach, you are being active. Your body is moving and your mind is engaged. Your students, on the other hand, are probably much less involved. That said, if you want students to stop looking at the clock and start focusing on their lessons, you need to get them into the position where they are actively participating in their learning.

Although there are a variety of options to pursue, in this chapter we learned that one way to get students involved in the learning process is to intellectually stimulate them. And, how do you do that? Of course, you now know that to intellectually stimulate your students, you need to: create class lessons with an interactive teaching style, challenge your students to really know the course material, and ask students to come to their own conclusions regarding what they are learning. Ultimately, doing these things will help your students become engaged in the learning process and will help them enjoy the experience too.

In the beginning of this chapter we encountered the idea that some teachers think students are not willing to give their full attention when it comes to school. The way we framed the issue was that it can sometimes seem like students are really only interested in experiencing college lite. However, we argued that this conclusion might not be entirely correct. It is not that students dislike doing work. Like you and me, they dislike doing work that is not purposeful. As I noted in the chapter on self-determination, students can be internally motivated to learn. However, the classroom experiences they encounter often suppress this internal drive. Thus, if we want to help students learn to their potential, it is our job to facilitate students' internal motivation by creating teaching practices that help students become engaged with and like what they are doing. In my opinion, most people only want less of something if they think it is bad and if they are forced to have it. Thus, if your students say that they want college lite, it probably means they want less of what you have to offer. Why not create such a terrific learning experience that students can't wait to come to your class? By employing some of the ideas in this chapter, you might be able to make that scenario a reality.

END-OF-CHAPTER QUESTIONS

1. Which aspect of intellectual stimulation do you think you struggle with most in the classroom? Why?

2. As a student, which component of intellectual stimulation do you think benefits you the most? Which component is the most motivating for you?

3. What do you think about the two positions articulated in the beginning of the chapter? Do you agree that students desire college lite? Or, do you think that students can be motivated to work hard as long as they see purpose in their efforts?

KEY TERMS

College lite: The expectation that instructors should make college easy for students

Interactive teaching style: Behaviors that get students engaged in, and excited about, their academic experiences

Challenging students: Behaviors that challenge students' ideas to help them build their academic proficiency

Encouraging independent thought: Behaviors that enable students to come to their own conclusions

Cold calling: Calling on students without advance notice

Warm calling: Alerting students to the possibility of being called on, giving students time to prepare their responses to discussion prompts

REFERENCES

Allred, C. R., & Swenson, M. J. (2006). Using technology to increase student preparation for and participation in marketing courses: The random selector model. *Marketing Education Review, 16,* 15–21. doi:10.1080/10528008.2006.11488932

Bass, B. M. (1985). *Leadership and performance beyond expectations.* New York, NY: Free Press.

Bolkan, S. (2015). Intellectually stimulating students' intrinsic motivation: The mediating influence of affective learning and student engagement. *Communication Reports, 28,* 80–91. doi:10.1080/08934215.2014.962752

Bolkan, S., & Goodboy, A. K. (2009). Transformational leadership in the classroom: Fostering student learning, student participation, and teacher credibility. *Journal of Instructional Psychology, 36,* 296–306.

Bolkan, S., & Goodboy, A. K. (2010). Transformational leadership in the classroom: The development and validation of the student intellectual stimulation scale. *Communication Reports, 23,* 91–105. doi:10.1080=08934215.2010.511399

Bolkan, S., & Goodboy, A. K. (2011). Behavioral indicators of transformational leadership in the college classroom. *Qualitative Research Reports in Communication, 12,* 10–18. doi:10.1080=17459435.2011.601520

Bolkan, S., Goodboy, A. K., & Griffin, D. J. (2011). Teacher leadership and intellectual stimulation: Improving students' approaches to studying through intrinsic motivation. *Communication Research Reports, 28,* 337–346. doi:10.1080=08824096.2011.615958

Dallimore, E. J., Hertenstein, J. H., & Platt, M. B. (2004). Classroom participation and discussion effectiveness: Student-generated strategies. *Communication Education, 53,* 103–115. doi:10.1080/0363452032000135805

de Villiers, J. (2007). The interface of language and theory of mind. *Lingua, 117,* 1858–1878. doi:10.1016/j.lingua.2006.11.006

Frisby, B. N., & Martin, M. M. (2010). Instructor-student and student-student rapport in the classroom. *Communication Education, 59,* 146–164. doi:10.1080/03634520903564362

Frymier, A. B., & Houser, M. L. (2016). The role of oral participation in student engagement. *Communication Education, 65,* 83–104. doi:10.1080/03634523.2015.1066019

Gillmore, G. M. (2001). *What student ratings results tell us about academic demands and expectations.* Seattle: Office of Educational Assessment, University of Washington.

Heath, C., & Heath, D. (2008). *Made to stick: Why some ideas survive and others die.* New York, NY: Random House.

Infante, D. A., & Rancer, A. S. (1982). A conceptualization and measure of argumentativeness. *Journal of Personality Assessment, 46,* 72–80. doi:10.1207/s15327752jpa4601_13

Johnson, D. W., & Johnson, R. T. (2009). Energizing learning: The instructional power of conflict. *Educational Researcher, 38,* 37–51. doi:10.3102/0013189X08330540

Marsh, H. W. (2001). Distinguishing between good (useful) and bad workloads on students' evaluations of teaching. *American Educational Research Journal, 38,* 183–212. doi:10.3102=00028312038001183

Medina, J. (2008). *Brain rules; 12 principles for surviving and thriving at work, home, and school.* Seattle, WA: Pear Press.

Michael, J. (2006). Where's the evidence that active learning works? *Advances in Physiology Education, 30,* 159–167. doi:10.1152/advan.00053.2006.

Mottet, T., Parker-Raley, J., Beebe, S. A., & Cunningham, C. (2007). Instructors who resist "college lite": The neutralizing effect of instructor immediacy on students' course-workload violations and perceptions of instructor credibility and affective learning. *Communication Education, 56,* 145–167. doi:10.1080/03634520601164259

Prince, M. (2004). Does active learning work? A review of the research. *Journal of Engineering Education, 93,* 223–231. doi:10.1002/j.2168-9830.2004.tb00809.x

Rancer, A. S., Whitecap, V. G., Kosberg, R. L., & Avtgis, T. A. (1997). Testing the efficacy of a communication training program to increase argumentativeness and argumentative behavior in adolescents. *Communication Education, 46,* 273–286. doi:10.1080/03634529709379101

Rocca, K. A. (2010). Student participation in the college classroom: An extended multidisciplinary literature review. *Communication Education, 59,* 185–213. doi:10.1080/03634520903505936

Van den Broeck, A., Vansteenkiste, M., De Witte, H., Soenens, B., & Lens, W. (2010). Capturing autonomy, competence, and relatedness at work: Construction and initial validation of the work-related basic need satisfaction scale. *Journal of Occupational Psychology, 83,* 981–1002. doi:10.1348=096317909X481382

Wellman, H. M., Cross, D., & Watson, J. (2001). Meta-analysis of theory-of-mind development: The truth about false belief. *Child Development, 72,* 655–684. doi:10.1111/1467-8624.00304

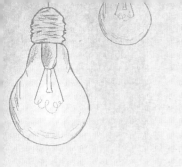

CONCLUSION

Does anybody actually read the conclusions in books? Whatever, I'll keep it short. In this book you learned a variety of principles and practices for effective instruction. Good for you. But, don't let your journey toward becoming a great teacher stop here. Remember that story I told you about G.I. Joe in the introduction? Learning is only half the battle, the other half involves you putting what you learned into practice. So, if you want to experience positive results in your classrooms, that means you actually have to change the way you teach. That said, don't get upset if you cannot change everything at once—in fact, this might not be the best way to move forward. Instead, think about the little ways you can improve your teaching and try to build from those as you develop your own personal best practices into the future. Crucially, while employing the behaviors outlined in this book will be beneficial for you personally, the real winners are going to be your students. When you signed up to be a teacher, you knew that your job was to help students learn to the best of their capabilities. And, by using some of the ideas presented in this book to inform your teaching you will be more likely to succeed in reaching this goal.

Next, let me mention that this book is only a start. What I mean is, if you are interested in any of the ideas I presented in this text, you should feel free to research them on your own. Becoming informed on the topic of, well really anything, is not difficult to do. And, if you want to become more knowledgeable about any of the subjects I covered in this book (or beyond), you should know that doing so is easier than you might imagine.

Finally, I want to conclude by saying that after reading this book you now know what it takes to be a successful teacher. In a general sense, like I mentioned regarding student success, it is going to take COWs. I imagine you probably already have the opportunity to teach successfully, and now that you have read this book you should have the capability to teach as a great instructor as well. That said, to become a terrific teacher, all that's left is the willingness, or motivation, to put what you have learned into practice. At the end of the day, the decision to be great is really up to you.

INDEX

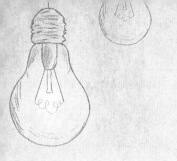

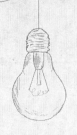